Drawing with Charcoal
For Beginners

Step By Step Guide to Drawing
Landscapes – Portraits – Animals

I0476733

Paolo Lopez de Leon
And
John Davidson

Learn to Draw
Book Series
JD- Biz Publishing

All Images Licensed

By: Paolo Lopez de Leon

Learn How to Draw Books for The Absolute Beginner

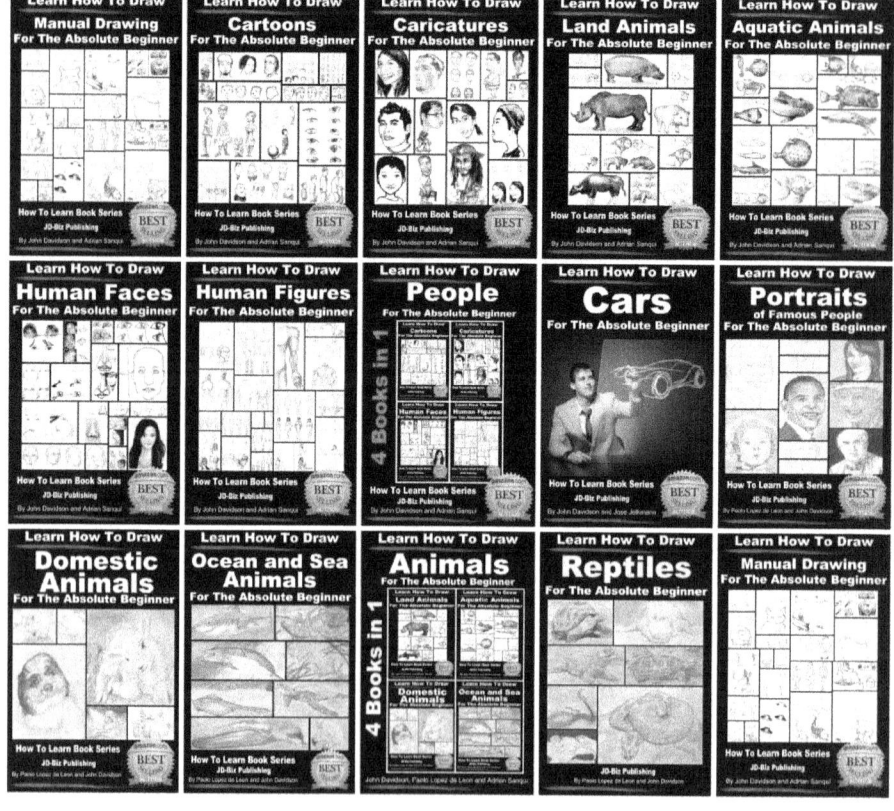

TABLE OF CONTENTS

Introduction:

Ever wonder how an artist draw a beautiful landscape, how with ease uses his chosen medium and finished his masterpiece. Well let me tell you, that can do it too, picking this book is the first step you showed your interest to draw Landscape. I promise you if you read and do the instructions step-by-step in this book in no time you will be drawing your Landscape masterpiece in no time. Imagine that you will not just amaze yourself but also your friends and others by your skill in drawing as well rendering it adding tones to make in realistic. Both in pencil and Charcoal, as what I always tell beginner artist, you must be dedicated, persevere and be patient, if your first drawing attempt is not the same as you seen in the examples, don't be discourage, try to relax or take a break and after that do it again with your calm mind.

This book will be showing you how easy it is to draw landscapes, people and animals so let's begin the journey and adventure of the world of drawing with your pencil and charcoal, and remember have fun and free your creative mind.

Rendering Harry Potter in Charcoal

We will start out with a complex charcoal example to show what can be done in charcoal and then we will step back and show you in the next chapters how to build up your skills to be able to accomplish great charcoal painings of your own. We are going to render Harry with Charcoal, so prepare your materials: shaved charcoal of different grades (Soft, Medium and Hard), Charcoal pencils and the brushes (Flat and round).

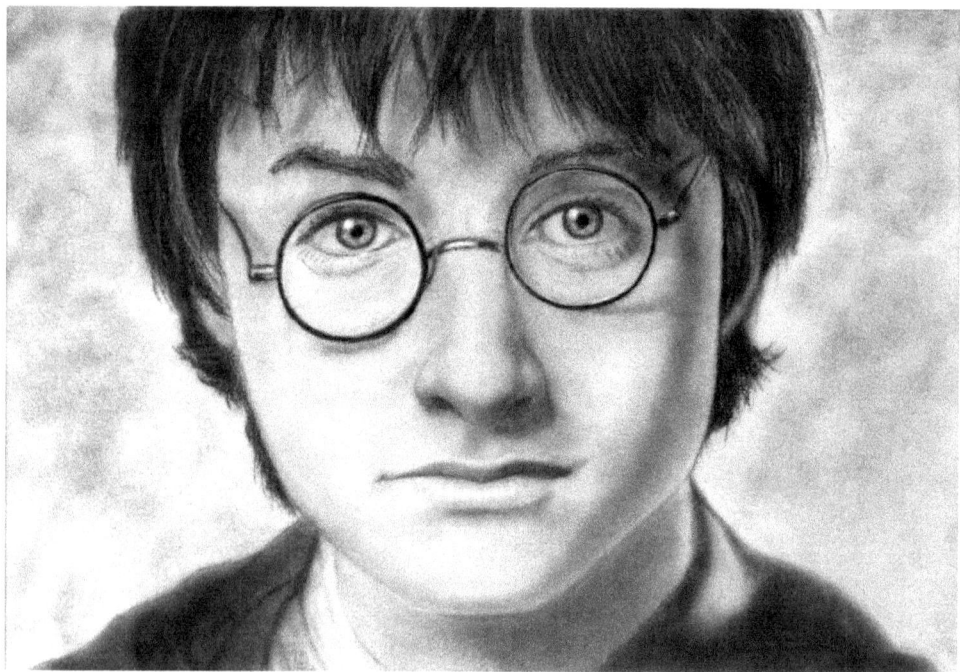

Transfer the image below to your Bristol pad (use 4H pencil or HB), just like we did before when we were rendering with pencils. Just copy the important contour and map the shades, including details.

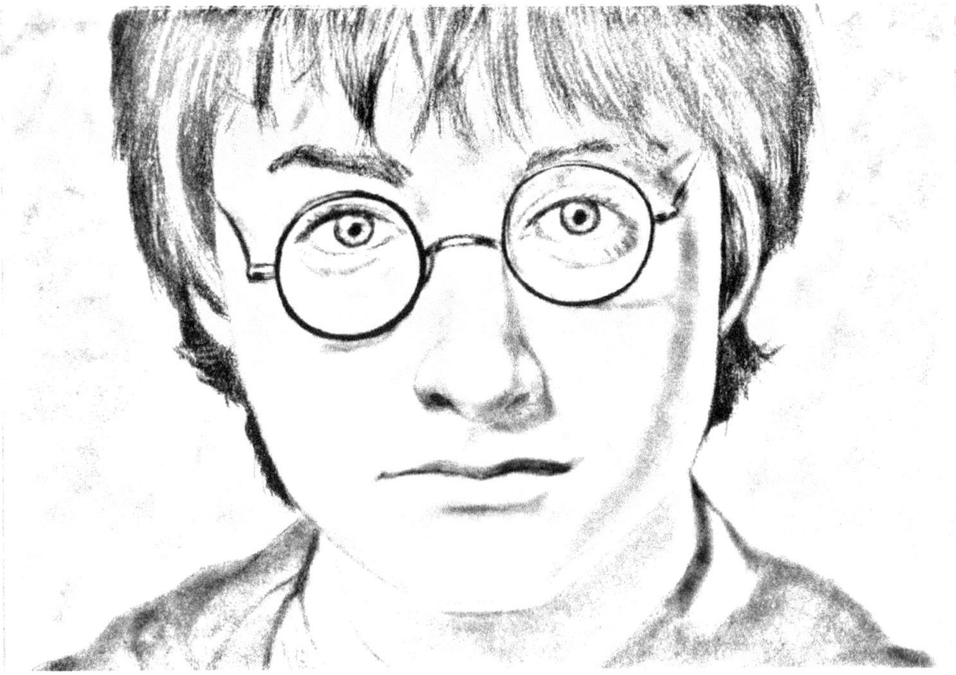

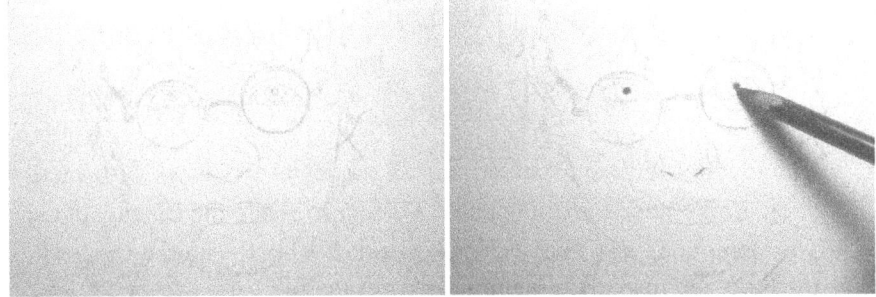

Steps:

1.   Begin by shading the pupils and nostrils using your Soft Charcoal pencil.

-     You may use your Templates for this, to have a perfect circle for the pupils.

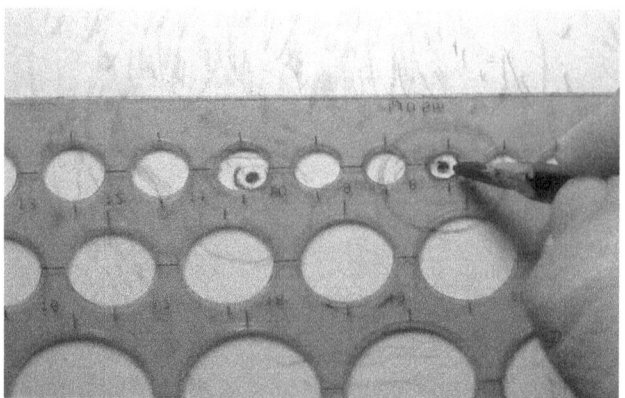

- Also draw the dark line between the neck and the robe.

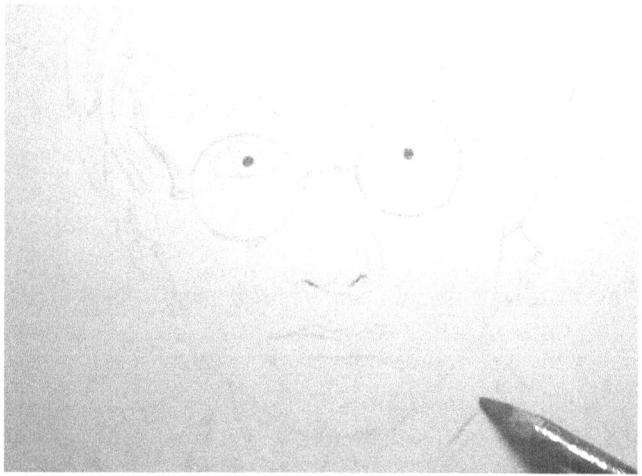

2. Using your Medium Charcoal pencil, shade the eyebrows with small short strokes (see the guide below), and also shade the iris (again use your template), and glasses. Then begin shading the hair at the back of the head and also draw the line between the lips.

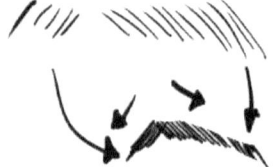 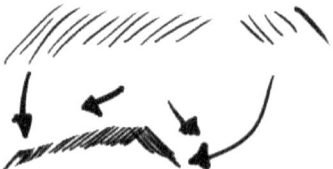

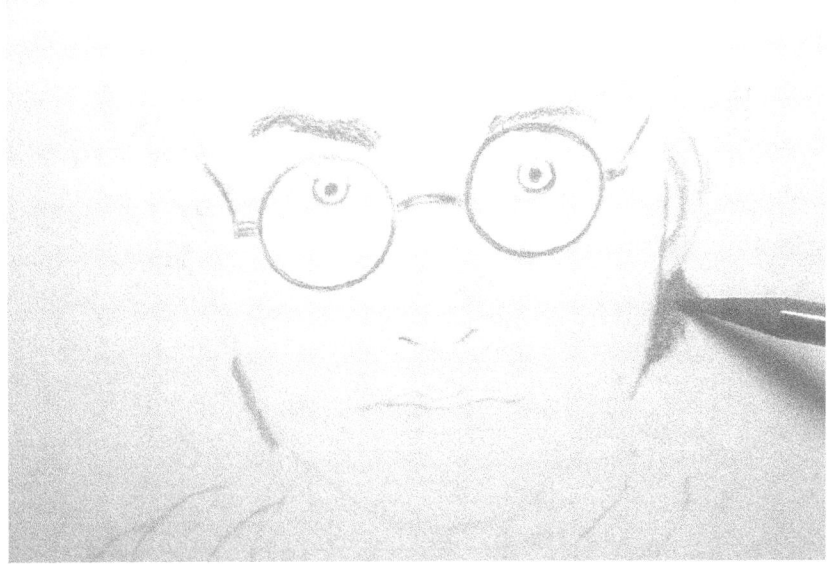

3. Fill the front side of the head, the bangs, and the side with hair strands, using the same grade of pencil (medium).

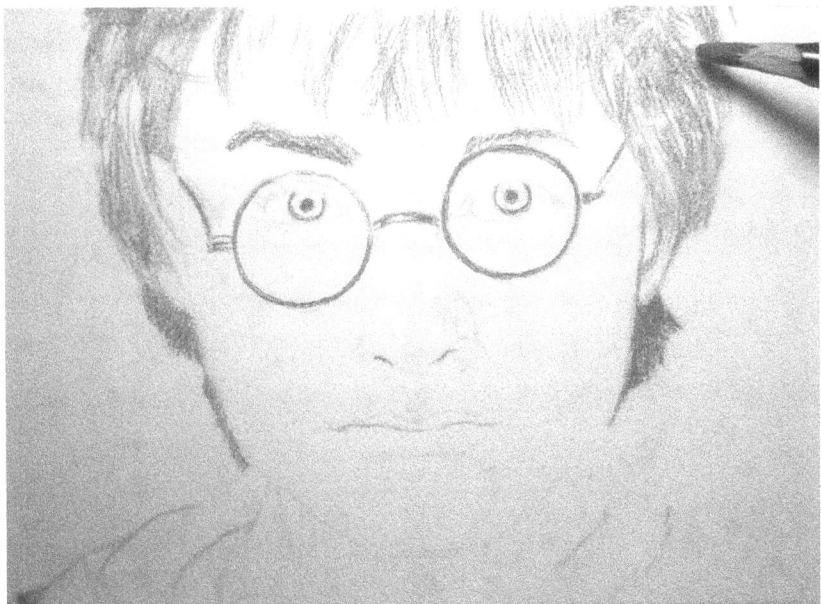

4. Draw a line for the eyelids.

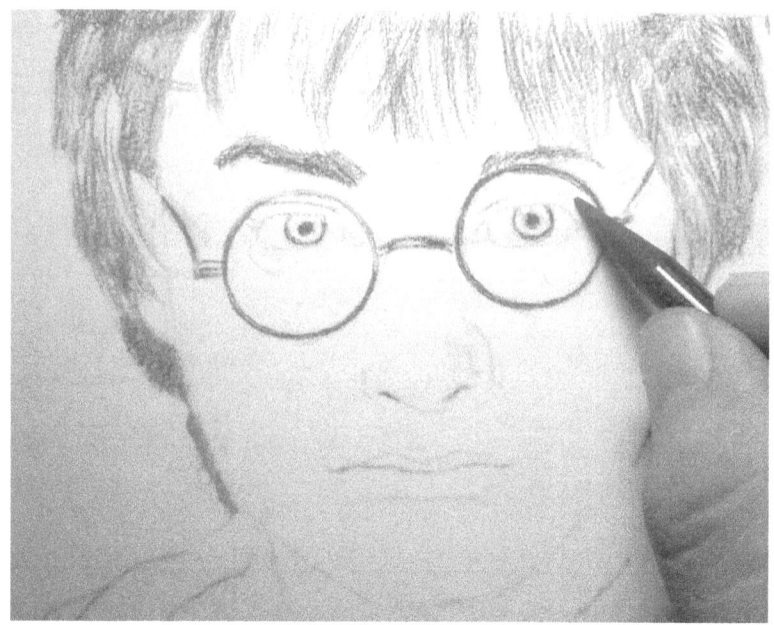

5.   Now shade the shadows around the eyes, nose, the areas between the nose and the mouth, lips (the upper lips are much darker than the lower lips), and on the side of the face to the chin (remember to leave some space for the reflected light). Use Medium shaved charcoal and apply with a Flat brush.

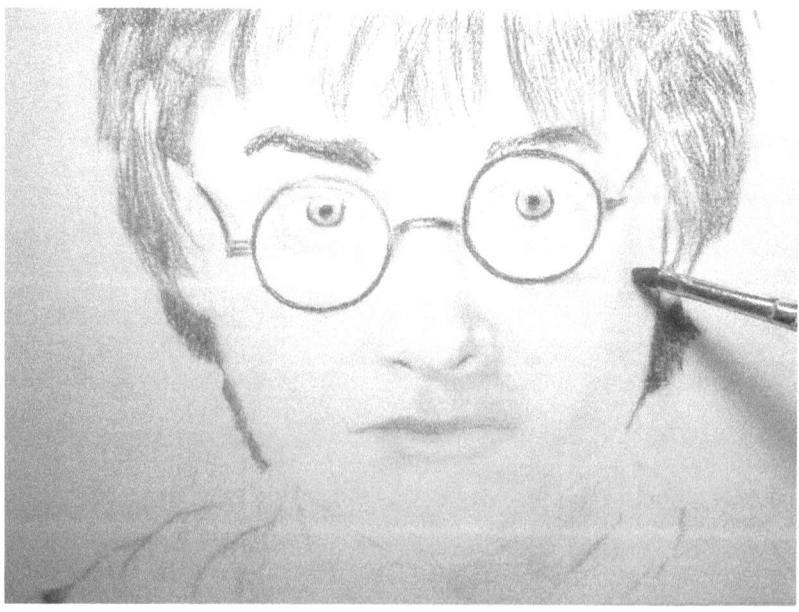

6.   Now use your Round Brush to dab lightly on the face with the same charcoal used to tone the surface of the face.

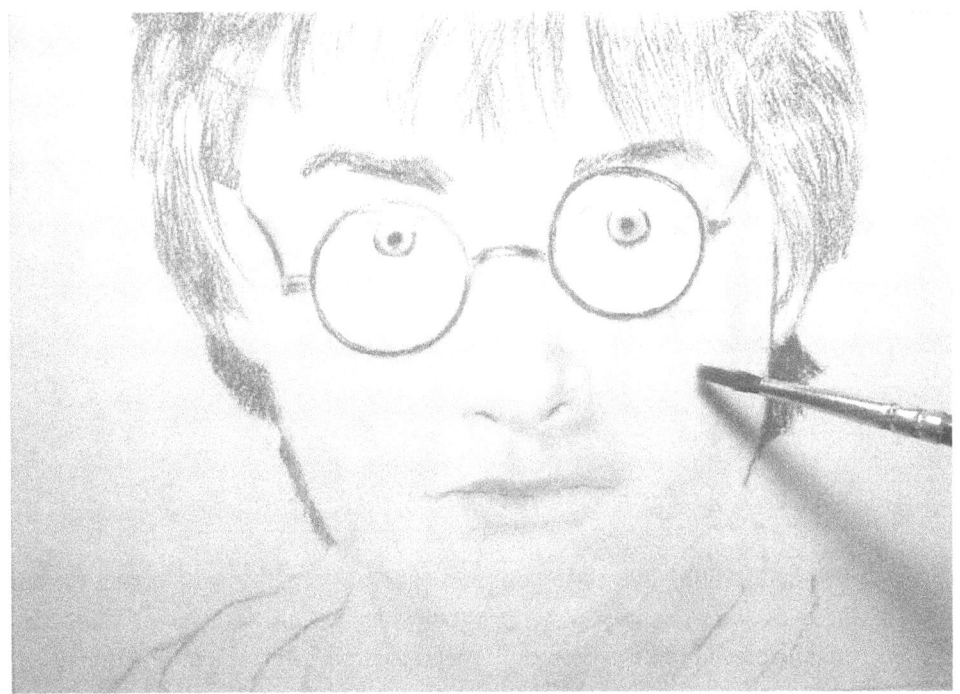

7.   Use cotton to blend the area, which will enhance and add a good texture to the face.

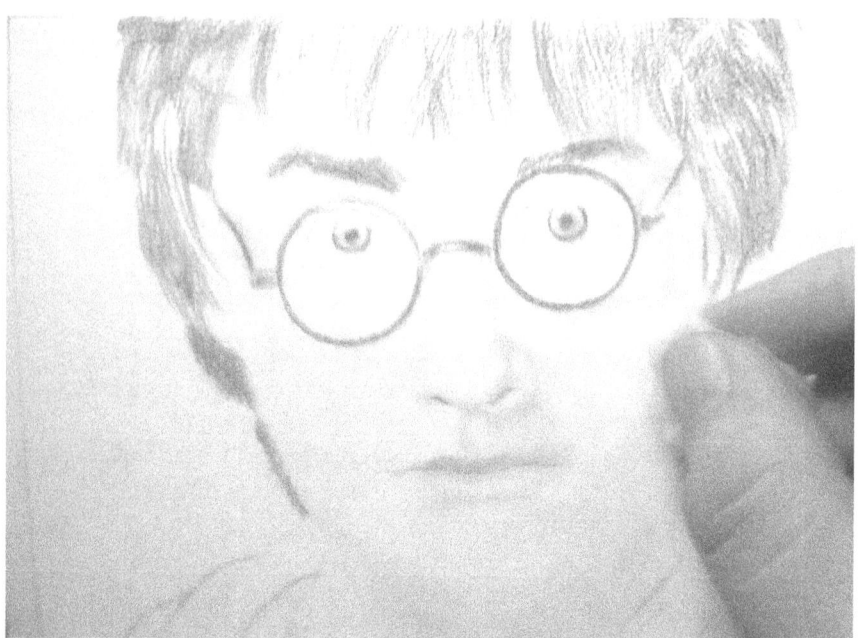

8.   Add detail in the eyes: use your soft charcoal pencil for the upper lines of the eyes, hard charcoal pencil for the eyelashes and some small lines for the muscles in the iris (you don't need to draw all of it just few lines). Next is to add a catch of light in both eyes using an electric eraser.

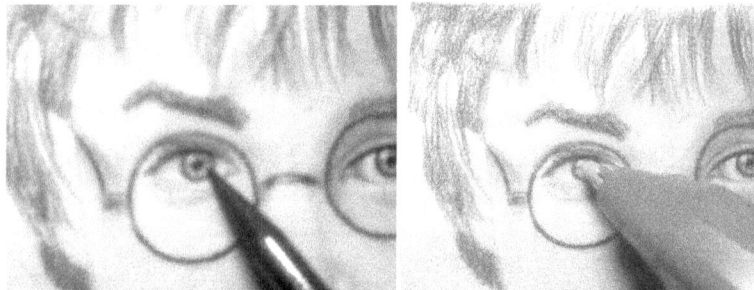

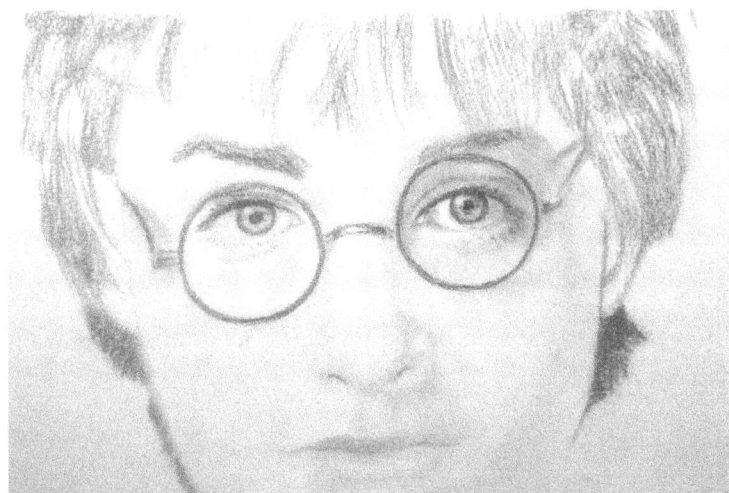

9. Moving on to the nose, finish the details by adding more shade including the Philtrum and lips.

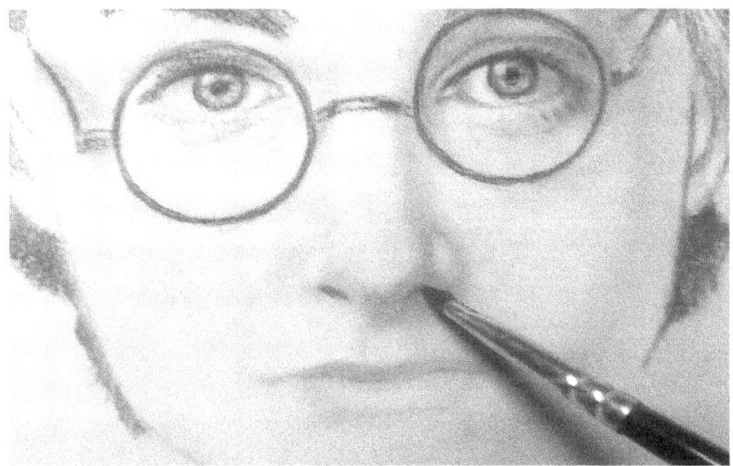

10. Shade the shadow on the neck with dabbing Medium charcoal shaved using your Round brush.

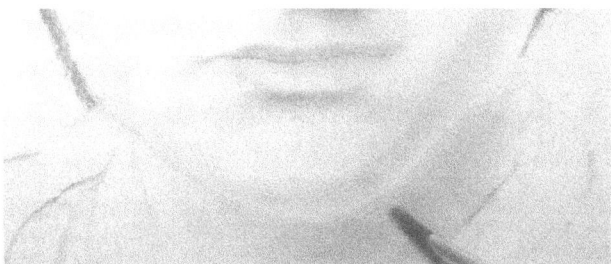

- And blend the area with a flat brush.

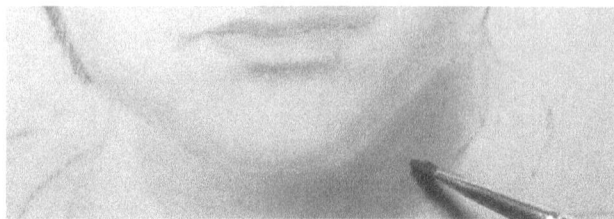

11.	Moving back to the hair, on the side add a layer of strokes with Soft charcoal pencil.

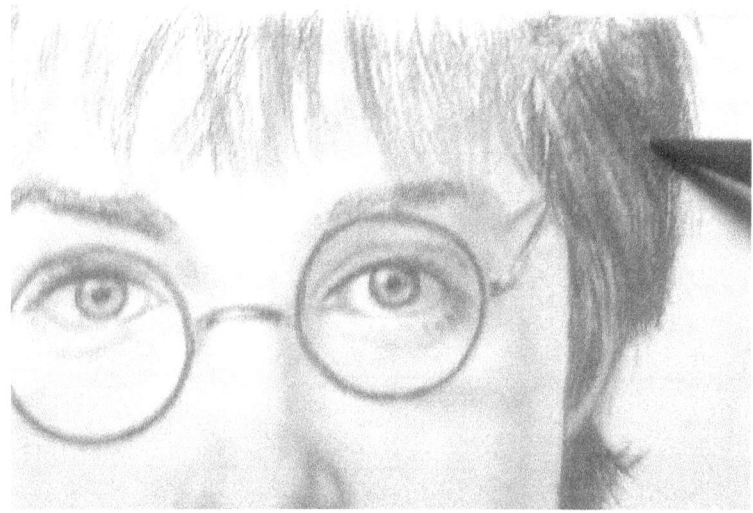

- Blend it with your Flat brush.

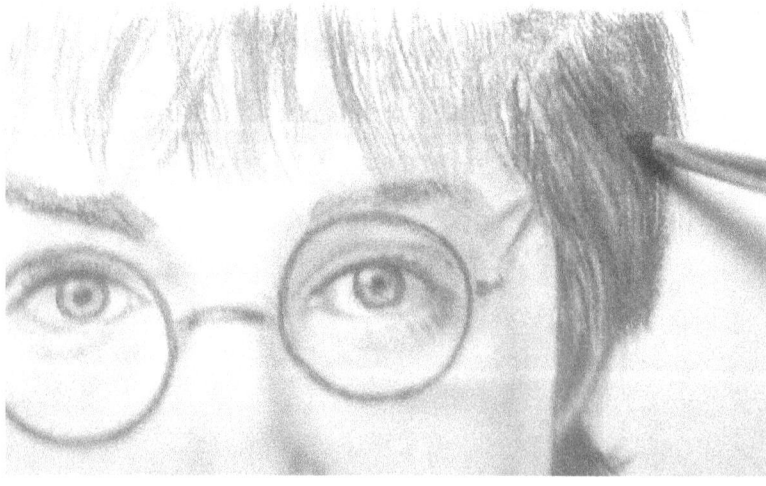

- Do the same to the other side.

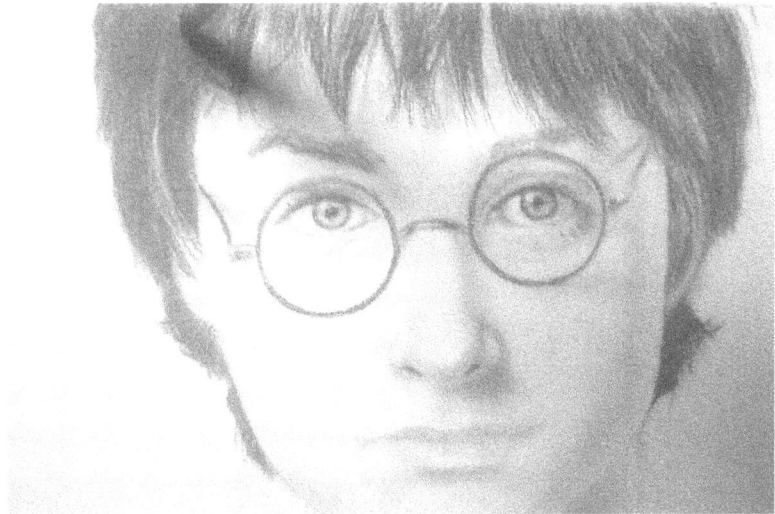

- And don't forget to also add hair on the forehead or bangs.

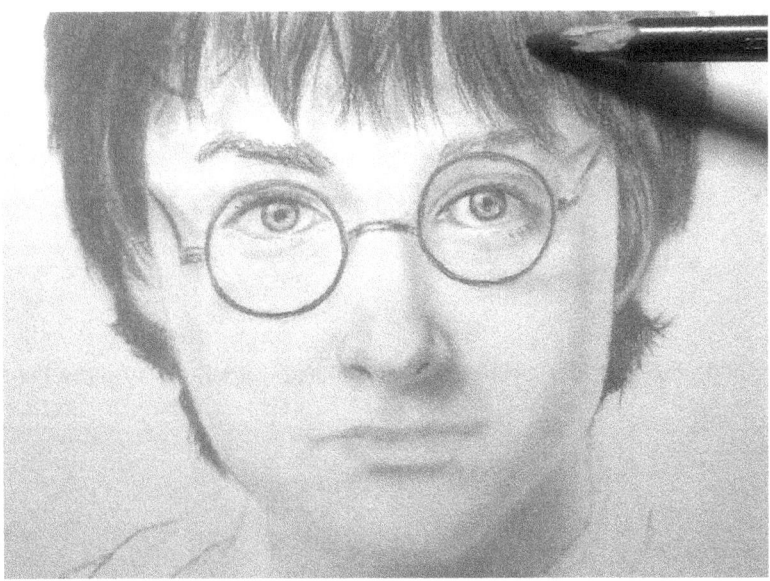

12. Add a thin shadow below the glasses, with Medium charcoal shavings and flat brush.

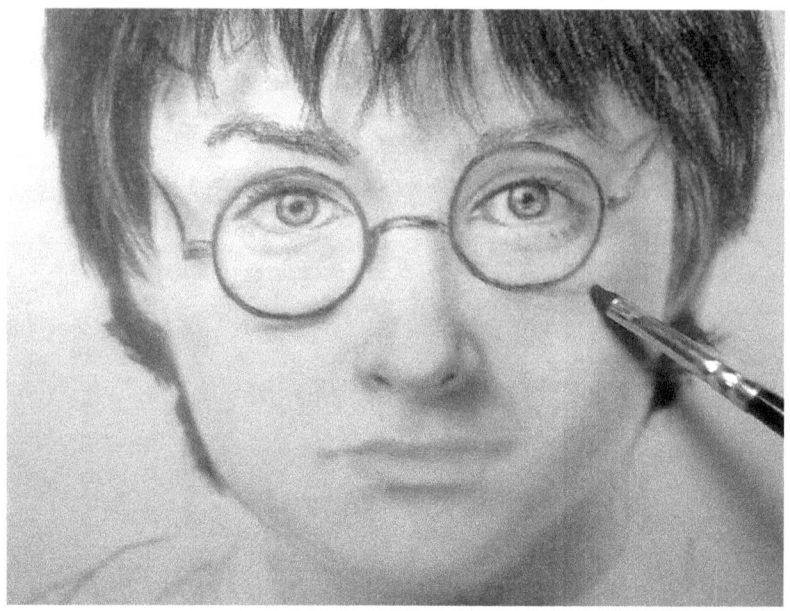

13.   Shade Harry's coat by following the instructions below:

-    Shade the darker area with Soft charcoal shavings using your Flat brush; shade the rest of the robe with Medium charcoal.

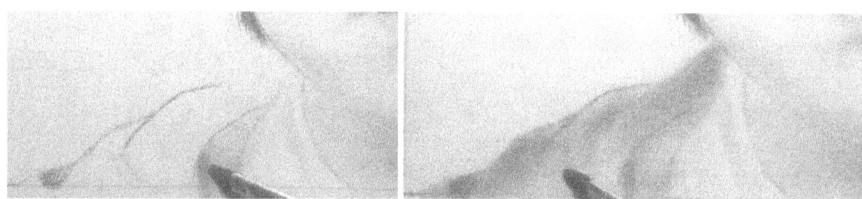

-    Shade the next darker area and do the same for the rest using the steps above.

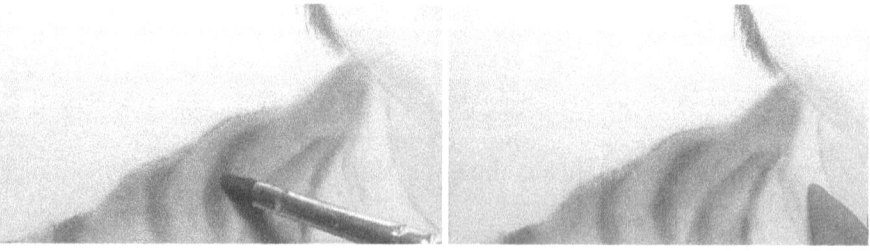

-    Add details for the inner shirt with your Medium Charcoal pencil and apply a darker tone (soft charcoal) on the other side, as the area is away from the light.

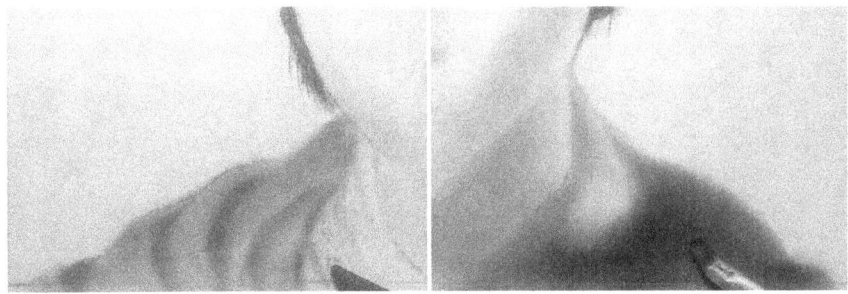

14.   For the background: Dab some shaved Hard Charcoal with your Round brush, randomly.

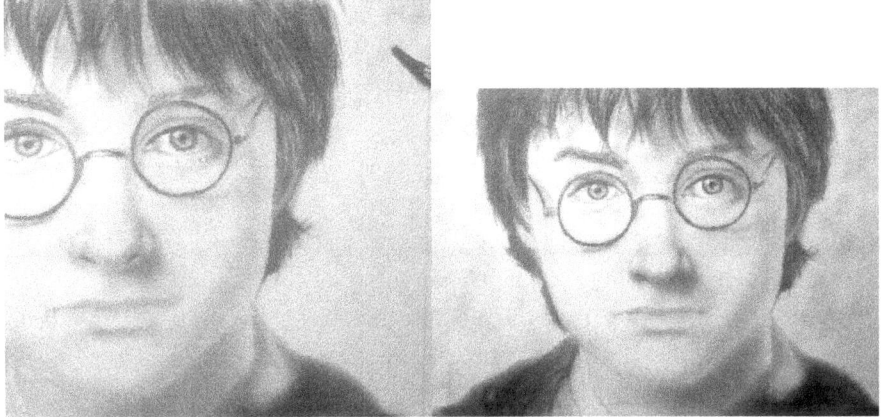

-    You're finished! Be sure to spray your work with fixative. Good job!

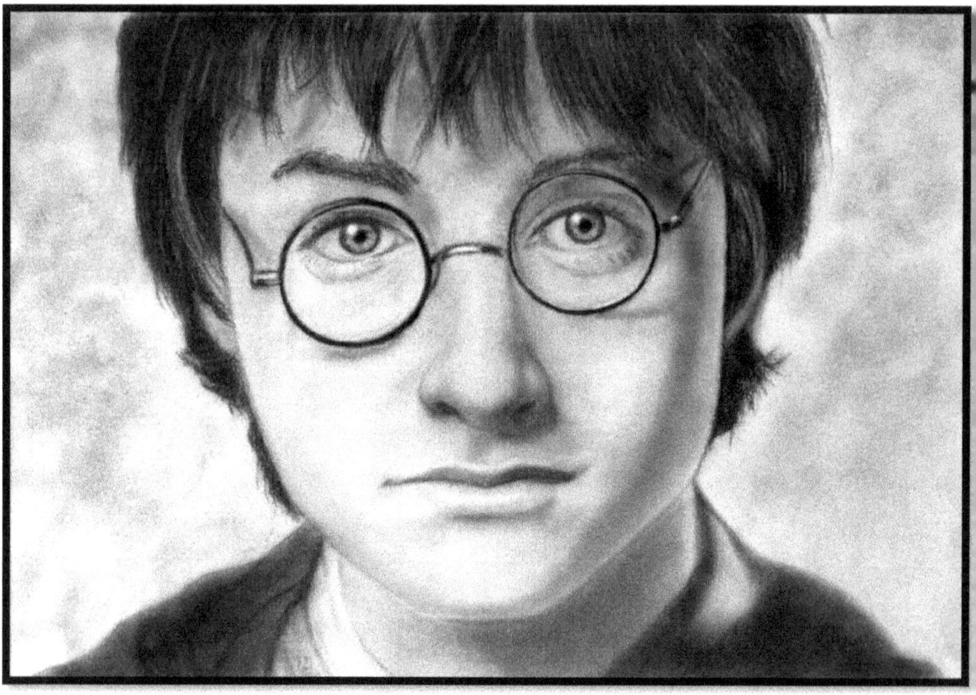

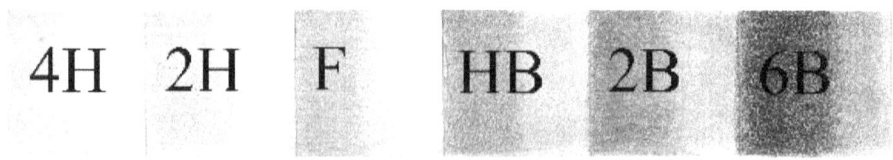

Take a break and after that, read the next section as we're going to paint our next exercise with colors.

The Basics:

I know you are eager to make your beautiful Masterpiece now, and I promise that you will, after you learn how to render. This is the part that will make a big difference as an artist. So, get your Pencils, Kneaded erasers, and smudge stick ready for our lecture.

This is our value scale this will help us select the right tone

4H 2H F HB 2B 6B

You can make your own Value Scale to have a reference. Take note that I blend (using the smudge stick) to the right, so that you will have an idea, how will it look.

Sphere

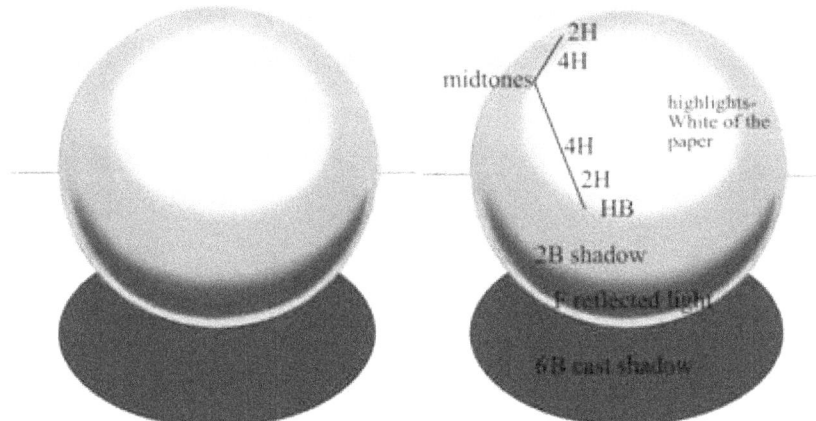

On the right side is our guide of what pencil to use to get the following tones of an object. The light source is coming from above.

Cast shadow 6B - It is the shadow cast by the object, depending on the placement or location of light; it's the place where no presence of light can be seen.

Reflected light-1.F or 2.Other times a light sliding stroke of your kneaded eraser can be used. Leave it blank and just blend the area depending on the tone of your subject picture. It's a bouncing of light up a reflective surface at the exact angle at which touches the surface. Like in our example, the light hit the table then reflected with an angle to the sphere. Reflected light is important in any drawing, because it also add realism to it.

Shadow 2B - It is where the light source cannot reach, and is always opposite to the light source.

Midtones HB, 2H, and 4H - It's the place where the transition of light is evidently present, so that is why we will be using different grades of pencils for this. Our orientation for this is from dark to light when rendering.

Highlights - this is the part that we're going to use the white of the paper or a kneaded eraser, if ever there is a presence of tone from shading.

Step1. Draw a circle, using your 4H or 2H pencil, with your circle template. For the cast shadow, use your ellipse template. Draw a line in the middle of the circle, as this will be the table.

Step2. Erase the unnecessary lines.

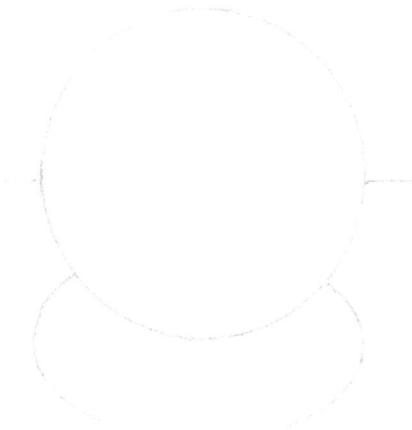

Step3. Let's start rendering the cast shadow using 6B, as this is the darkest part of our drawing. Remember that we are going to render this from dark to light, building the pencil lines gradually up and down, matching the value of our example. Then, blend the cast shadow using your smudge stick. It is better if you only use this smudge stick for this tone alone.

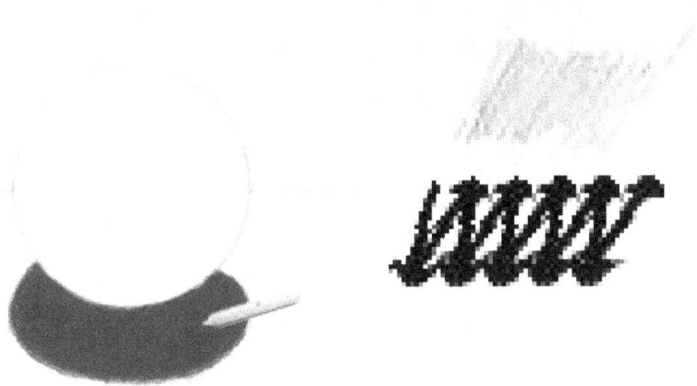

Step4. Using your 2B pencil, we're going to draw the shadow. Do shading strokes around the ball and remember to leave some space below it for our reflected light.

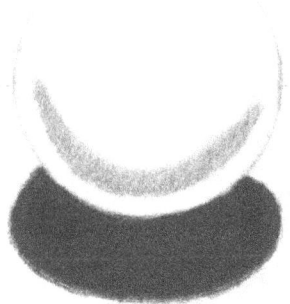

Step5. Next is the reflected light. Use F pencil and apply shading strokes below the shadow, like you did in Step4.

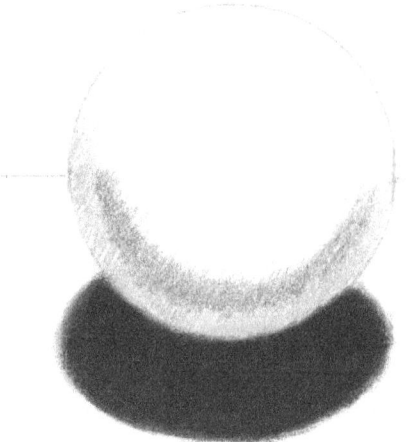

Step6. Working with our Midtones, we will be using HB, 2H and 4H. Starting with HB, apply strokes above the shadow.

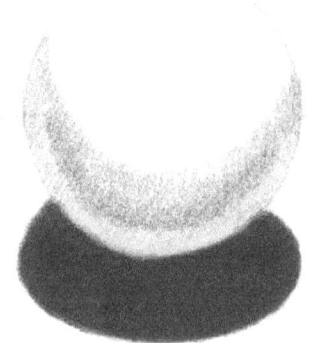

Then apply 2H above the HB stroke and also apply light strokes in the upper part of the inner circle.

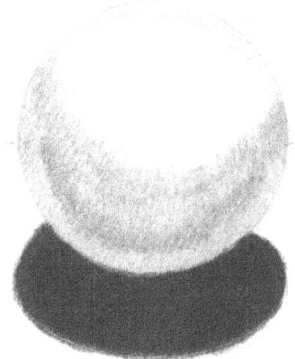

Do the same, using 4H, just above and below the 2H, then also apply light strokes below the 2H and also above.

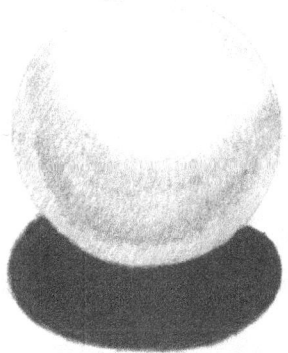

Step7. It's time to Blend these tones, and we will be working from light to dark. Be sure to clean your smudge stick first, as there must be no graphite to it. A new one would be better or just use sand paper to polish it, so not to darken any of our light tones.

Starting at the upper part, blend the 4H tone (going upward then downward) to the 2H tone; your stroke will be the same as when using a pencil.

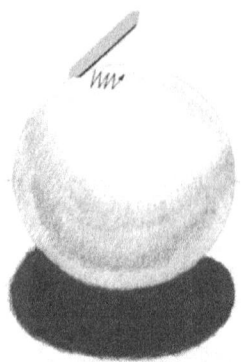

Do the same with the rest. Start blending from the 4H tone to 2H then HB, slowly and gradually. For the shadow with 2B tone, lightly blend it upward to HB. For the F tone (reflected light) blend it starting from the left side going circular to the right side, not to have contact with the 2B tone. After that, clean your work using your eraser.

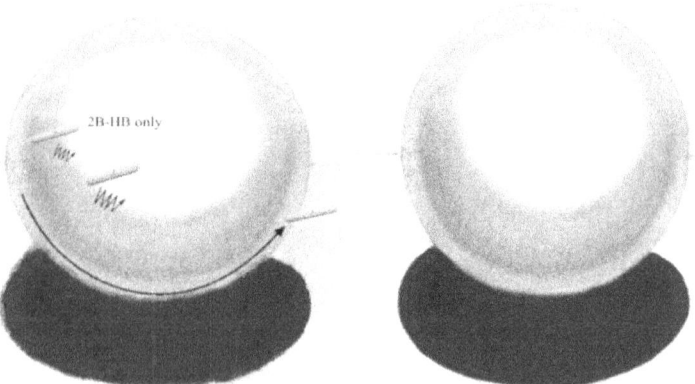

Now there you have it! You have learned how to render the Sphere.

Tips:

- If you accidentally blend or erase some dark tone, just redo it with your pencil lightly.

- Use your pencil to fill any uneven light spots and for any uneven dark spots just lift it with kneaded eraser.

Cone

Step1. Copy the shape below. You can trace it if you want or you can draw it by drawing a vertical line first and a short horizontal line. Use an ellipse template to draw the base and use a ruler for the slope starting at the top of the vertical line going to one end of ellipse. Do the same to the other one.

Step2. Begin shading the cast shadow (6B).

Step3. Then apply 2B to the shadow area, and also to F for the inner circular area of the base. You can extend the F tone until the top, but do it lightly. Your

stroke should be following the circular shape of the cone. But don't shade the right and left side near the slope, as that is where our highlights will be.

Step4. Next are our midtones. On the line where we shaded the 2B, apply shading starting with HB, lightly. Overlap the 2H tone and also the 4H, and do the same to the other side. Be careful and leave some space for our highlights for both sides.

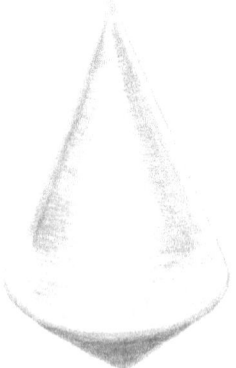

Step5. Now, let's blend everything one at a time starting from F at the bottom. Start your strokes at the left moving to the right until you reach the top. Be careful when blending with 2B tone, not to smudge much. For 2B to midtones,

slowly blend the 2B to HB, 2H and 4H going to the outer side for both sides. Make sure highlights can be seen, so pull out the highlights using the kneaded eraser on that side. Also, just between the 2B tones near the tip, erase so that it will look evident and draw a line at the back of the cone.

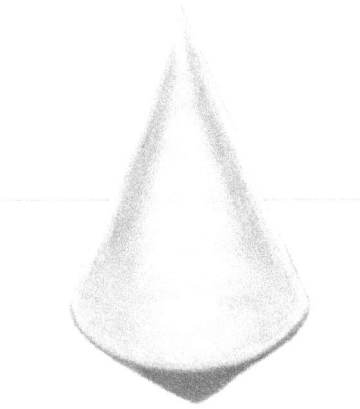

Cube

Step1. Copy the cube outline, you can trace or do it manually. You have to draw the line 30° on the left and on the right, with both sides forming a letter "V". Draw 3 lines vertically; one on the left end of the "V", one on the right end, and one in the center. On the top of it is another "V" shape connecting to an inverted "V" shape again, forming a diamond shape.

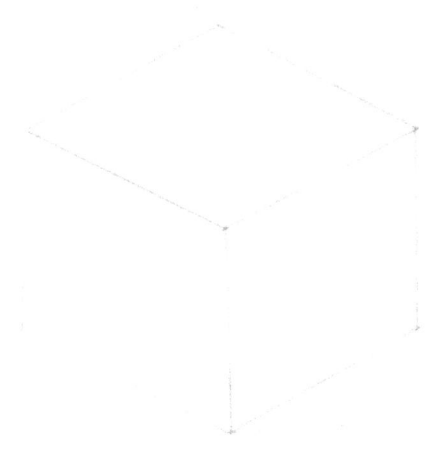

Step2. Start shading with the cast shadow. In this example, the cast shadow on the right side is darker than the backside, and that's because the light source comes from the left side giving light to it.

Step3. Apply the shadow (2B), and also the reflected light (F) on the lower part of this side.

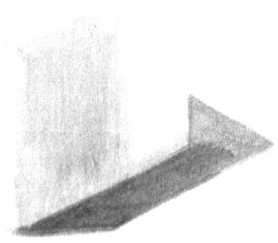

Step4. Add the midtones, HB, 2H and 4H, beside the shadow, and also shade a portion of HB below the front side.

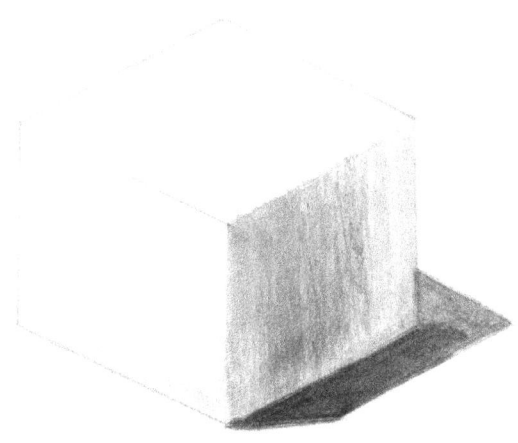

Step5. Shade the front side with 2H until you fill half of this side, then switch to 4H and fill the rest.

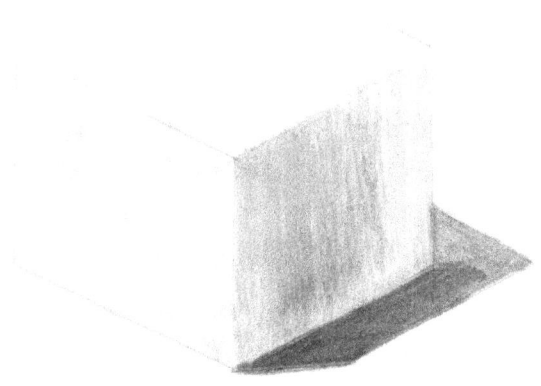

Step6. Slightly shade a small tone on the right side at the top.

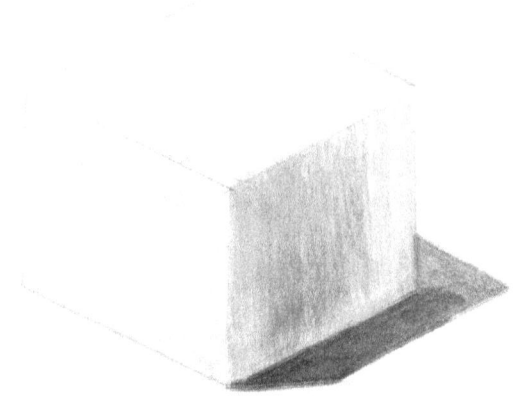

Step7. Blend all respective sides accordingly with your smudge tool.

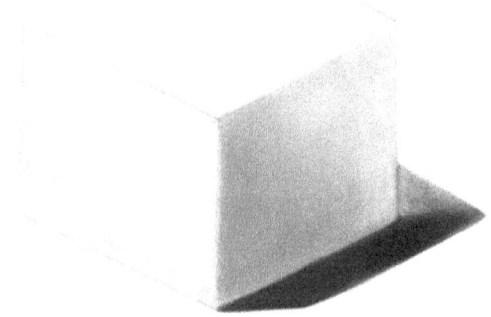

Cylinder
Step1. Copy the outline or do it manually. The parts are composed of two ellipses and two vertical lines. The light is coming from the left side, so the shadow would be at the back; opposite the light source.

Step2. Begin shading the cast shadow (6B) at the back.

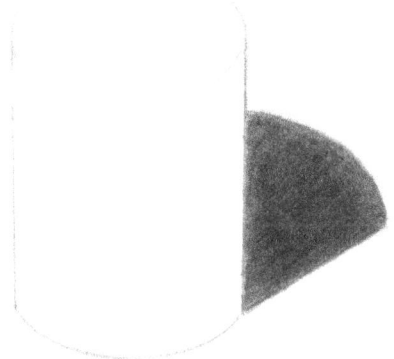

Step3. Next, apply the Shadow (2B) and take note of the roundness of the cylinder shape. There will be two shadows running vertically, as seen in the illustration. Lightly apply F on the left side of the cylinder, vertically beside the shadow.

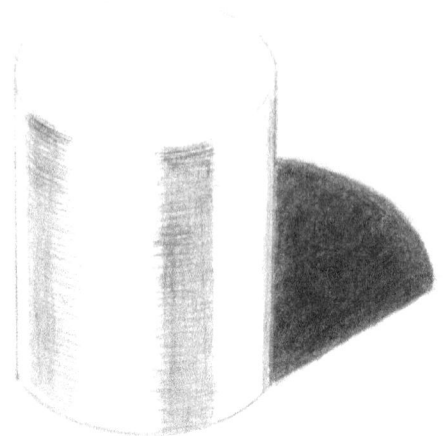

Step4. Work your midtones beside the two shadows, starting with HB, 2H and 4H. Also do it to the other side of each shadow. Apply these tones on the top of the cylinder as well.

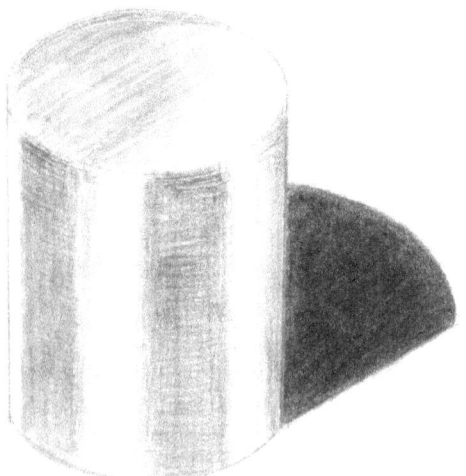

Step5. Blend the cast shadow and shadows with the midtones (careful to leave empty space for the bands of highlights; we have three). Blend the top as well, and we're done.

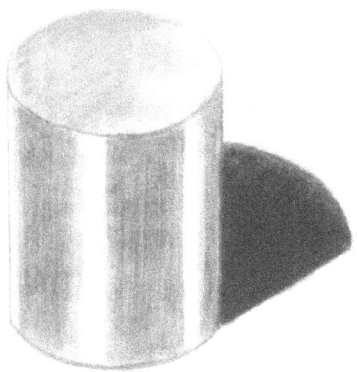

You may wonder why we need to learn all of this or what the connections of these shapes are to the human face. Let me explain; the Sphere shape is seen in the face, eyes, ears, and nose. The Cone shape can be seen in the nose (from the nasal bridge to septum). The Cube shape can be seen in the mouth (a cube when elongated turns to rectangular shape) and teeth. And, if your drawings have arms and a finger, that's a cylindrical shape, so take note that the upper and lower extremities are cylindrical.

How to render a Harry Potter with pencils:

Let's render Harry using different grades of pencil:

We will be using 4H, 2H, F, HB, 2B and 6B. This will be similar to how we rendered the Sphere, Cube, Cone, and Cylinder in our topic in "The Basic".

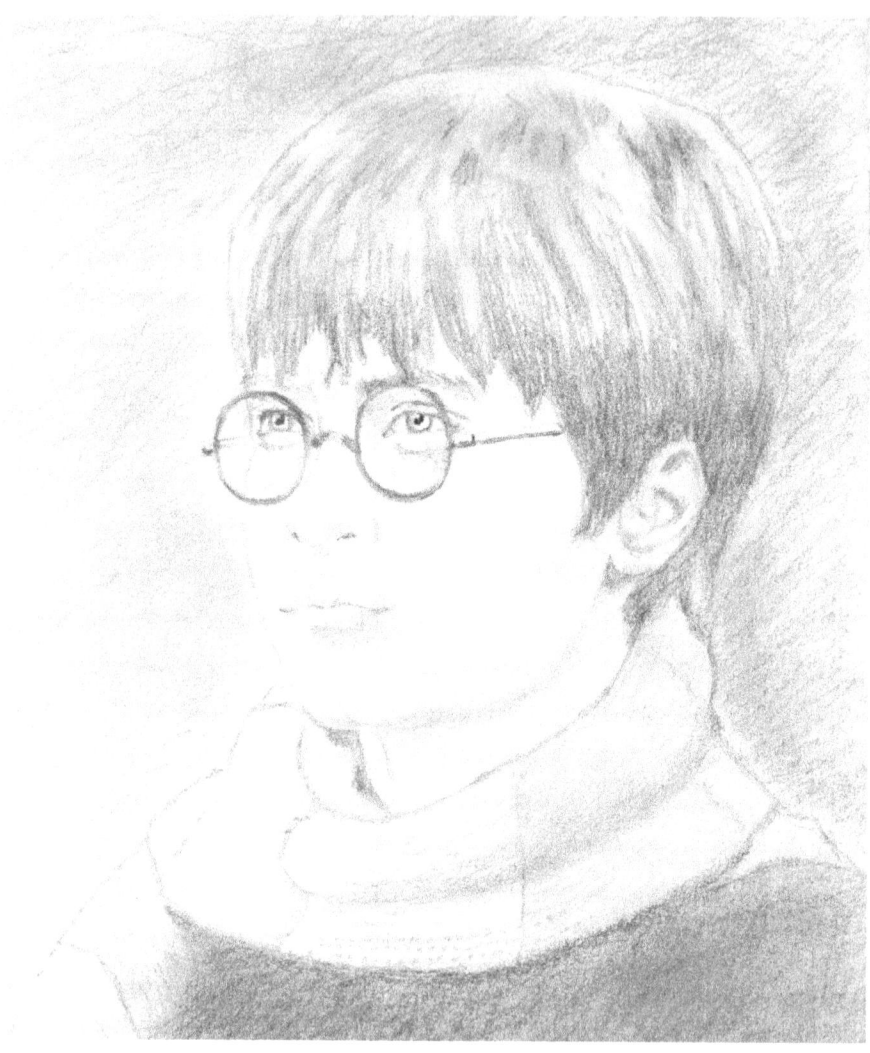

Scan the image below and print a copy using your printer. You may enlarge it to around 130-150%, as the larger is your work is, the better you can add details to it to make it realistic. Transfer or trace the image below to your working paper, or you may draw the image by using the Basic shapes. You can also use the method I mentioned earlier using Tracing Table or Light Table / Flexi-glass with Bendable Lamp , but be sure to include the important details.

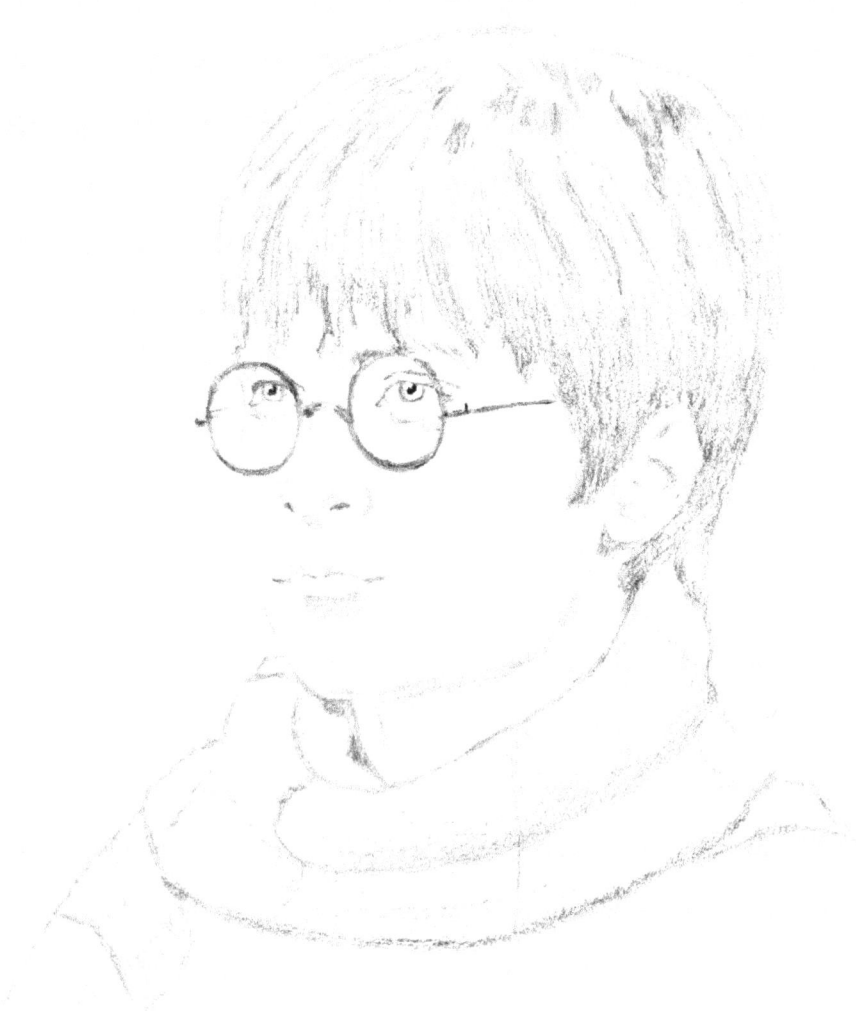

Steps:

1.   After you have transferred the image, begin by shading the darkest areas. Use 6B to shade the pupil of the eye and nostrils.

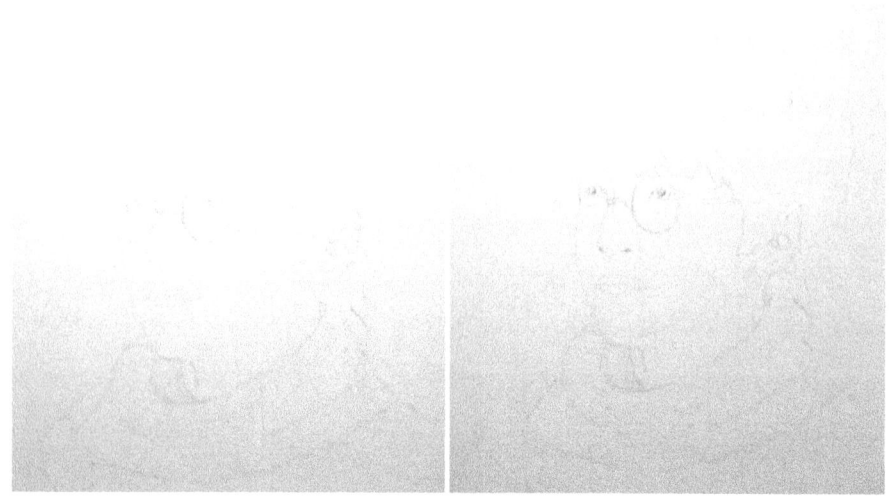

2.   Next is to shade the darker areas or the areas with cast shadows such as the area below the neck, under the lower lip, eyebrows, outline of the eyes, glasses, and the area behind the ear, with 2B.

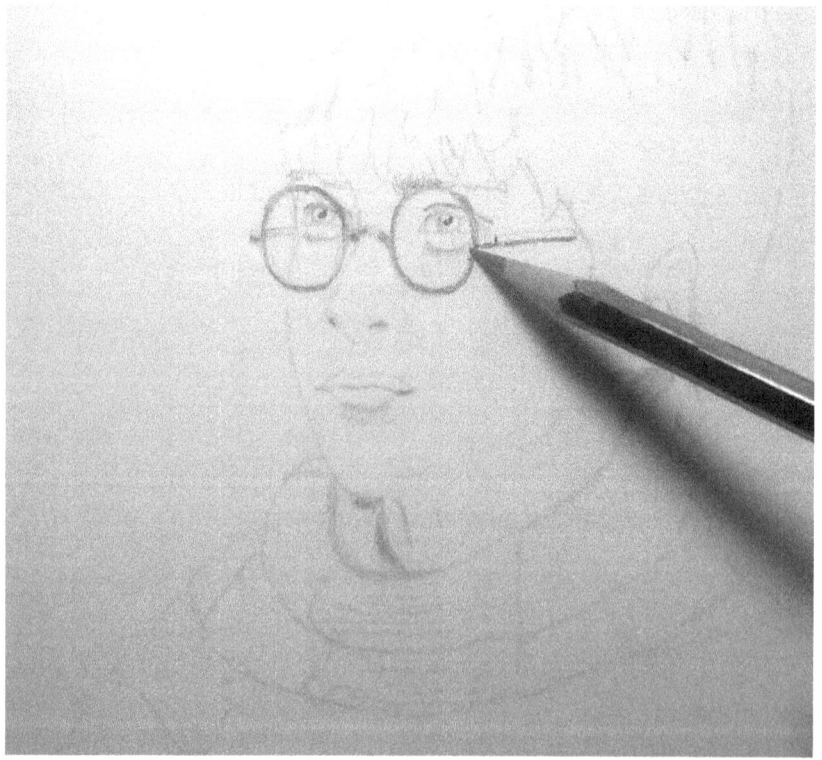

3.   Shade the area on the chin with F, as this is the area with a reflected light.

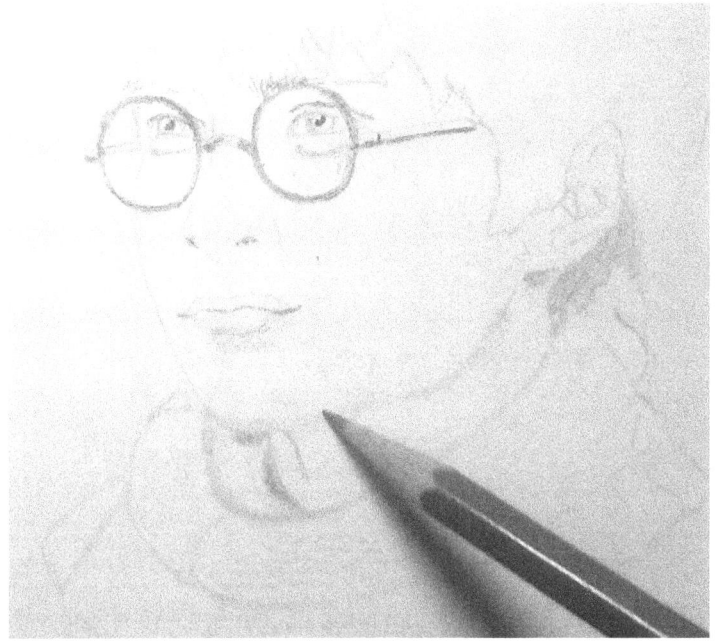

4.   Shade the darkened nose, ear, and neck areas (light shadow) with HB.

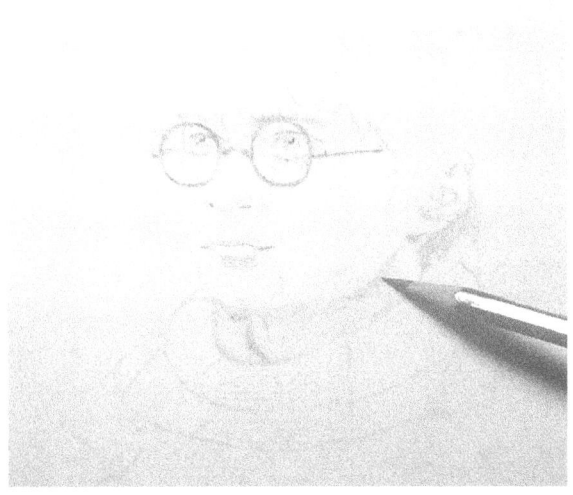

5.   Shade the entire face with 4H to tone it.

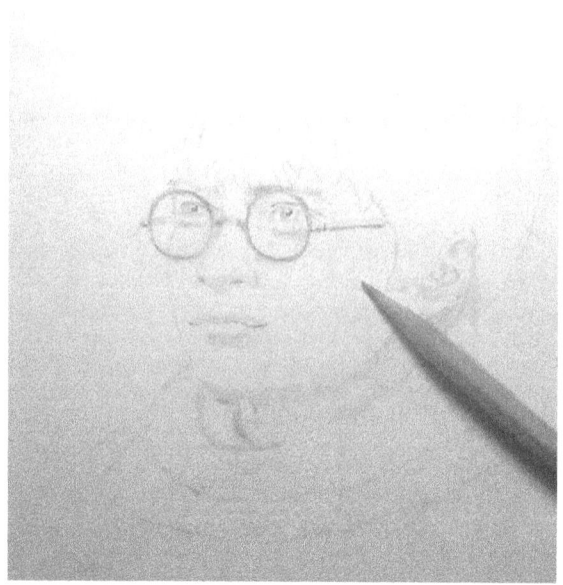

6.   Then shade 2H to create a transition of lighter to light tone value of the
      skin.

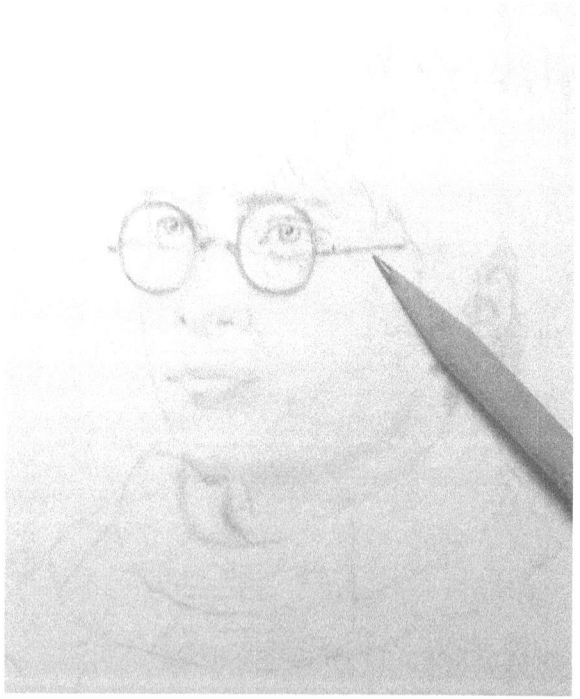

7.   Use your kneaded eraser to create the highlights or the white areas of the
      skin.

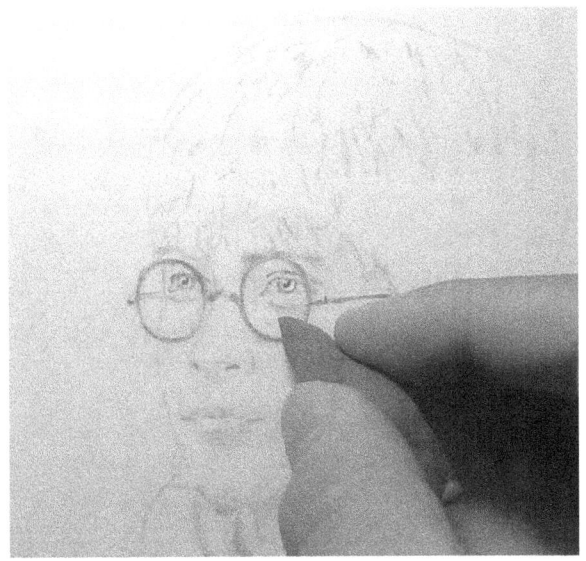

8. Begin shading the hair; bangs, the side, and back.

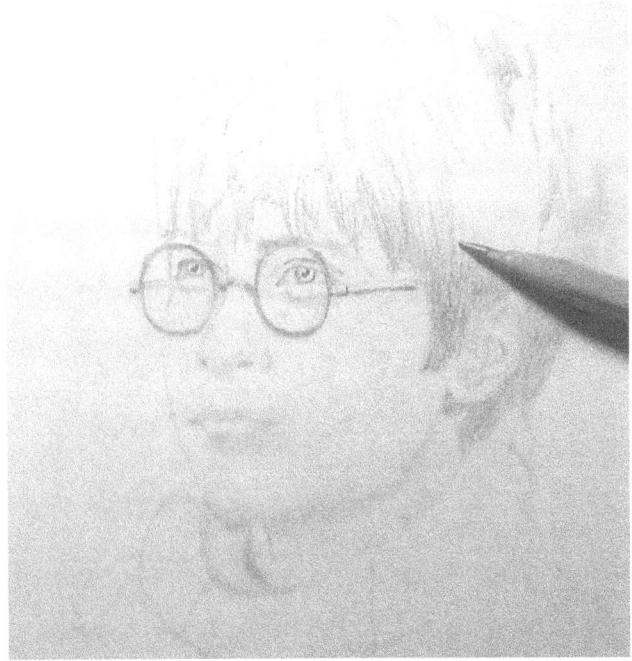

9. Continue filling the area, but leave some space for the highlights.

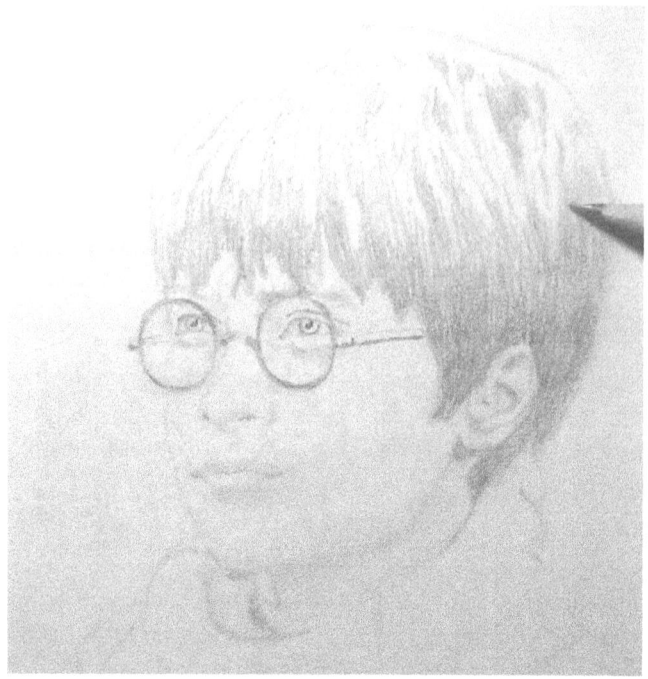

10.   Blend the top of the hair with cotton to tone the area.

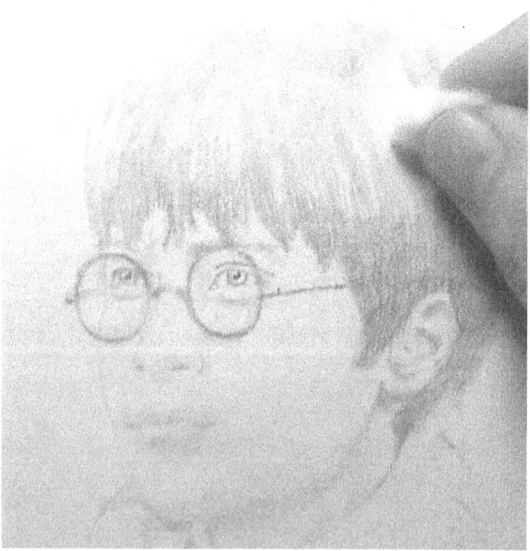

11.   Create the highlights using your kneaded eraser. Making it into the shape of a knife by pressing it side by side.

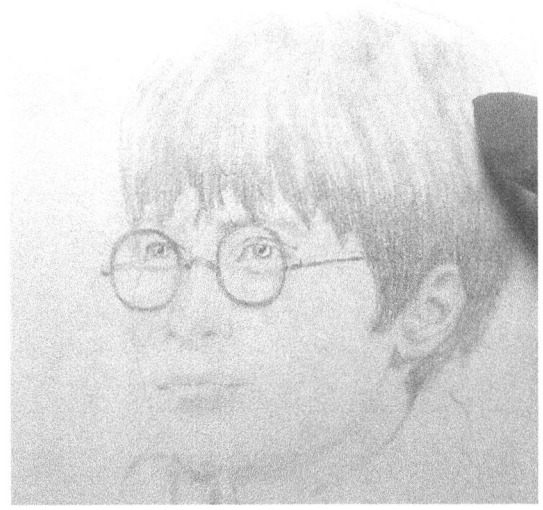

12.   Shade the knitted scarf with HB, and press harder when adding texture on the surface.

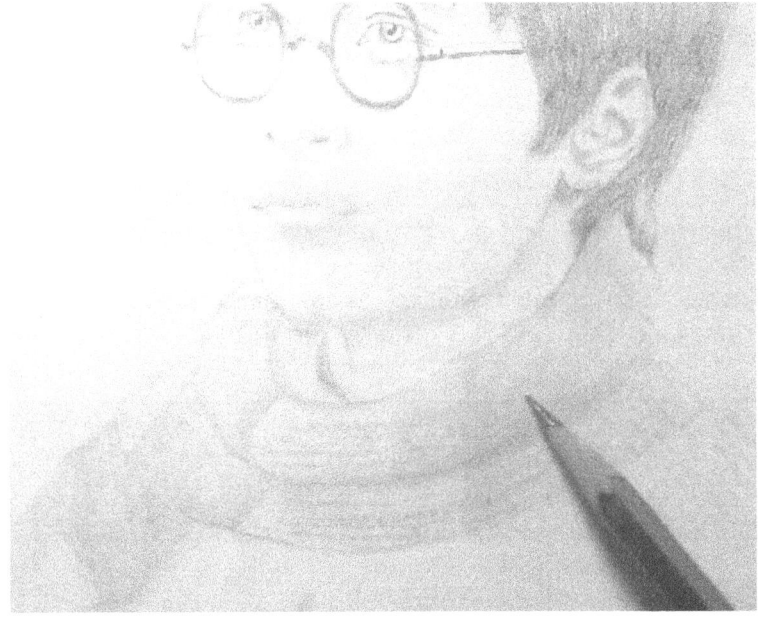

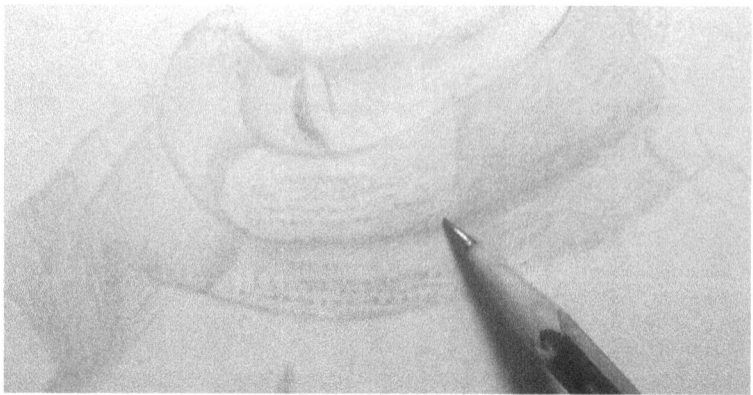

13.   Shade the uniform with 2B, below the scarf.

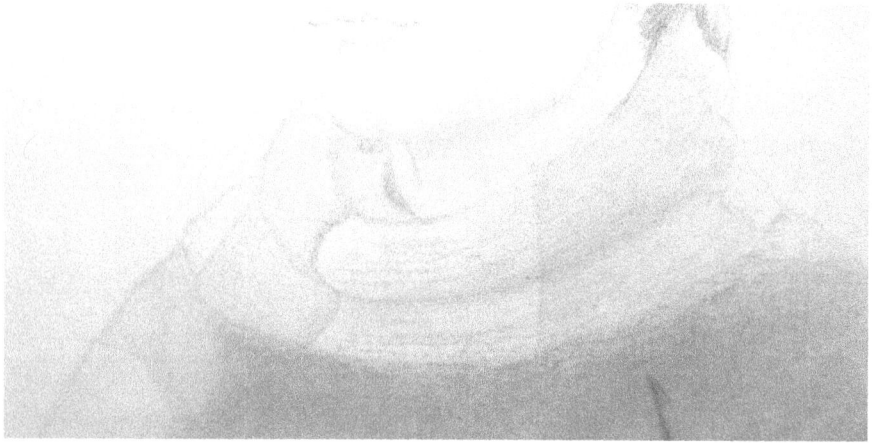

14.   Create the background with various cross-hatch strokes, using HB and
       2B pencils.

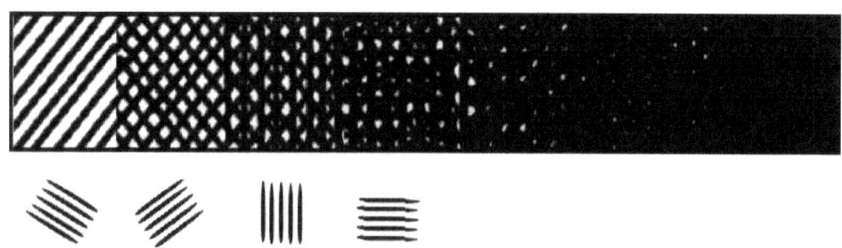

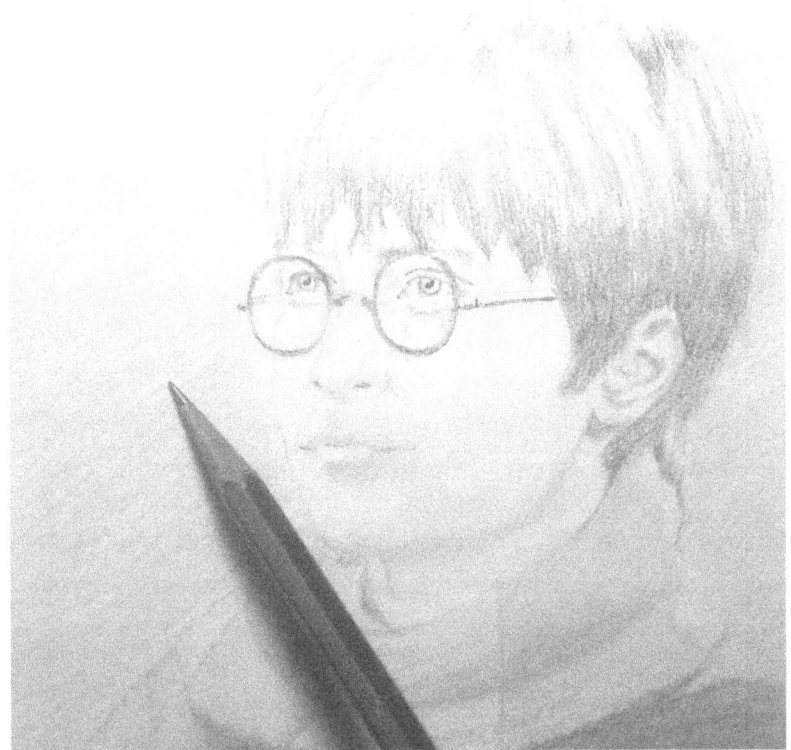

It's easy right? Before anything else, spray your work with Fixative spray. If you want to frame your work and hang it, it's up to you. Also, you might want to sign your signature on the bottom right corner, so that everyone will know that it's your work.

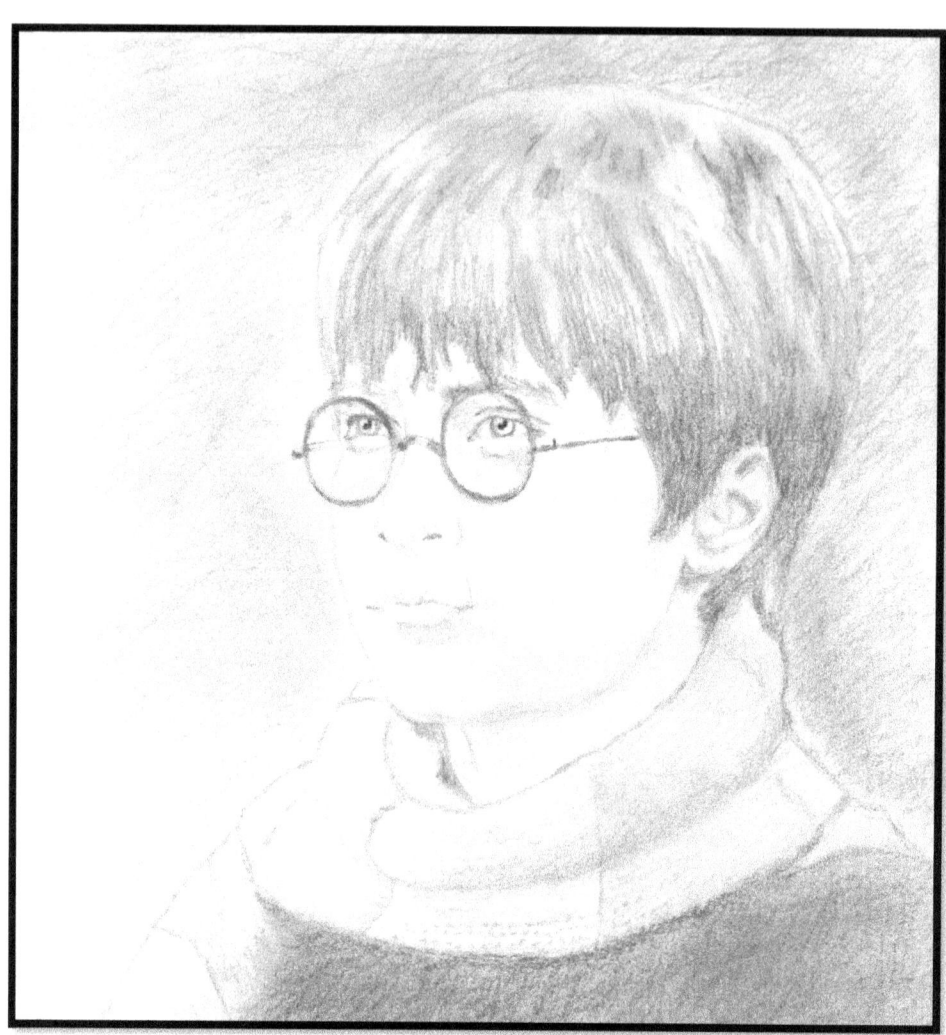

How to Draw a Horse

Below is a picture of the horse that we are going to draw.

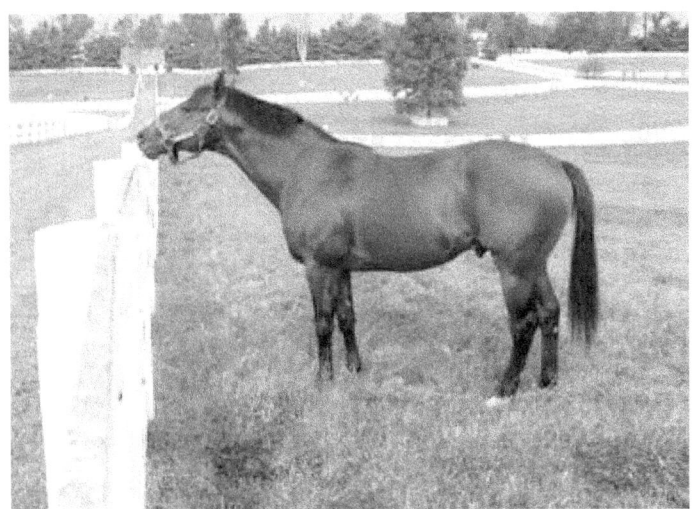

So, take your HB pencil, and let's draw this horse step-by-step.

Steps:

1. See thru the basic shapes: Sphere, Cube, Cone, and Cylinder on the horse.

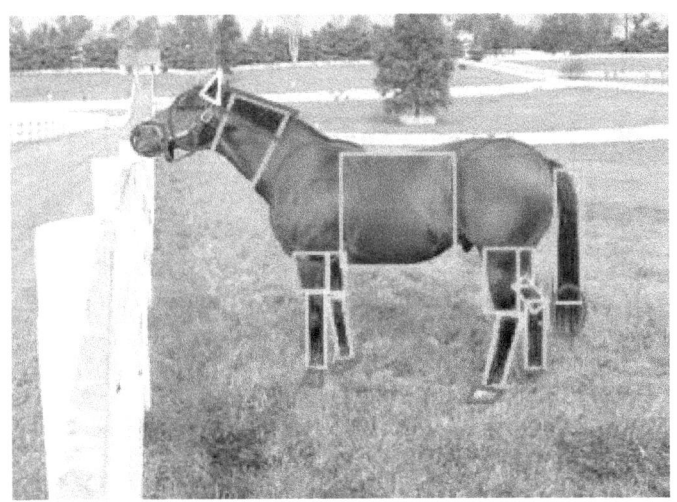

Legend: =Cone =Sphere =Cube/Rectangle

2. Now, draw these shapes on your paper.

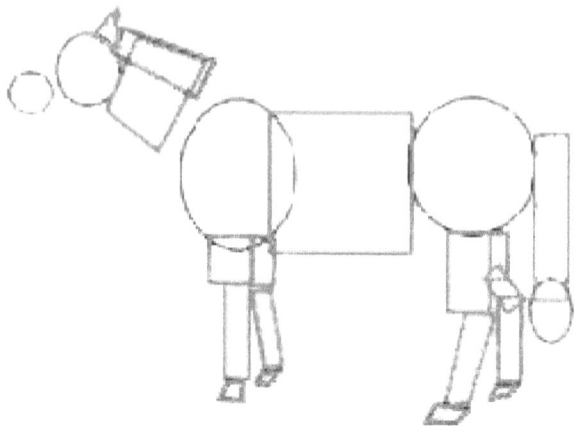

This will serve as the framework when you are building the parts of the horse.

3.   Draw lines that will connect the shape to other shapes, just like drawing a line when connecting dots.

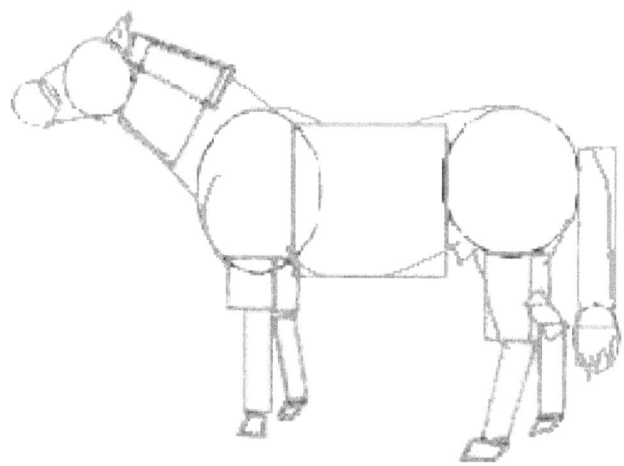

4.   Erase the excess of unwanted lines and shapes in your drawing, and continue to refine the outline of the horse.

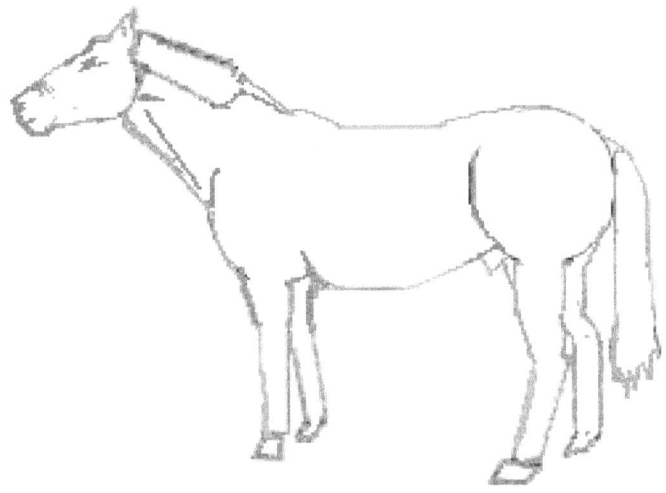

5.   Add the important details in the features such as the mane, the contour of the muscles, and the bit collar or head harness.

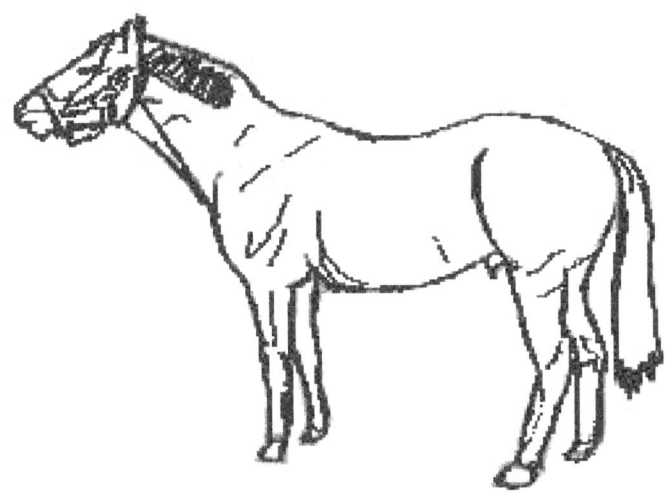

If you find this hard, just keep on practicing, and takes note of the angle of the lines, and the size of the shapes in relation to the other shapes, in order to have a good proportion.

Drawing Horses in Different Poses

The steps are the same as what we did above:

(a.)   Find the basic shapes and draw them as the base for your framework.

(b.)   Flesh out your drawing by connecting the lines from one shape to another.

(c.)   Erase the lines and shapes that are not needed, and then add more details to your drawing. Also consider shading the shadow.

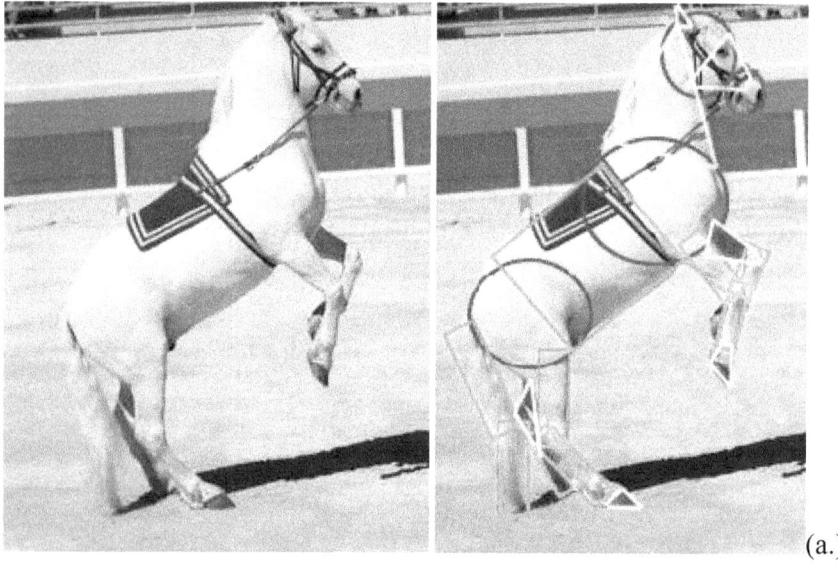

(a.)

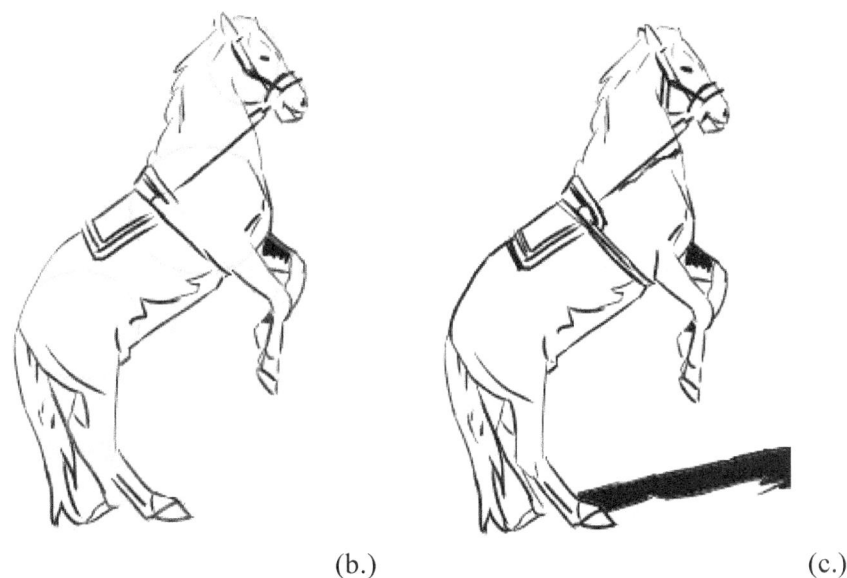

(b.)   (c.)

Let's try another one, but we're going to include the background:

So here, we have two subjects for you to draw:

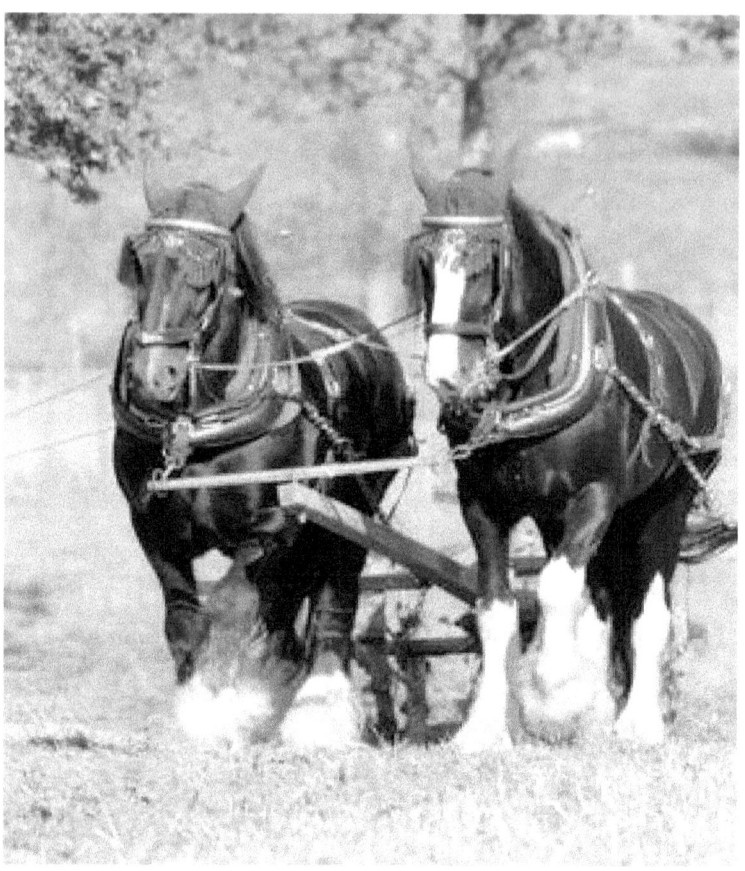

Find the basic shapes by starting with Spheres.

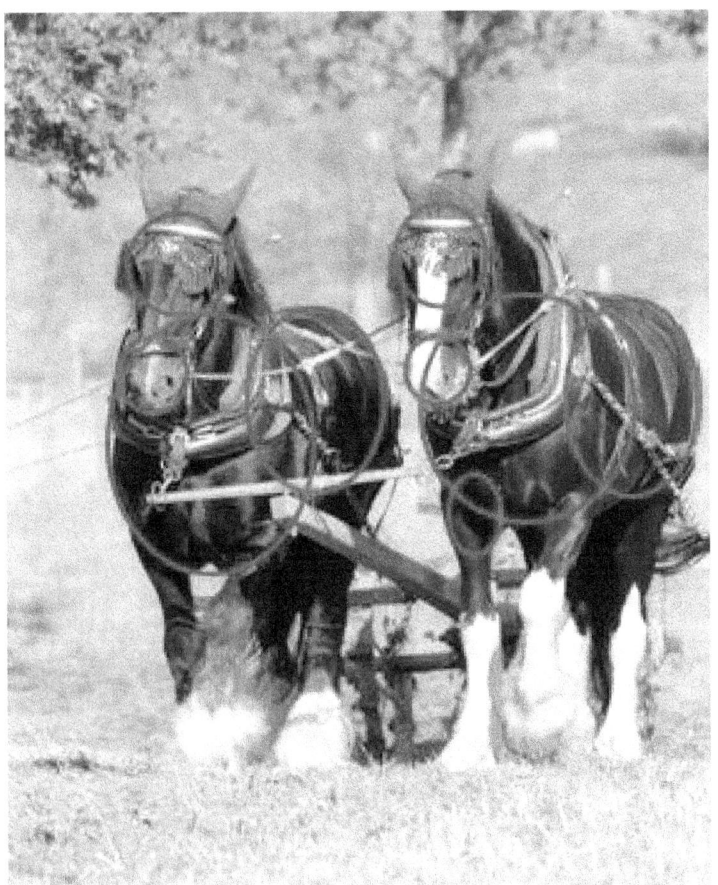

Next is to draw some cubes.

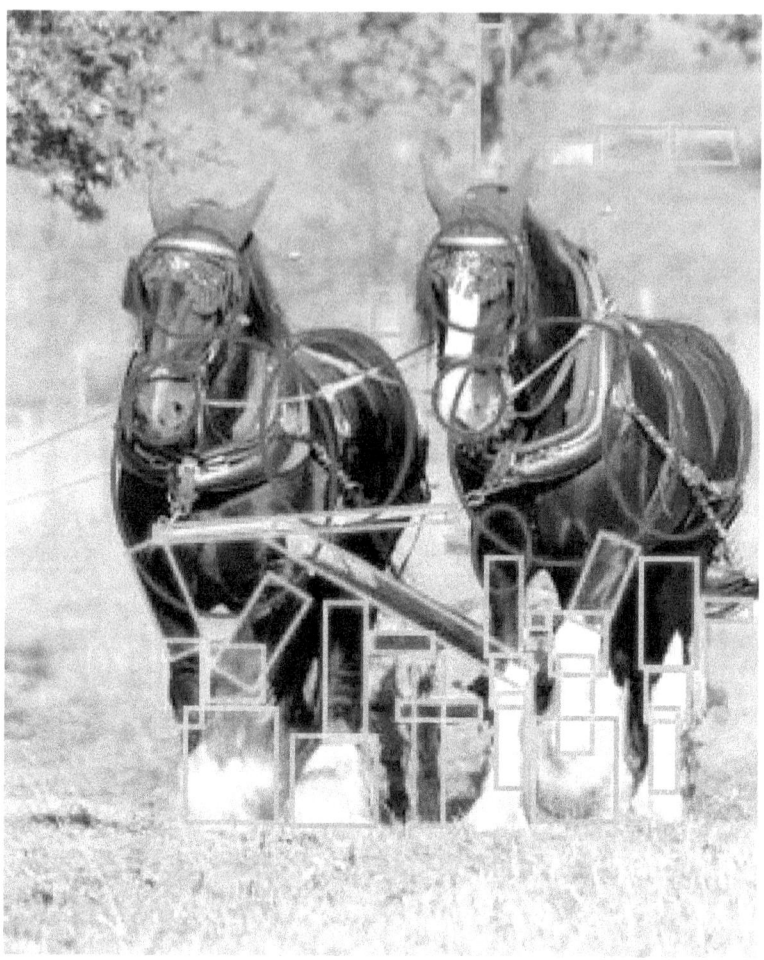

Then draw the cones. In the picture, I also included lines and some foliage of the tree with a Blue color.

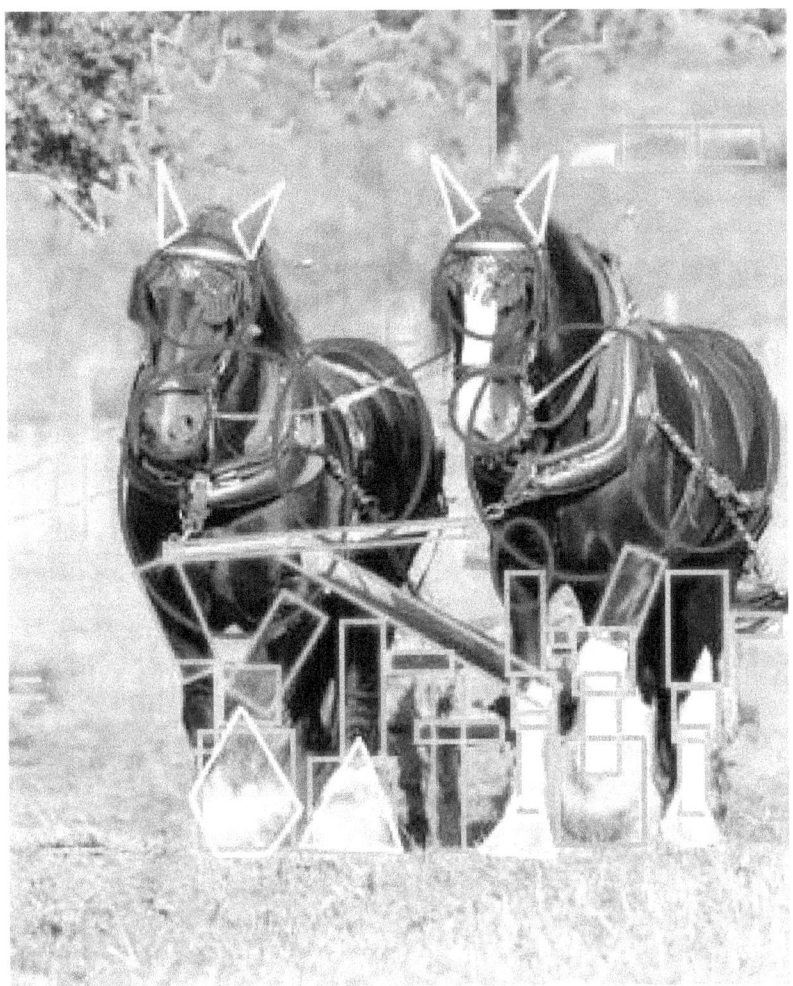

Now, draw the outline of the horses and also include the background.

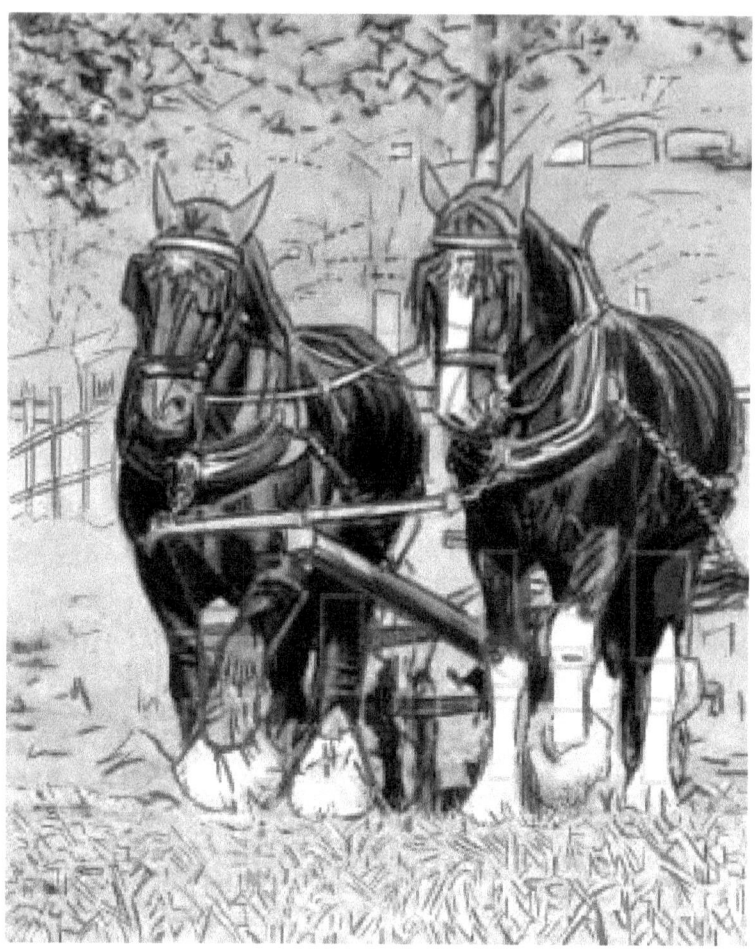

Erase the unwanted lines, and also make your work clean. You may make some adjustments on your strokes to have thick and thin lines, and also vary your pressure by applying heavy pressure on the subject and light pressure on other areas. In my example below, I drew the outline similar to what you see in some Graphics comic books, as if it was done with ink. You can render it with your own style if you want.

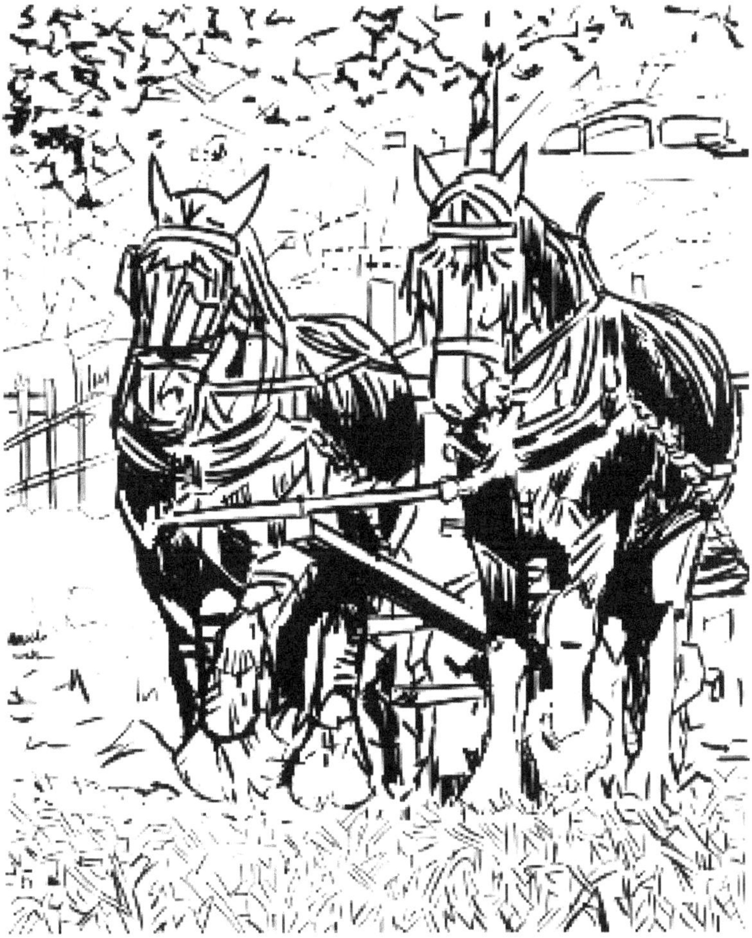

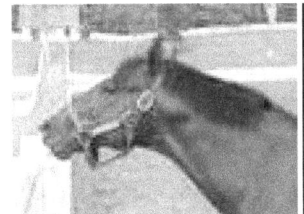

Tips:

- See through the shapes, including the negative of the image, as well as the positive, to help you visualize the shapes.

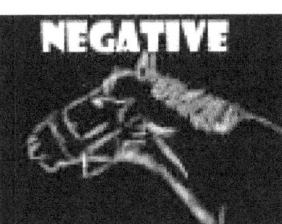
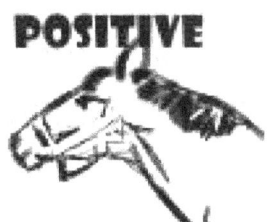

- Practice sketching basic shapes and making outlines, and it will help you improve your strokes and hand coordination. It can also give you confidence in your work.

- If you find it hard to get the right distance and sizes of the shapes, you can use a Ruler and Templates to draw accurately.

How to Render a Horse with Pencils

Let's render this running white horse using different grades of pencils.

We will be using 4H, 2H, F, HB, 2B, and 6B, similar to how we rendered the Sphere, Cube, Cone, and Cylinder in our topic in "The Basic".

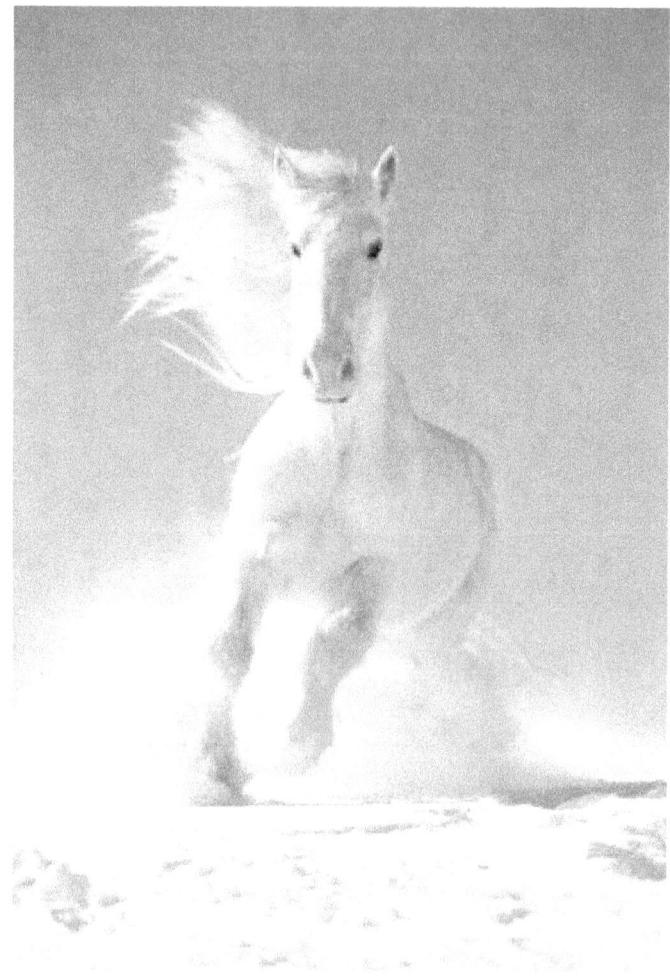

Scan the image below, and print a copy using your printer. You may enlarge it to around 130-150%, as the larger your work is, the better you can add details to it to make it realistic. Transfer or trace the image below to your working paper, or you may draw the image by using the Basic shapes, as we did with the horse in

"How to Draw a Horse:" You can use a projector, tracing table or the method I mention earlier, just be sure to include important details.

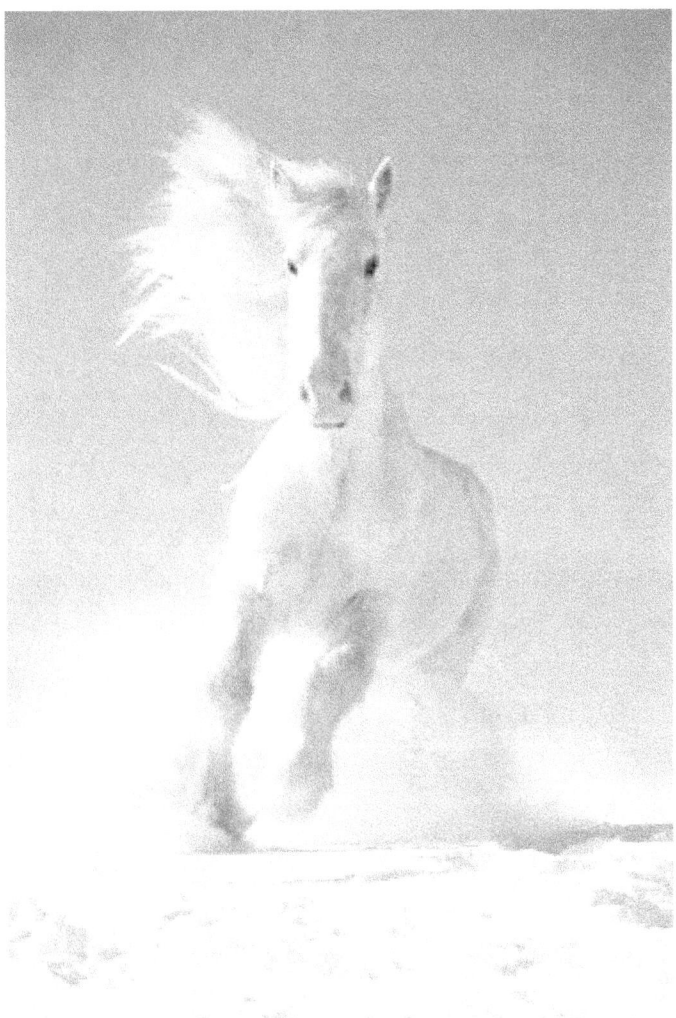

Steps:

1.   After transferring the image to your paper or board, darken the very dark parts of the drawing with 6B, and in our case, this will be the eyes and mouth.

2.   Shade the shadows with 2B: face, knees, back, and on the ground.

3. Next, using your HB pencil, shade the midtone areas of the drawing in order to give your drawing dimension and mass.

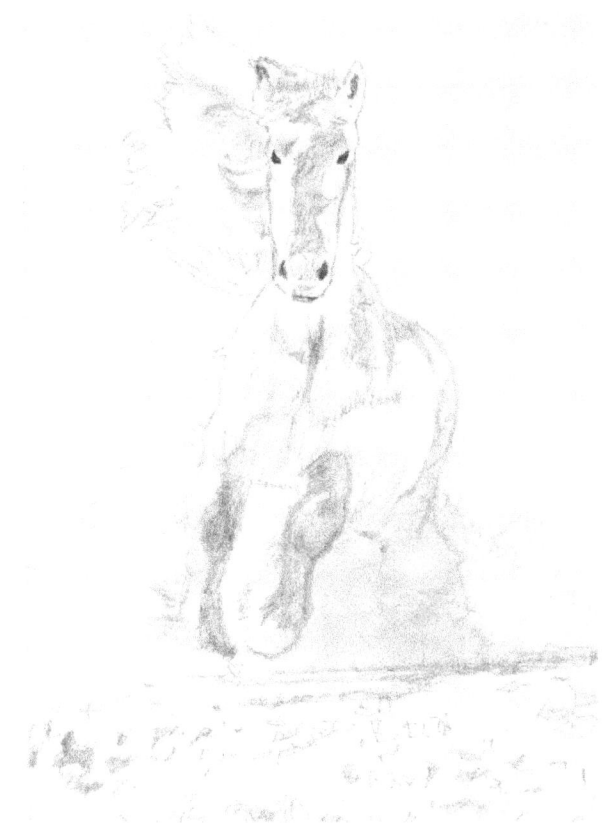

-Even toned areas can be achieved by first shading the area with a pencil and then blending it with a Tortillon/make up applicator/cotton swab.

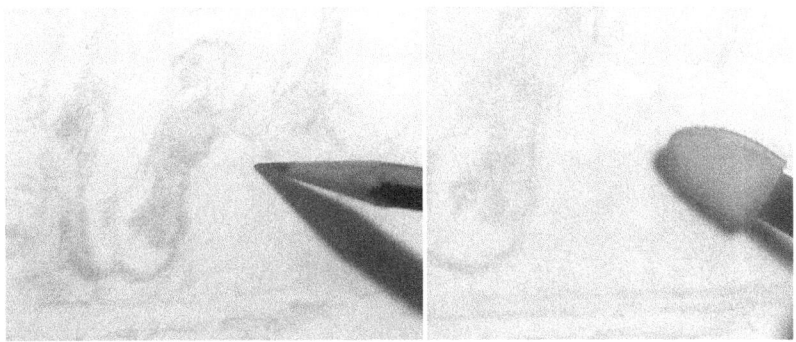

4.   Now, using your 4H (your lightest pencil) pencil, shade the background horizontally.

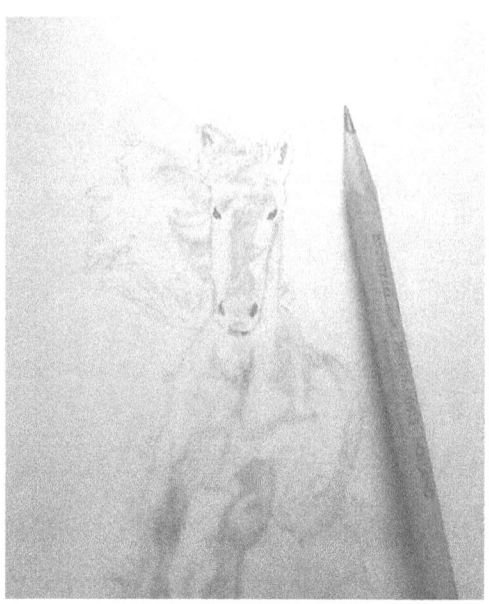

5. Next is to use the 2H (slightly darker than 4H) pencil on the background, especially on the top.

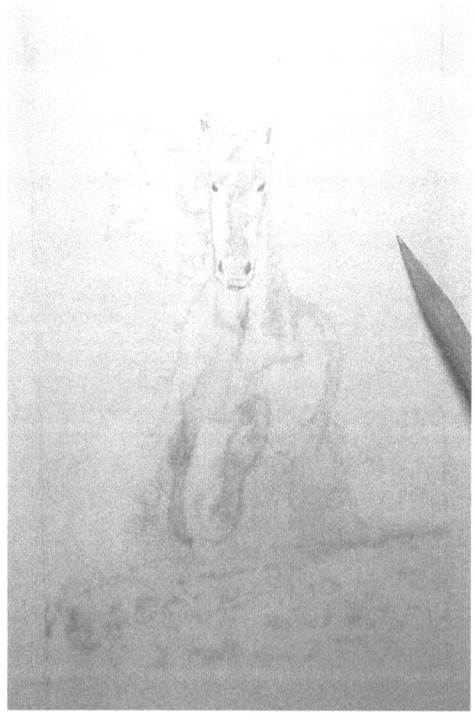

6.   Use your electric eraser to create the mane on the left side and the highlights, making the white of the paper show.

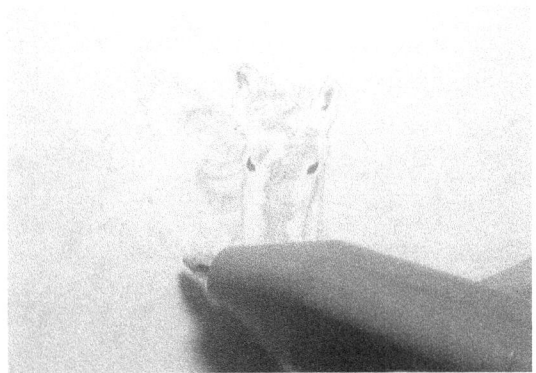

7.   Check your work, and if it needs dark tones, add more or if it's too dark, lighten the areas using your soft or kneaded eraser.

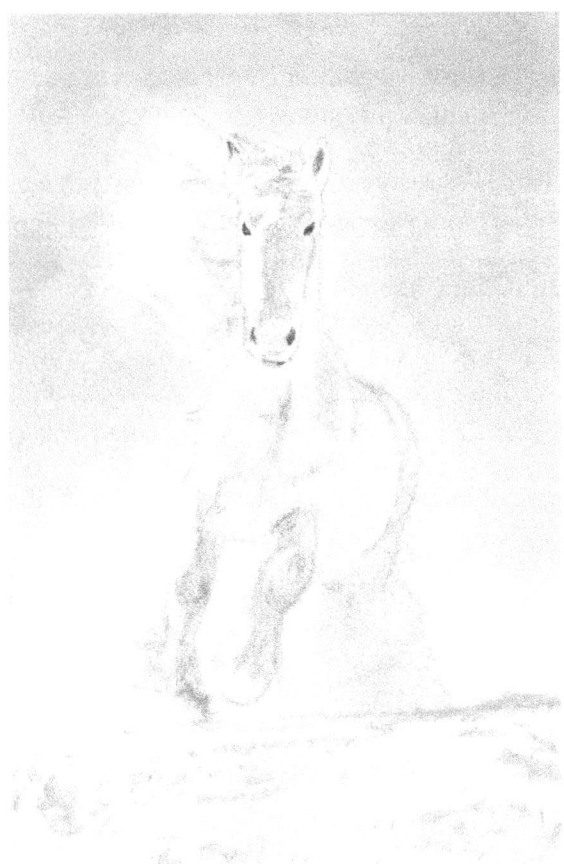

Charcoal Painting

- ### Shaving the Charcoal

So, before I teach you how to render using Charcoal, let me show you how to shave the Charcoal using a cutter.

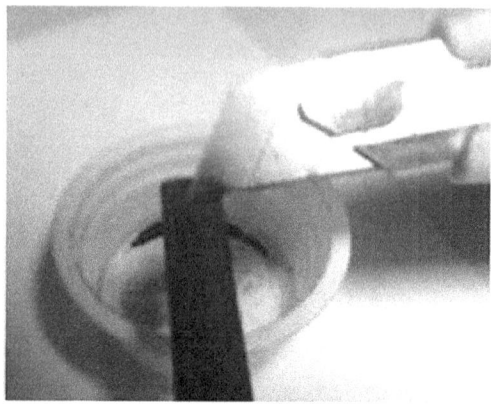

Shave your Charcoal using a one-way direction of strokes, and place it over your container or cup to accumulate the dust or powder to use.

Now we have a Charcoal dust and we're ready to begin. Let's copy the outline of the sphere from our previous exercise or make a new sphere for this exercise.

- ### Rendering Using Charcoal

Charcoal is similar to pencils, but there is a difference in terms shading. You're going to use a brush to fill the values (more area coverage), unlike using a pencil, which you have to make a lot of strokes to fill a specific area.

And Charcoal has a darker value compared to Pencil, even with various ranges of tones. Charcoal also has a matte texture, unlike Pencil which is Glossy in texture.

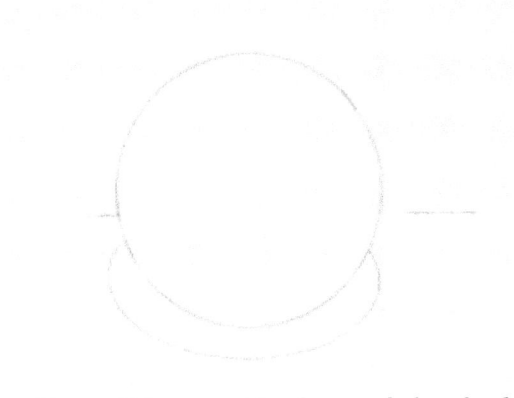

Draw a light circle inside the sphere. This will be our guide when rendering the shadow.

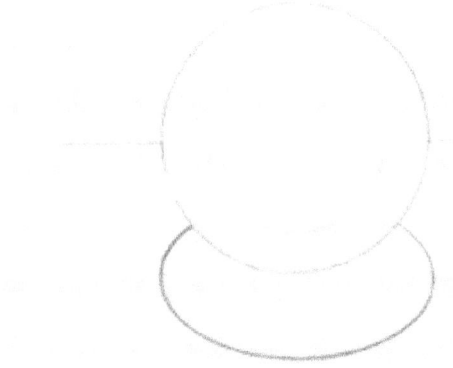

Let's use the Soft Charcoal, which has the darkest tone, to the cast shadow. Use your Small Flat Brush and fill the area with enough pressure to make a tone. The stroke should be the same when shading with Pencil or Tortillon.

Note: Tap your brush 2-3 times in the container to remove excess Charcoal dust in your brush, before applying it in your working paper.

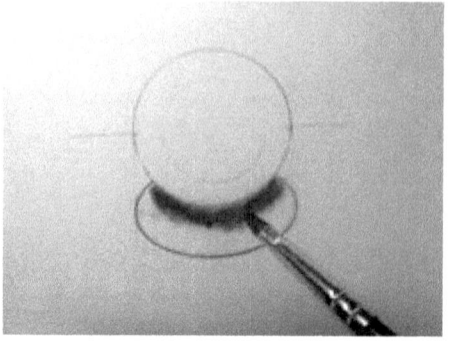 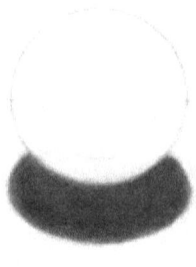

Next, we're going to render the shadow. Use your Small Round Brush and with dabbing strokes, fill the area in a circular motion going up.

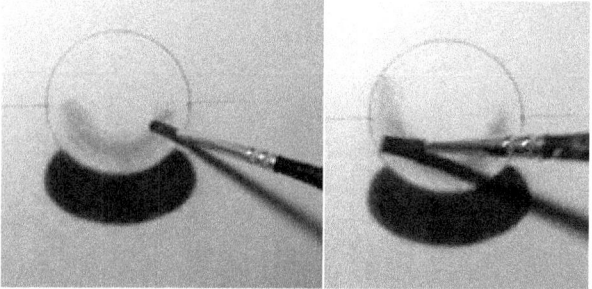

Then it's time to focus on the reflected light. Get your kneaded eraser and mold it to a point, and lightly erase some of the tone in a circular motion; enough to have a reflected light tone.

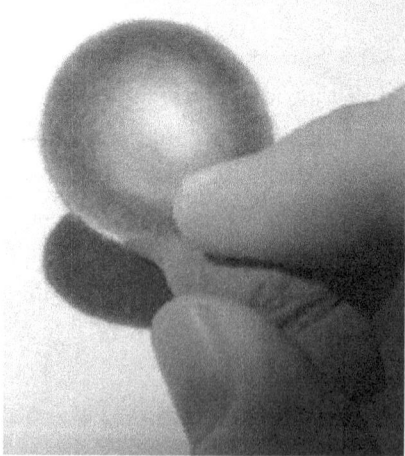

Erase the Charcoal dust outside the Sphere, and also clean your work using the dusting brush.

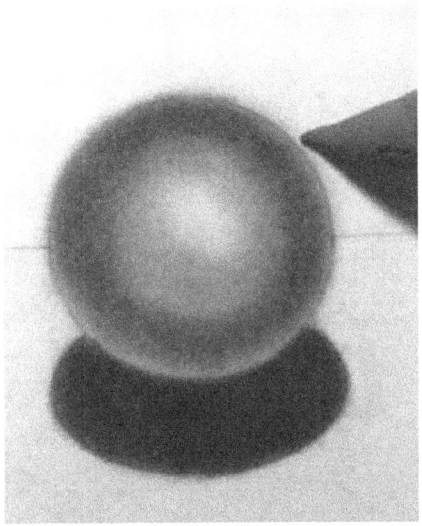

Time to render the ground where our sphere is placed. Use your Small Round Brush and dabb some Medium Charcoal beside the sphere and fill the area.

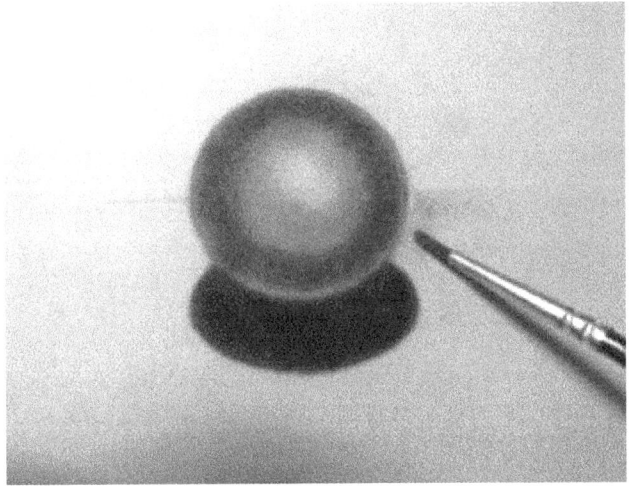

Add the highlights by lifting some tones using your kneaded eraser.

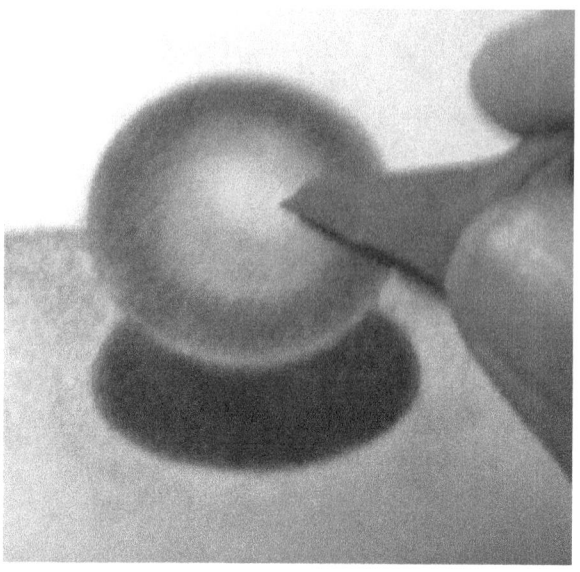

We just rendered a Sphere using Charcoal.-"FANTASTIC!"

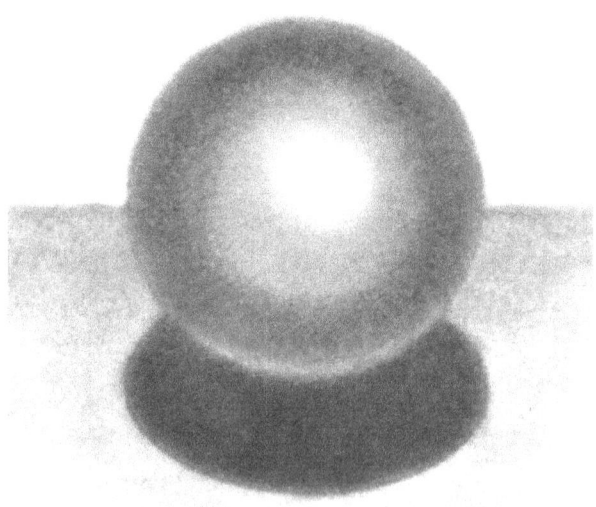

As you can see in the illustration, this is how you will likely render portraits. Shadows depend on the source of lights. Your very own observation of shadows, from their respective shapes, will help you in your drawing when trying to achieve realism. Remember that the value of tones changes as the object moves away the light.

Tips to Remember

- You must have a clear copy or photograph of your subject.

- Practice sketching simple basic shapes and it will help you improve your strokes and good hand coordination, as well as give you confidence in your work.

- Sometimes some parts in the photograph are blurred and it's hard to distinguish, so in that case, use your imagination.

- It's not a bad idea to pick up some magazines and newspapers to find a picture you want to draw, and also that interests you, for practice.

- Secure yourself a good lighting source when drawing.

- Watch the proportion of shapes to other shapes in a picture.

- Remember different textures have different techniques or strokes that you need imitate when drawing.

- If you find some parts of the face and other parts of the body difficult to draw, break it down to smaller components.

- It helps if you have a reference or a photograph handy, so that you will have a guide when drawing and shading. Especially if your confused of the shadows and cast shadow in your drawing.

- If you're having issues with smudges or fingerprints, caused by the oil from your hand, on your work, you can prevent this by placing an extra sheet of paper under your working hand, specifically the side of your palm.

- Constant practice drawing and rendering will for sure make you succeed.

Rendering the Horse in Charcoal

Transfer the image below to your paper or board.

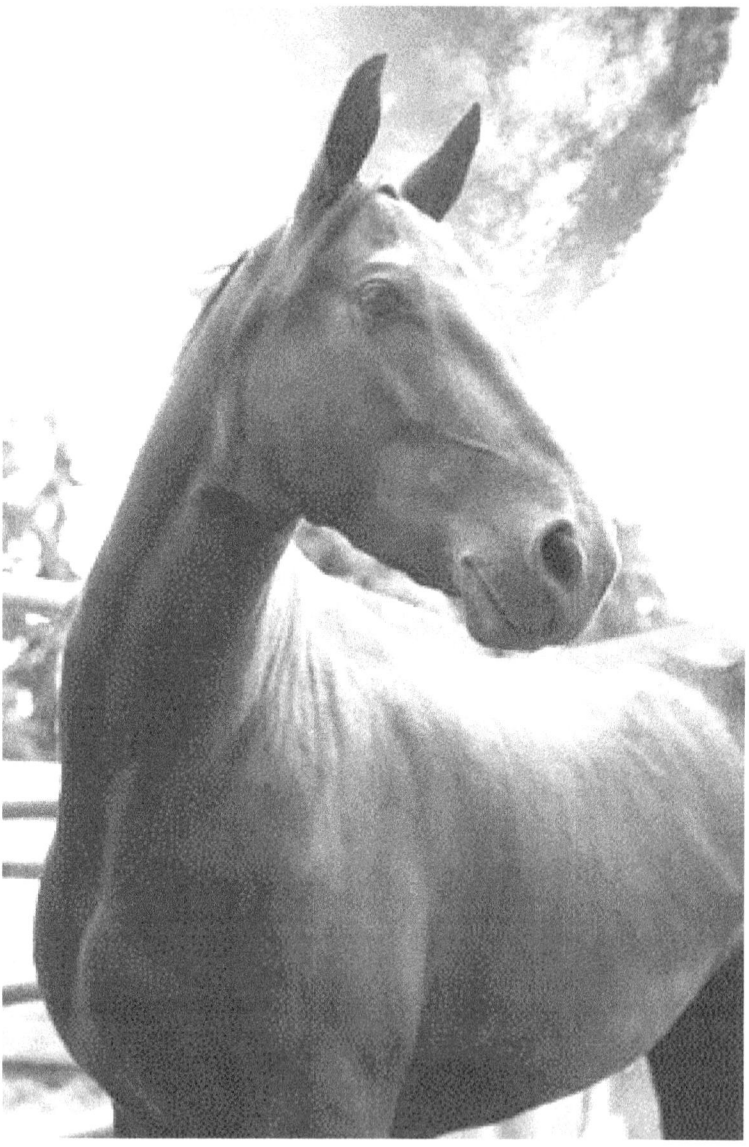

Steps:

1. After transferring the image, erase the hard lines, but be careful not to ruin your paper.

2.	Using your Soft charcoal pencil, darken the accents, like in the nostril and the dark line on the top of the head.

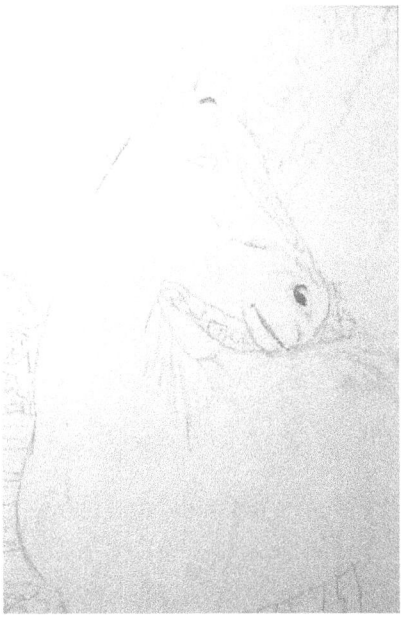

3.	Darken the shadow on the ear and neck with Medium charcoal shavings, using your flat brush.

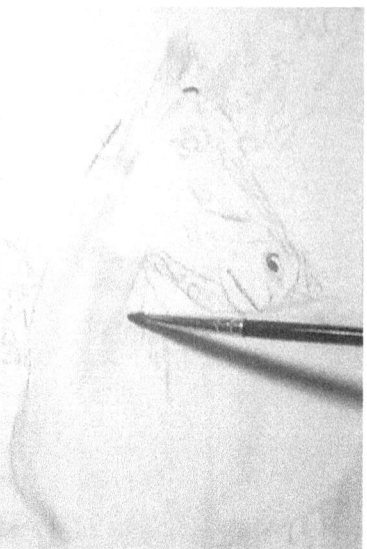

4. Now, to make an even tone with this charcoal, use a round brush and apply it with dabbing strokes. Also, apply tones to the background.

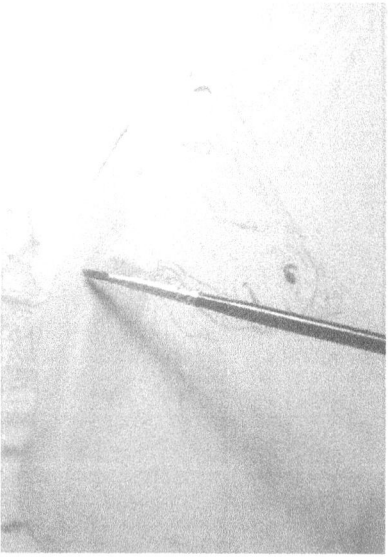

5. Do the same on the rest of the body, darkening the shadows.

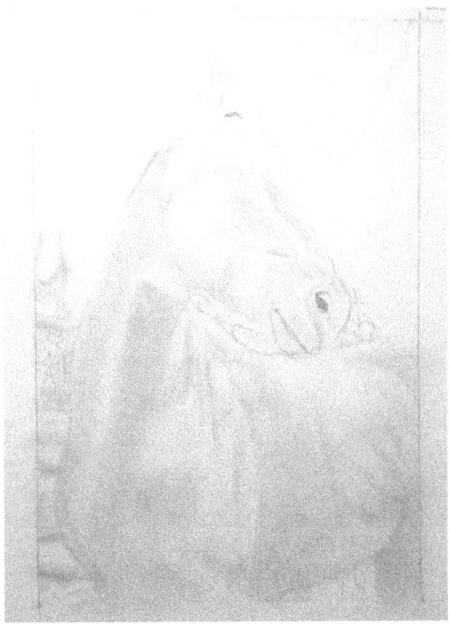

6.   Define and add details on the ears using the round brush, and add another layer of shaved Medium charcoal.

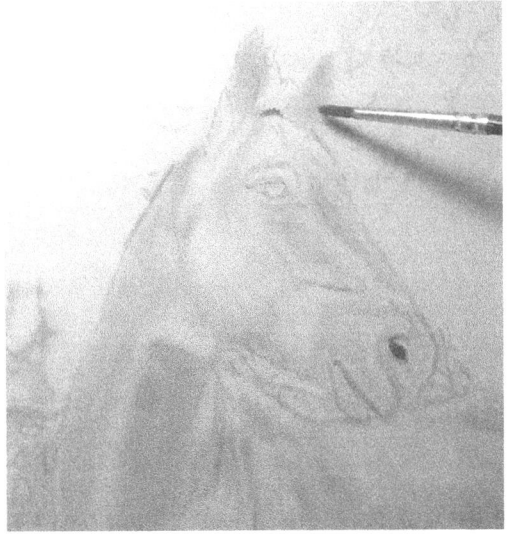

7.   Create highlights on the ear.

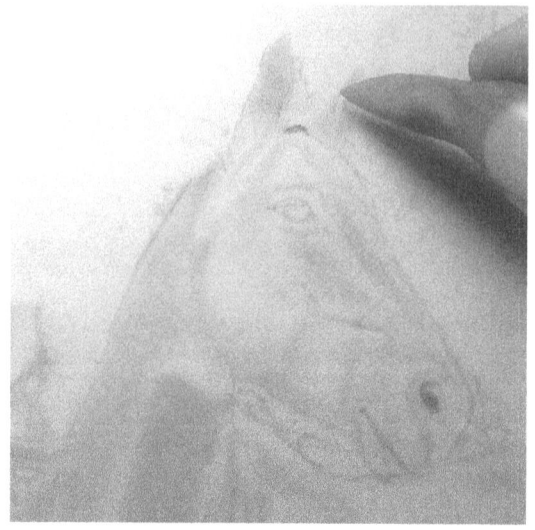

8.   Darken the outline of the ear with a Medium charcoal pencil.

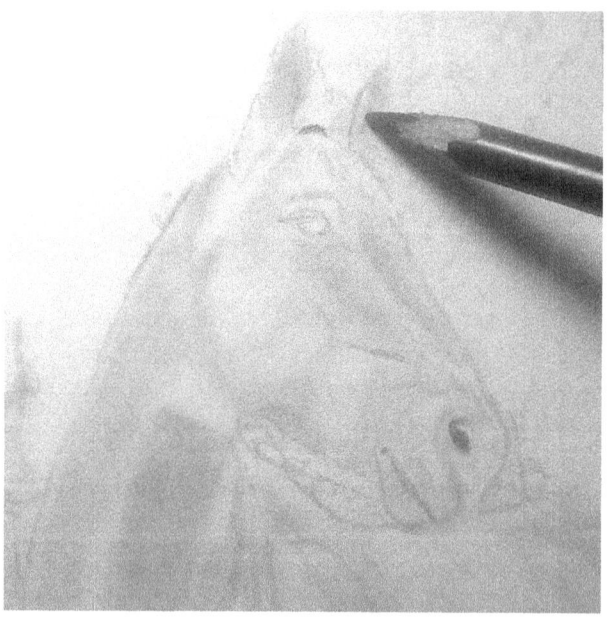

9.   Next is to add details on the eyes, using this charcoal pencil.

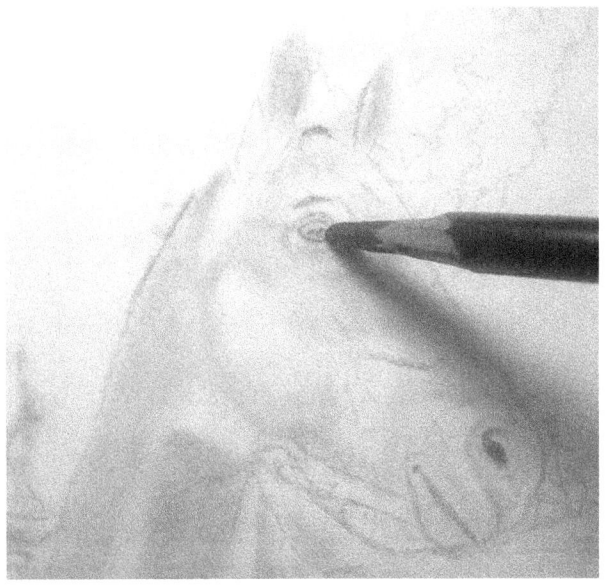

10. Continue to add details such as the wrinkles on the back and other fine lines. Also, start adding tones to the sky on the upper right.

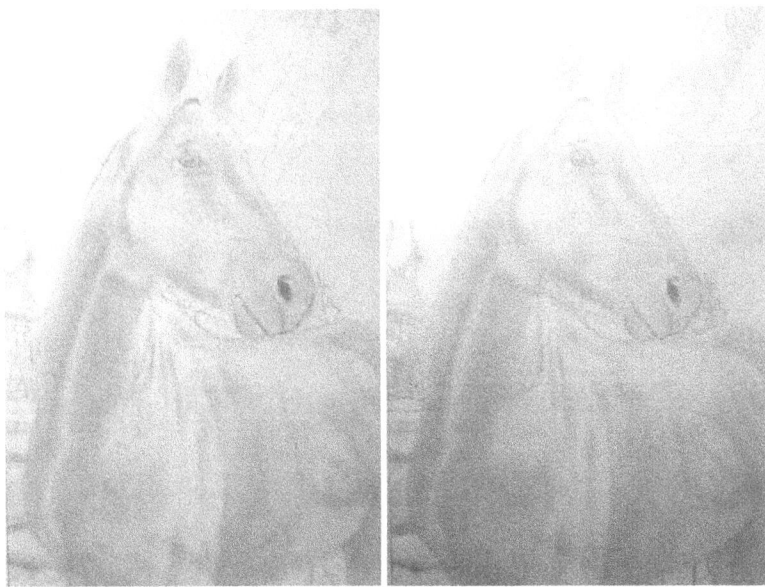

11. Create the cloud effect using the electric eraser.

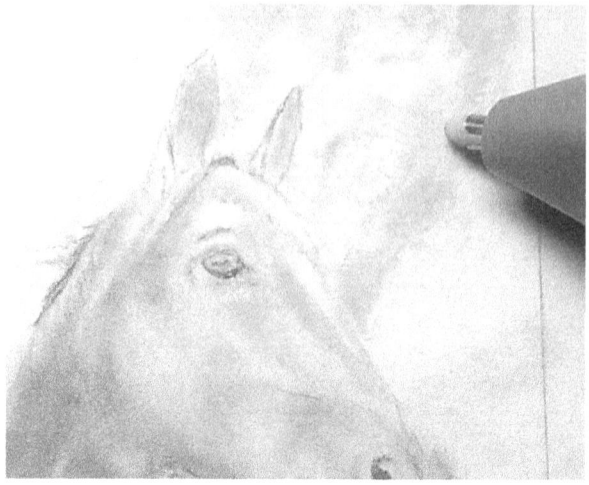

12. Apply a last coat of shaved Soft Charcoal, to darken the tone of the horse.

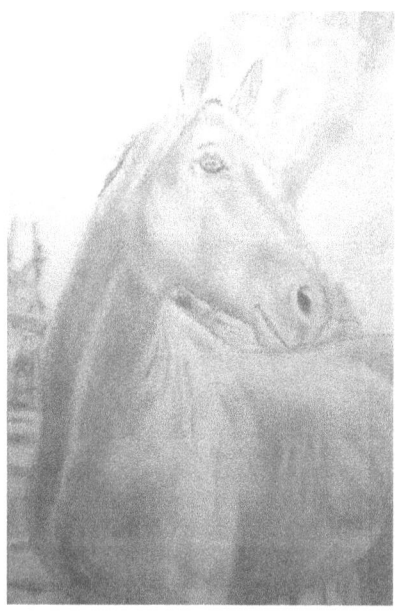

13. Finish the rest of the details, especially the highlights, using your kneaded eraser. Make your eraser shaped like a knife by pressing it on both sides and shaping it thinly. Then apply it to the area with single strokes. For the catch light, just shape your kneaded eraser like a needle, by rolling it and shaping the tip like a pin, then apply it by picking up the tone. Check your work for any needed corrections. If you need to darken

a tone, apply another coat, and if you find it too dark, lightly pick up the tone, carefully, with your kneaded eraser.

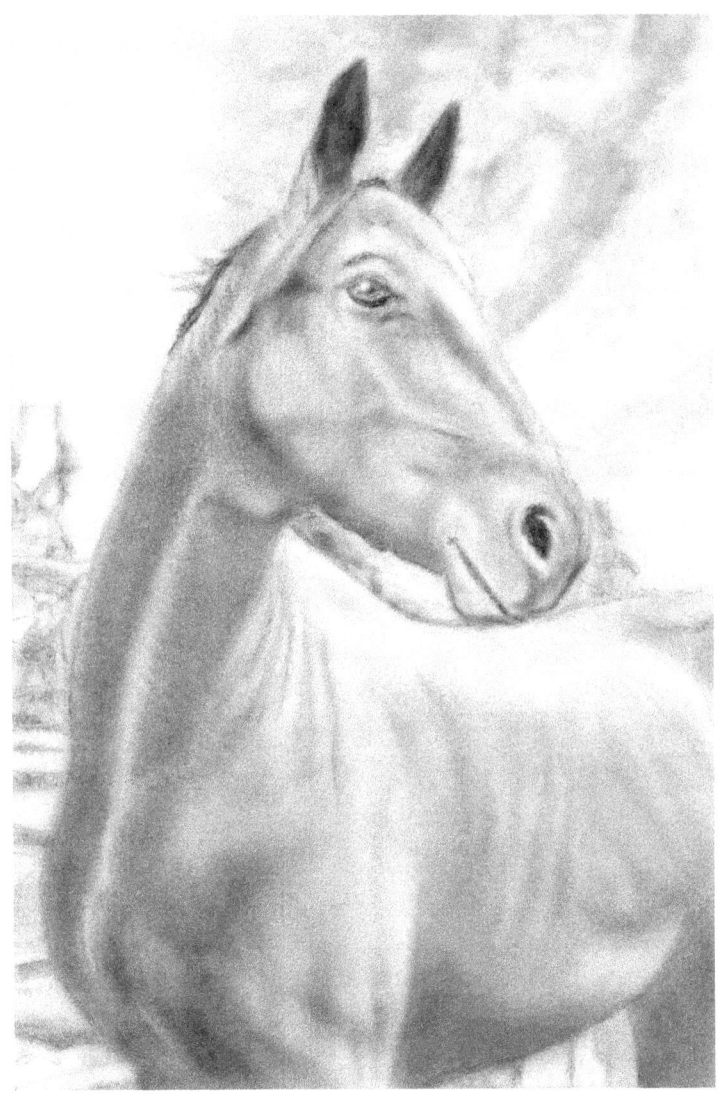

Drawing Materials

Pencils

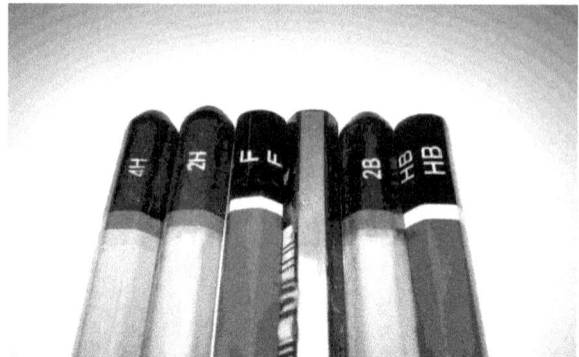

The most important tool, made from Graphite with a mixture of Clay, soft pencils like B have little amount of clay or not at all, used for outlining and giving texture to your drawing, comes in different scales: H(Hard), F, HB, and B(Soft) varying grades like 9H(lightest)to 9B(darkest)range.

For our drawings we need the following: 4H, 2H, F, HB, 2B and 6B, but if you're short of supplies, you can use HB only, just apply pressure when you want a darker tone and light pressure for light tone.

Mechanical Pencils

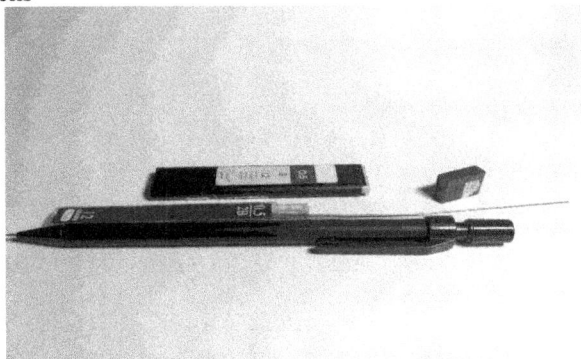

Like Pencils the lead is also made of Graphite, Good for details, come in handy especially for tight areas, the difference is it doesn't need a sharpener if the lead breaks, just press the cap on the end of the pencil and it's good to go, it comes in different sizes: 0.2mm to 5.6mm, for our drawing 0.5 will just be suffice.

Charcoal

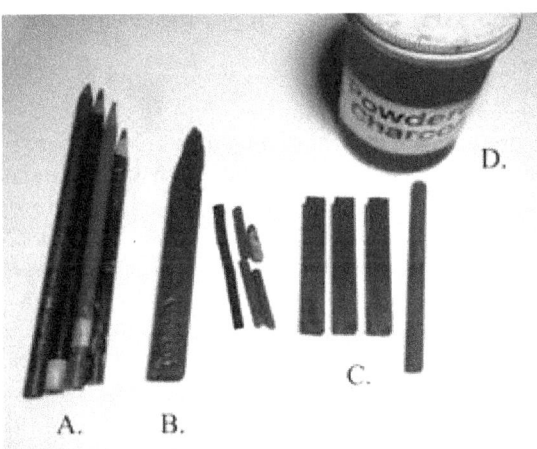

Said to be the oldest medium for drawing, use by Art Masters all over the world, and when smudge can create wonderful effects.

A. Charcoal pencils-Comes in different range: Hard, Medium and Soft, good for giving details in any charcoal work.

B. Vine Charcoal- They also comes in different range and also sizes, you can apply it directly or shave it with your cutter and use the accumulated dust in your working paper.

C. Compress Charcoals- The same as other charcoal, with different range and in shapes, available in bar or cylindrical shape, they have more darker tone and can easily adhere to any drawing paper.

D. Powder Charcoal-They comes in cans or plastic bottles, very fine and useful for any charcoal work specially for toning, can also be use for transferring your drawing or outlines to working paper.

Brushes

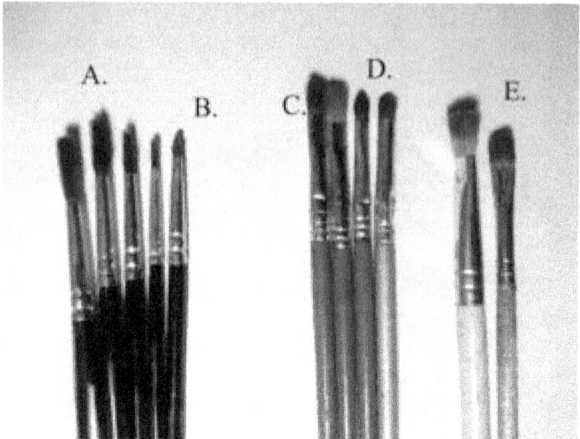

They come in natural and synthetic, natural brush was taken from animal hair: squirrel, weasel, Pony and other land mammals. While synthetic brush is made of synthetic fibers like Nylon. Advantage of synthetic brush includes, less deterioration in terms of time and easy to clean.

For our works, we're going to use the following:

A. Rounded Nylon Brush- Use when applying a light pressure of Charcoal tone that has soft edges. Choose a fine kind of this brush and since sizes varies depending to the manufacturers, just get a brush that have these following width in my case it .2cm width-that would be my small brush, for my med-size brush it measure .3cm, and for the large one it's almost.5cm. You can add another range of brush to have variety of sizes. I seen other artist uses sizes with even numbers-0,2,4,6,8,10 and 12, so see what works for you.

B. Flat Nylon Brush- Use it to apply darker tone and hard edges, usually use when doing aggressive strokes. For the sizes you can use the even numbers to get different kinds of range. In my case, I used no.4 flat Nylon brush mostly on my works.

C. Large Flat Nylon Brush (long handle) - Used for areas that need dark tones.

D. Old Used Brushes- Used as scrubbers, when we need to achieve specific dark tones so that the charcoal dust will adhere to the working paper. Use aggressive strokes and be careful not to ruin the painting surface.

E. Long Soft Hair or Synthetic brush- Use to cover large dust tones in large areas, like hair on the head.

Erasers

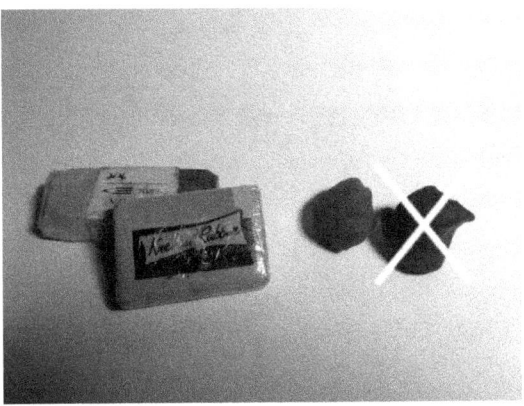

- **Kneaded Eraser**

This is like a clay or putty eraser, which can be mold to any difference shape and thickness, depending to your needs, it can lift Graphite in the paper without any damage, good for tight areas, can lighten areas in your drawing, and used for making highlights in your drawings to make it more realistic. Need to be replaced if it is already dark due to accumulation of Graphite.

- **Vinyl Eraser**

This kind of eraser does not smudge the surface of the paper; it can erase hard and tough areas totally especially for large areas, and does not harden.
There are other types of Erasers like Pink Eraser, Typewriter Erasers and Peel-Off type Eraser, you can also use those, as it depends on the availability of the materials in your area, feel free to experiment what works best for you.

Sharpener

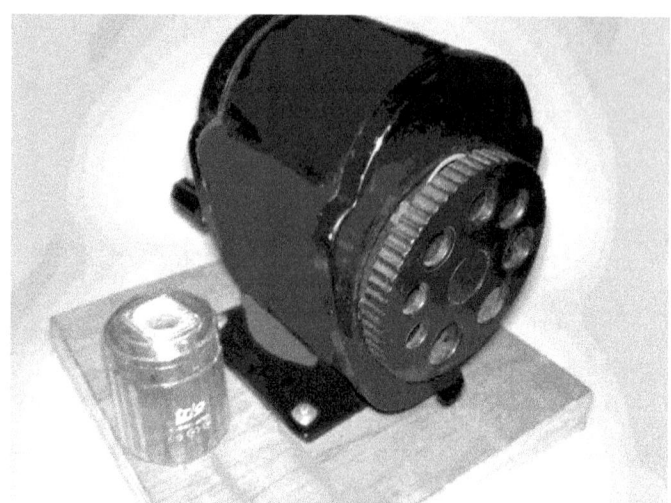

There is manual Sharpener, Wall-Mounted Sharpener and Electric Pencil Sharpener, Any type of Pencil sharpener will do, just make sure that it is safe to use. Use to sharpen the Pencil and Charcoal Pencil.

Cutter

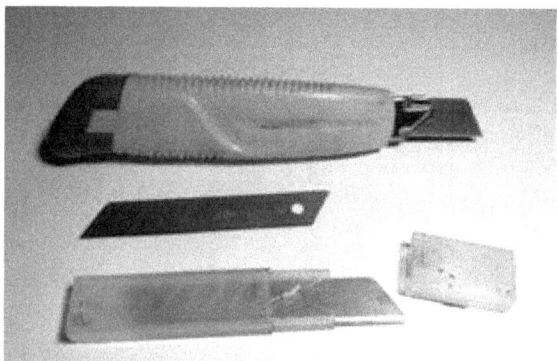

Use to shave the Charcoal and use the accumulated dust on your work. Can be use to sharpen your pencil and Charcoal pencil also, but make sure to be careful not to cut yourself.

Sandpaper

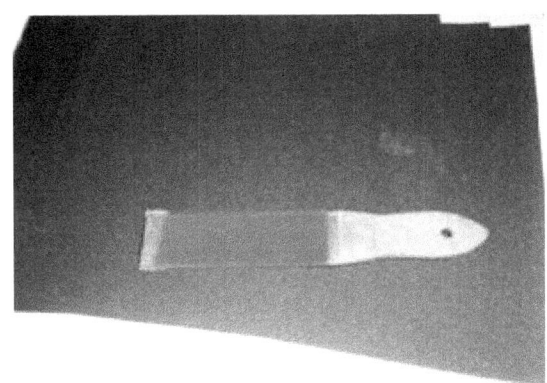

Can be use to sharpen your Pencils and Charcoal. Use 220 grit and cut it to small pieces that you can use. In my case, I place a piece in my old Sandpaper Pencil Pointer.

Spray Fixative

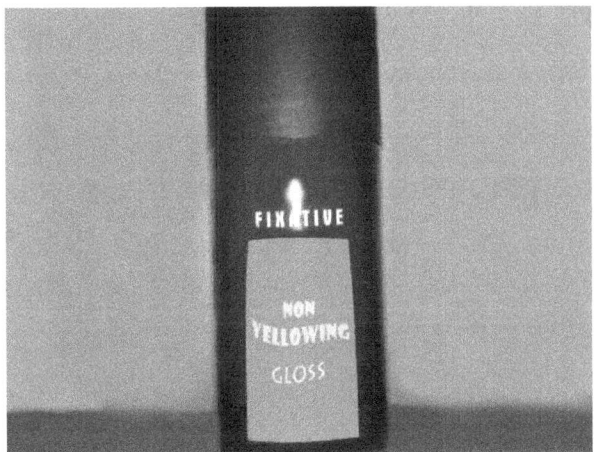

These are available in spray cans, it will make you're drawing fix to the paper, so that it will not smudge and to have professional looks, they comes in Matte or Gloss Finish, better to choose a trusted brand and a non-yellowing.

Smudge Sticks or Tortillon

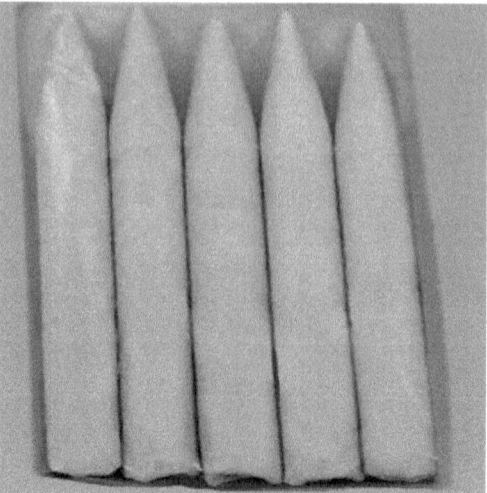

Used to blend your drawing, smear one tone to another (this is the only time you are allowed to smear your work) when making even tones, especially in facial areas. You can use fine sand paper to make polish the pointer, when it's ruin. Also when you use this, position the tortillon at an angle of 45° (Slanting "/") from your working paper.

Paper and Board

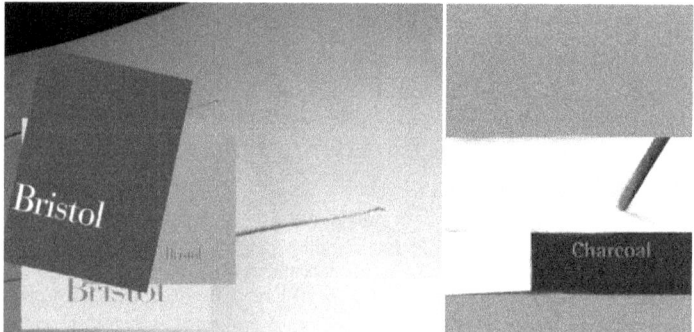

For our drawings Bristol paper will be used, they come in board and pads 2-ply, the front has a Plate surface, a smooth finish and has an egg shell texture, while the back has the Vellum surface texture, I used the Vellum surface which is good for shading. Both Pencil and Compress Charcoal, come in different sizes, a good suggestion is to make sure it's marked as acid free(so that your work can last a long time aside from spraying Fixative)..

You can use other type of paper, but make it's the right one for drawing using pencils and Charcoals.

Illustration board is also good for Pencil and Charcoal works, use the cold press since it has tooth and texture, which make the pencil and charcoal adhere to the surface.

Ruler and Template

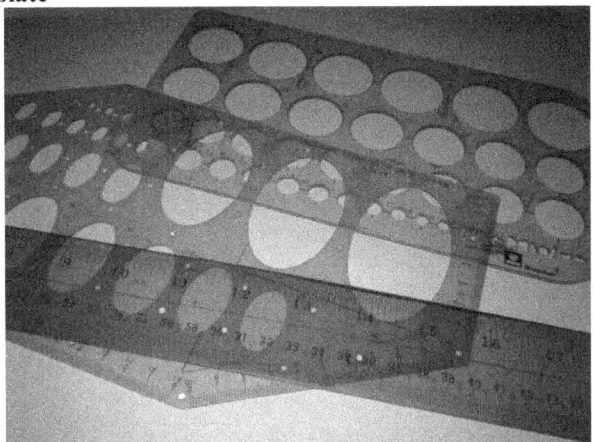

Ruler helps you draw straight lines, measure distance, you can use plastic or wooden for our drawings.

Templates can be use to draw circles or ellipse accurately, especially when drawing the parts of the eyes. Which demand a good form of shape.

Plastic Container

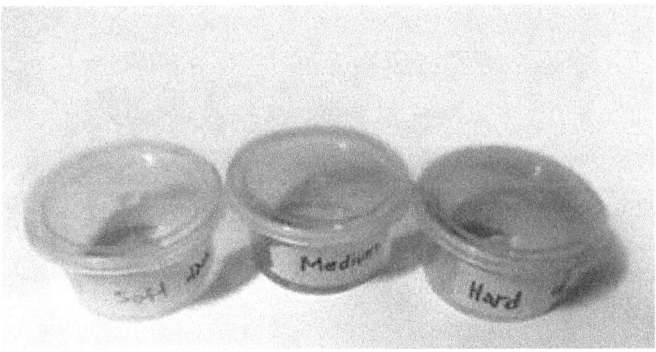

Serve as your container for your accumulated dust, after shaving the charcoal.

Magnifying Lens

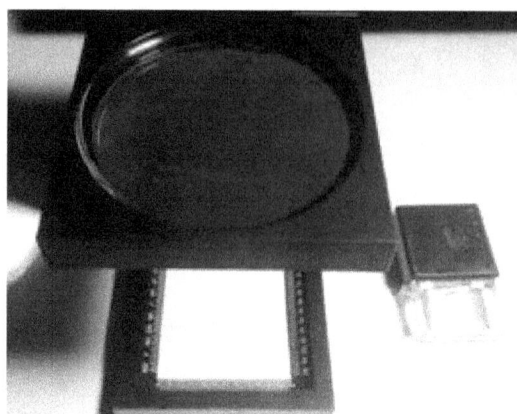

To magnify the image you are copying, so that your work will have more details; since we want it to look real.

Dusting Brush

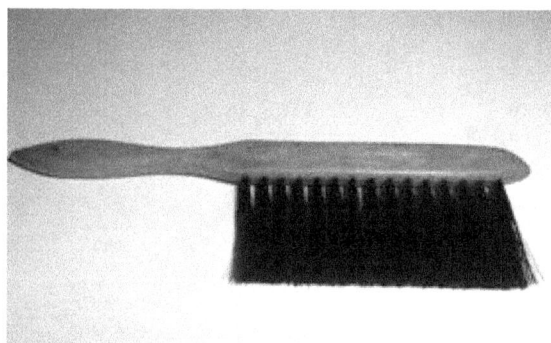

Use to take unwanted dirt and eraser particles in your work, and keep your work clean.

Rendering

Pencil

I know you are eager to make your beautiful Masterpiece now, and I promise you that "you" will after you learn how to render, this is the part that will make a big difference as an artist. So be ready of your Pencils, Kneaded erasers, and smudge stick for our lecture. This is our value scale this will help us select the right tone

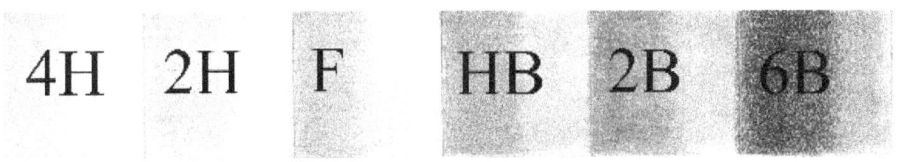

 You can make your own Value Scale to have a reference, take note that I blend (using the smudge stick) to the right, so that you will have an idea, how will it look like.

Sphere

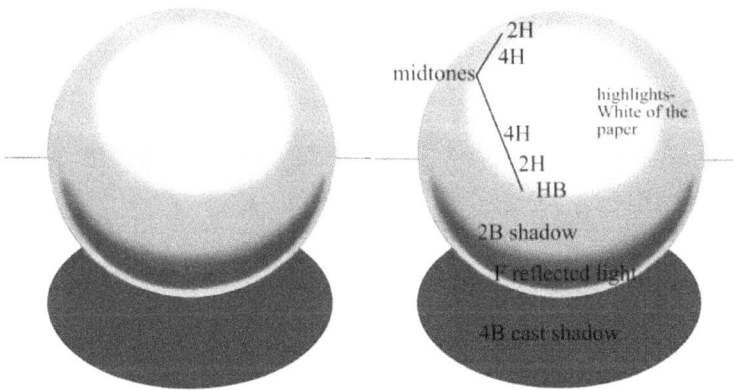

On the right side is our guide, of what pencil to use to the following tones of an object. Light source is coming from above.

Cast shadow-4B, it is the shadow cast by the object, depending on the placement or location of light; it's the place where no presence of light can be seen.
Reflected light-1.F or 2.Other times a light sliding stroke of your kneaded eraser can be used 3.Leave it blank and just blend the area depending to the tone of your subject picture, it's a bouncing of light up a reflective surface at the exact angle at which touches the surface, like in our example the light hit the table then reflecting with an angle to the sphere. Reflected light is important in any drawing, because it also add realism to it.

Shadow-2B, it is where the light source cannot reach, and always opposite to the light source.

Midtones-HB,2H and 4H, it's the place where the transition of light is evidently present, that is why we will be using different grade of pencils for this, our orientation for this is from dark to light when rendering.

Highlights-this is the part that were going to use the white of the paper or a kneaded eraser if ever there is a presence of tone from shading.

Step1. Draw a circle using your 4H or 2H pencil, use your circle template, for the cast shadow use your ellipse template, draw a line in the middle of the circle, this will be the table.

Step2. Erase the unnecessary lines.

Step3. Let's start rendering the cast shadow using 4B, as this is the darkest part of our drawing, remember that where going to render this from dark to light, building up the pencil lines gradually up and down matching the value of our example. Then blend the cast shadow using your smudge stick, it is better if you only use this smudge stick for this tone alone.

Step4. Using your 2B pencil, we're going to draw the shadow, do shading strokes around the ball, and remember to leave some space below it for our reflected light.

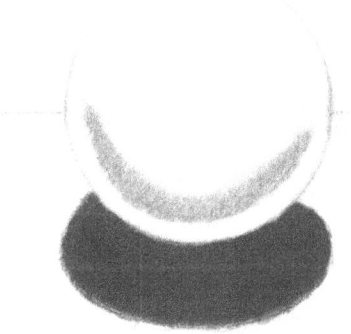

Step5. Next is the reflected light. Use F pencil, apply shading stroke below the shadow, same as you did in Step4.

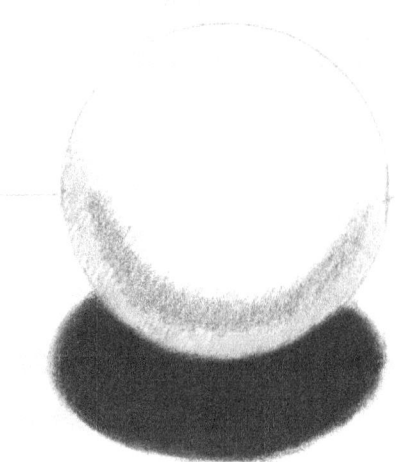

Step6. Working with our Midtones, we will be using HB, 2H and 4H. Starting with HB apply stroke above the shadow.

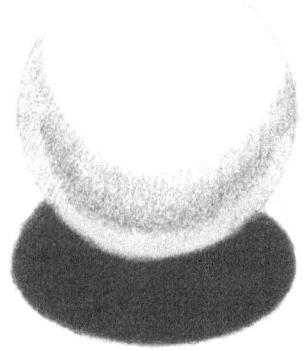

Then with 2H above the HB stroke and also apply light strokes in the upper part of the inner circle.

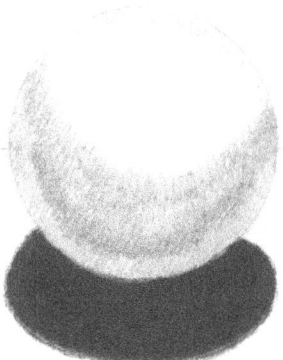

Do the same using 4H, just above the 2H below and also apply light stroke below the 2H above.

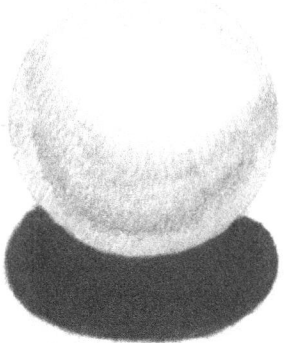

Step7. It's time to do the Blend these tones, we will be working from light to dark, be sure to clean your smudge stick first, there must be no graphite to it, new one would be better or just use sand paper to polish it, so not to darken our any light tone.
Starting at the upper part blend the 4H tone (going upward then downward) to 2H tone, your stroke will be the same like when using pencil.

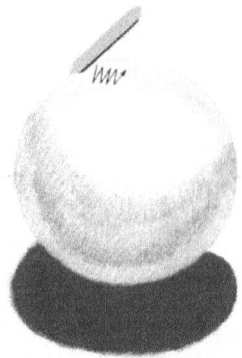

Do the same with the rest, start blending from the 4H tone to 2H then HB, slowly and gradually, for the shadow with 2B tone, and lightly blend it upward to HB. For the F tone (reflected light) blend it starting from the left side going circular to the right side not to have contact with the 2B tone. After that, clean your work using your eraser.

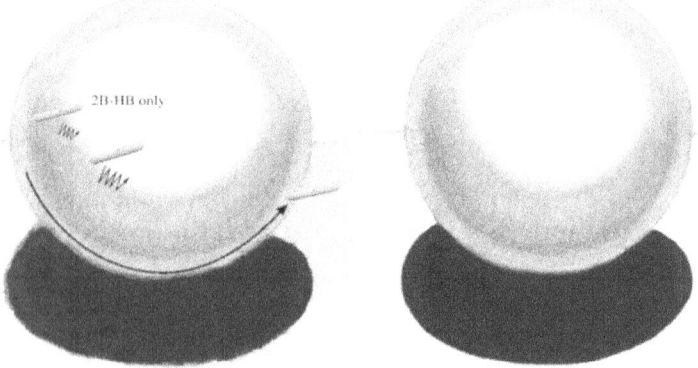

Now there you have it, you now learned how to render the Sphere.
Tips:
- If you accidentally blend or erase some dark tone, just redo it with your pencil lightly.
- Use your pencil to fill any uneven light spots and for any uneven dark spots just lift it with kneaded eraser.

Cone

Step1. Copy the shape below: you can trace it if you want or you can draw it by drawing a vertical line first and a short horizontal line, use an ellipse template to draw the base, and use ruler for the slope starting at the top of the vertical line going to one end of ellipse, do the same to the other one.

Step2. Begin shading the cast shadow (6B).

Step3. Then apply 2B to the shadow area, also F to the inner circular area of the base, you can extend the F tone till the top but do it lightly, your stroke would be like following

the circular shape of the cone. But don't shade the right and left side near the slope that where our highlights will be.

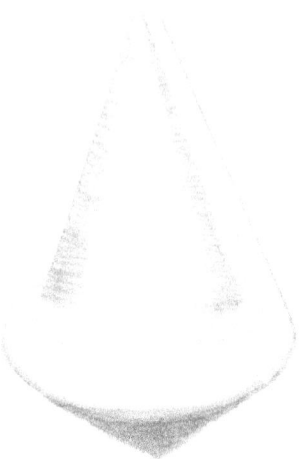

Step4. Now for our midtones, on the line where we shade the 2B, apply shading starting with HB lightly, overlap the 2H tone also the 4H, to the same to the other side. Careful, leave some space for our highlights for both sides.

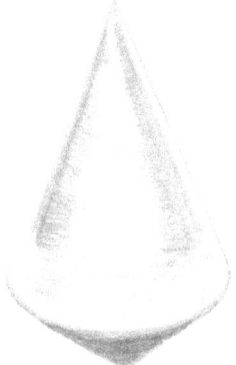

Step5. Now let's blend everything one at a time, starting from F at the bottom, start your stroke at the left moving to the right till you reach the top. Careful when blending with 2B tone, not the smudge much. For 2B to midtones, slowly blend the 2B to HB, 2H and 4H going to outer side for both sides. Make sure highlights can be seen, so pull out the highlights using the kneaded eraser in that side, also just between the 2B tone near the tip, erase so that it will look evident. And draw a line at the back of the cone.

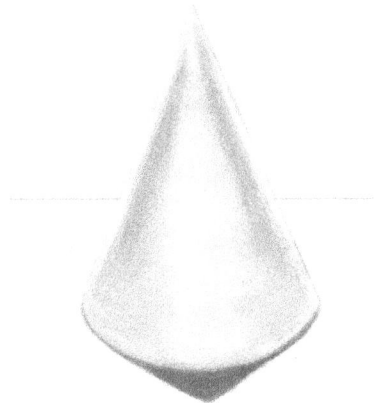

Cube

Step1. Copy the cube outline, you can trace or do it manually, you have to Draw the line 30° on the left and on the right both sides forming a letter v, draw 3 lines vertically; one on the left end of the v, right end and center, on the top of it is another v-shape connecting to inverted v shape again, forming a diamond shape

Step2. Start shading with the cast shadow, in this example, the cast shadow on the right side is darker than the backside, that's because the light source came from the left side giving light to it.

Step3. Apply the shadow (2B), and also the reflected light (F) on the lower part of this side.

Step4. Add the midtones-HB, 2H and 4H beside the shadow, also shade a portion of HB below the front side.

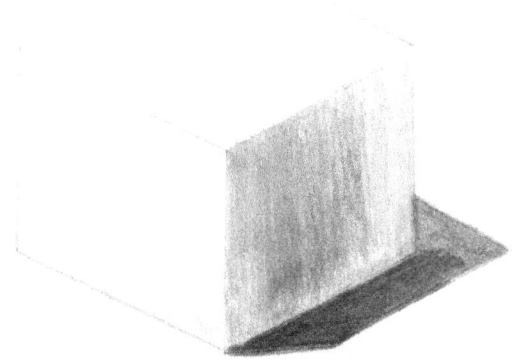

Step5. Shade the front side with 2H till you fill the half of this side, then switch 4H and fill the rest.

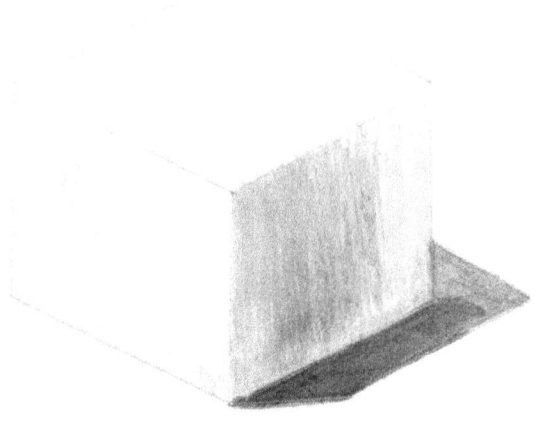

Step6. Slightly shade a small tone on the right side at the top.

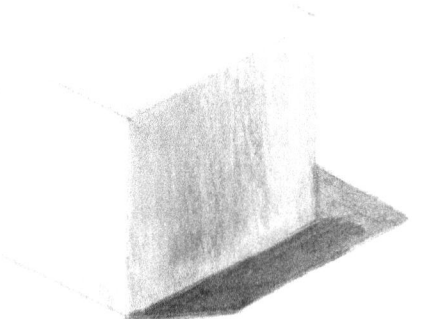

Step7. Blend all respective sides accordingly with smudge tool.

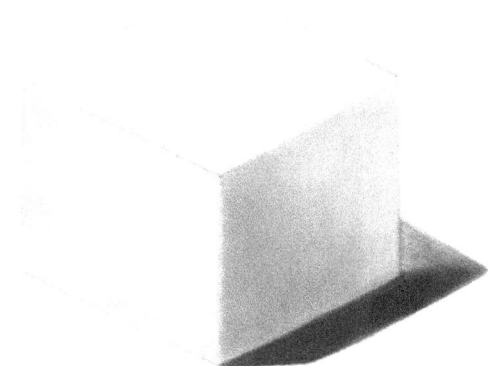

Cylinder

Step1. Copy the outline or do it manually, parts are compose of two ellipse and two vertical lines. The light is coming from left side, so the shadow would be at the back opposite the light source.

Step2. Begin shading the cast shadow (6B) at the back.

Step3. Next apply the Shadow (2B), take note of the roundness of the cylinder shape, there will have a two shadow running vertically as seen in the illustration, lightly apply F on the left side of the cylinder vertically beside the shadow.

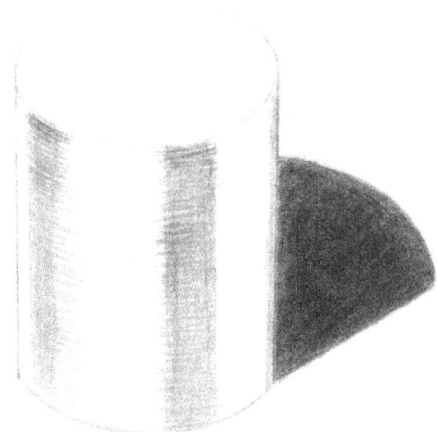

Step4. Work your midtones, beside the two shadows, starting with HB, 2H and 4H, do it also to the other side of each shadow, apply also these tones on the top of the cylinder.

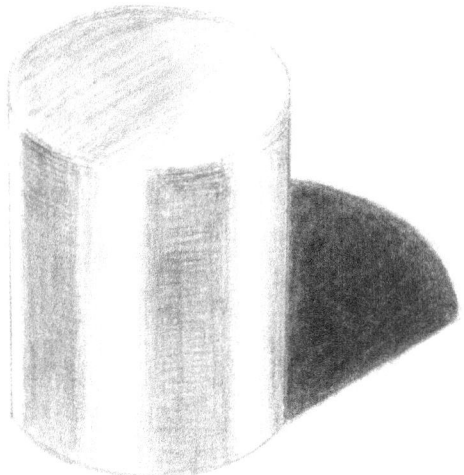

Step5. Blend the cast shadow and shadows with the midtones (careful to leave empty space for the bands of highlights, we have three). Blend the top as well, and were done.

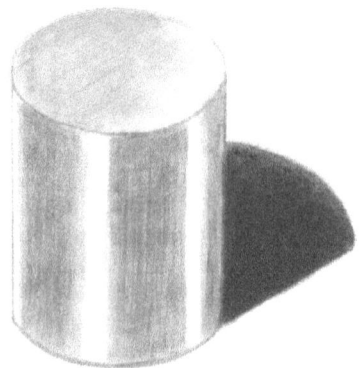

You will wonder, why we need to learn all of this, what's the connection of this shapes on the human face. Let me explain, the Sphere shape, we usually see these in the face, eyes, ears and nose. The Cone shape can be seen in the nose (from the nasal bridge to septum). The Cube shape can be seen in the mouth (cube when elongated turn to rectangular shape) and teeth. And if your drawings have arms and a finger, that's cylindrical shape, so take note that upper and lower extremities is cylindrical.

Charcoal

For Charcoal, principles are the same, but there is difference in terms shading, since you're going to use a brush to fill the values (more area coverage), unlike using pencil which you have to make a lot of strokes to fill a specific area.
 And Charcoal has a darker values compare to Pencil even with various ranges of tones; also Charcoal has a matte texture unlike Pencil that has Gloss.

So, before I teach you how to render using Charcoal. Let me show you how to shave the Charcoal using cutter first.

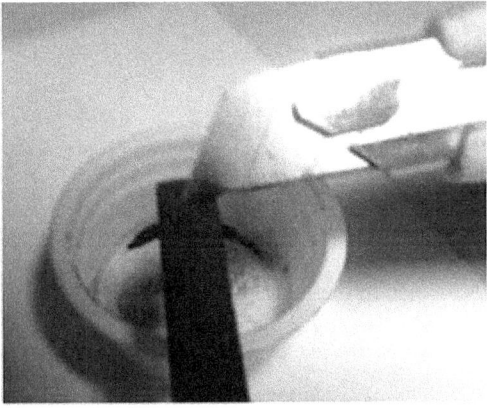

Shave your Charcoal using a one -way direction of strokes where you place it to your container or cup to accumulate the dust or powder to use.

So now we have a Charcoal dust and we're ready to begin, Lets copy the outline of the sphere from our previous exercise or make a new sphere for this exercise.

Draw a light circle inside the sphere; this would be our guide when rendering the shadow.

Let's use the Soft Charcoal, which has a darkest tone to the cast shadow, use your Small Flat Brush and fill the area with a pressure enough to make a tone; the stroke should be the same when shading with Pencil or Tortillon.

Note: Tap your brush 2-3 times in the container to remove excess Charcoal dust in your brush before applying it in your working paper.

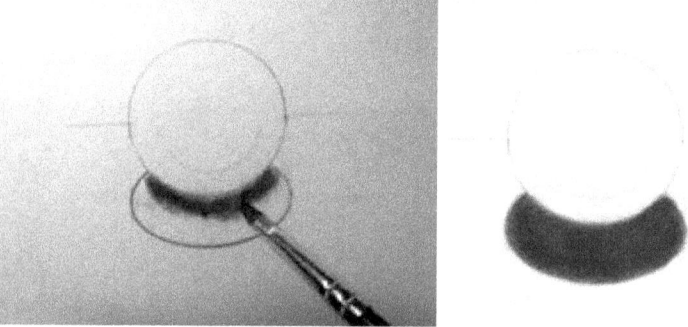

Next we're going to render the shadow, use your Small Round Brush and with dabbing stroke fill the area in a circular motion going up.

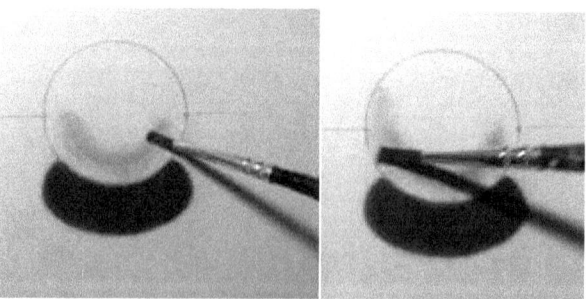

Then it's time to focus on the reflected light, get your kneaded eraser and mold it to point shape, and lightly erase some tone in a circular motion, enough to have a reflected light tone.

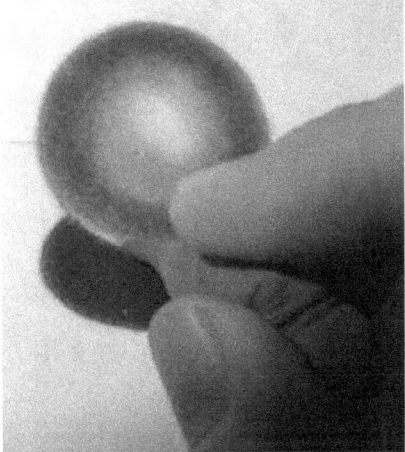

Erase the Charcoal dust outside the Sphere also clean your work using dusting brush.

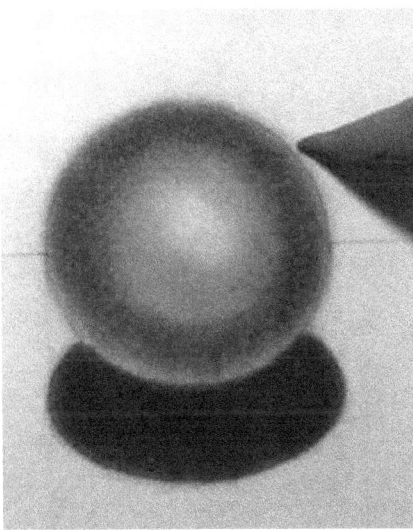

Time to render the ground, where our sphere is placed. Use your Small Round Brush and dabb some Medium Charcoal beside the sphere and fill the area.

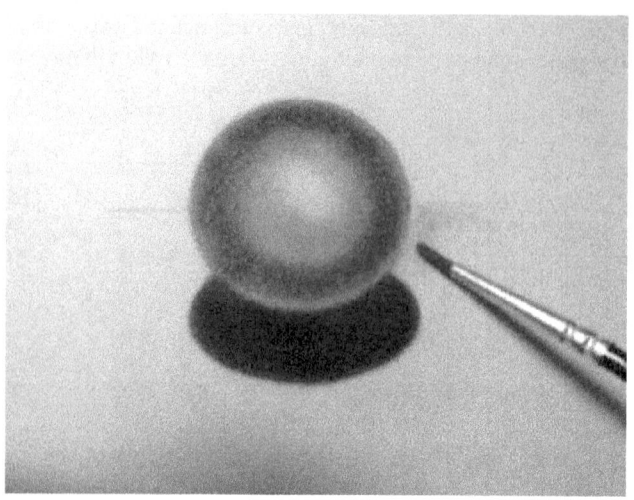

Add the highlights, by lifting some tones using your kneaded eraser.

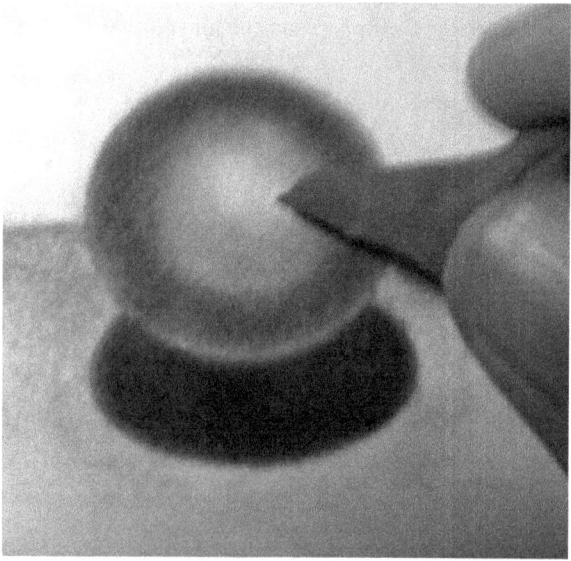

Finish Perfect, we just render a Sphere using Charcoal.-"FANTASTIC"

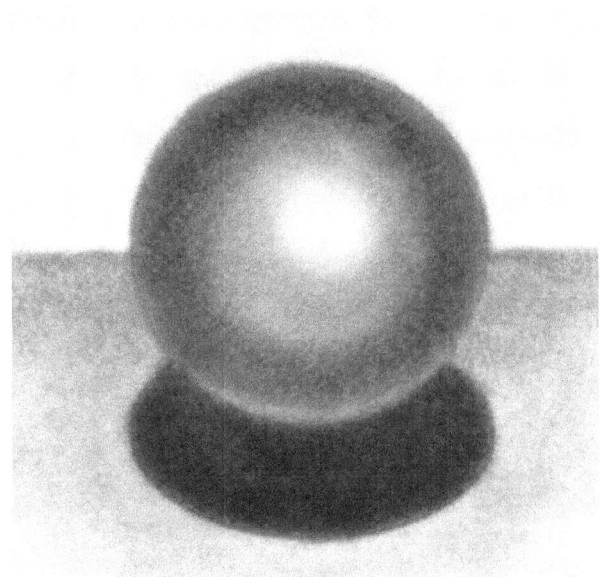

Application

Drawing an Outline

Outline is line of the shape of the object; other says that it is a mark of a boundary.
First draw the basic shapes, then if you're sure that draw them accurately and in correct proportion, draw the outline lightly in your drawing paper, then erase unnecessary lines and done.

Tips:
- See through shapes including the negative of the image as well the positive, to help you visualize the shapes.

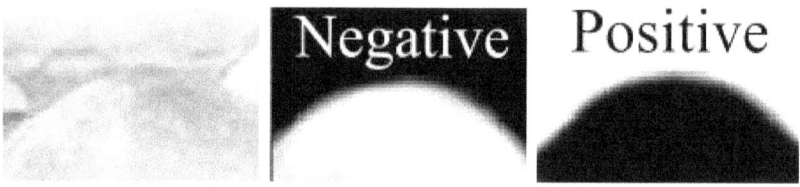

- Practice sketching basic shapes and making outlines, it will help you improve your strokes and good hand coordination, and it can give you confidence in your work.
- If you find it hard to get the right distance and sizes of the shapes you can use Ruler and Templates to draw accurately.

Grid System

If you find it difficult to draw the outline accurately, not to worry we have solution to that, "The Grid System", used by a German Artist named Albrecht Durer, he created this device to assist artist when drawing details, also by this he can re-scale his work. We don't need that device, what you will just make a grid measure 1/2" over the picture of the subject, and draw a desired inches of grid on your paper, same squares with picture of the subject, copy the picture from the Grid to your drawing paper, after that erase the grid in your working paper, Also I have to mention it would be better that the picture was a photocopy or scanned. Not to ruin the original picture.

Drawing and Rendering

Landscapes in Charcoal

Sahara Desert in Pencil

This picture of the Sahara Desert is the good way to practice the basic way of rendering a Landscape.

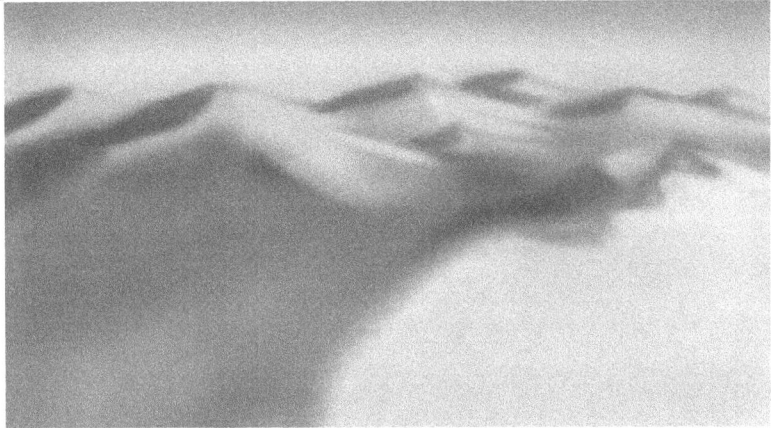

Here is the grid of the picture above. So let's start.

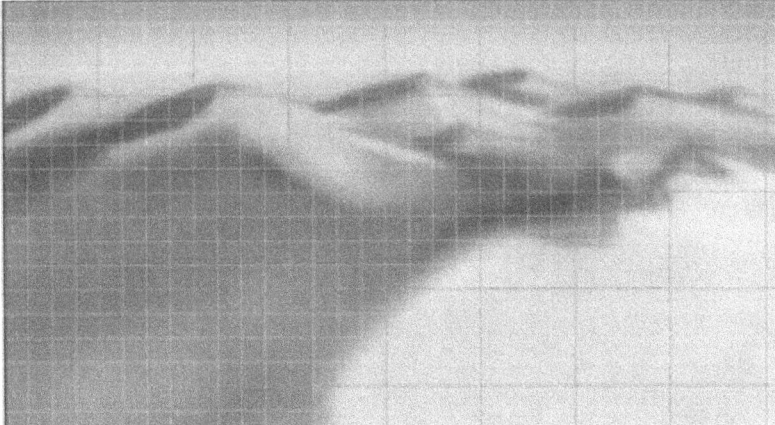

Let's draw the hills using my 4H pencil.

Use your 2B, shade the shadows on the areas of sand.

Now shade the darkest area by using 6B.

Now shade the darker area by shading your HB.

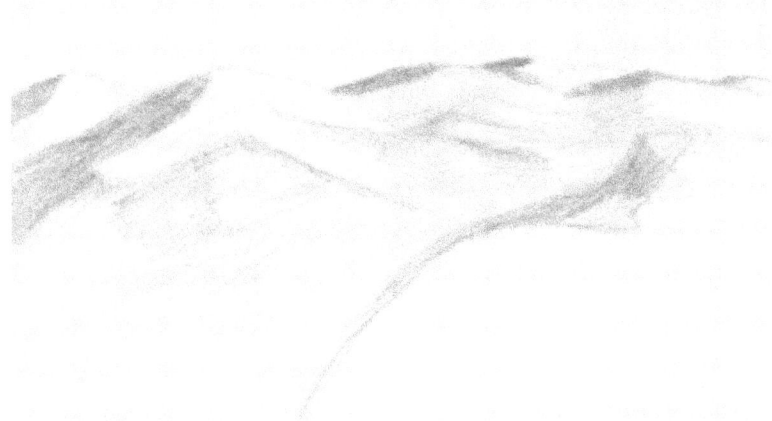

Now shade the entire working area with 4H to give tone to it.

Now shade 2H to darken areas to give more definition on the Landscape and also shade the sky.

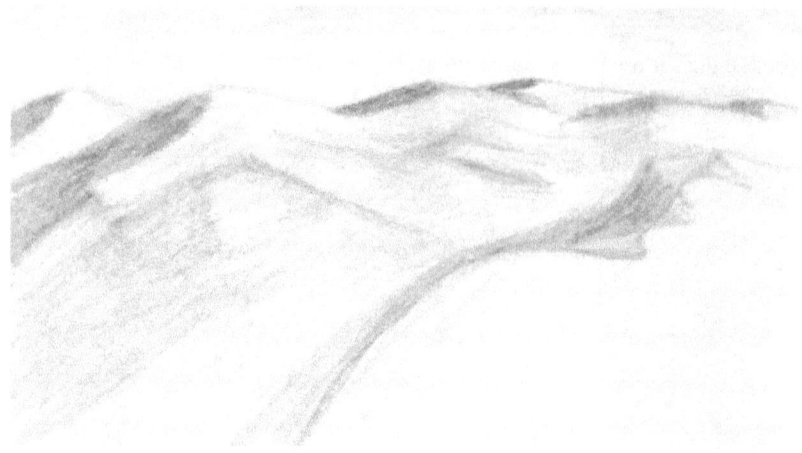

Now Blend All areas using your tortillon, by this the sand will have a smooth texture, making it more realistic, also give highlights on the right side of the slope using your kneaded eraser, after that spray your work with Fixative, and you are done. Take a break and prepare for the next exercise, because we're going to use Charcoal.

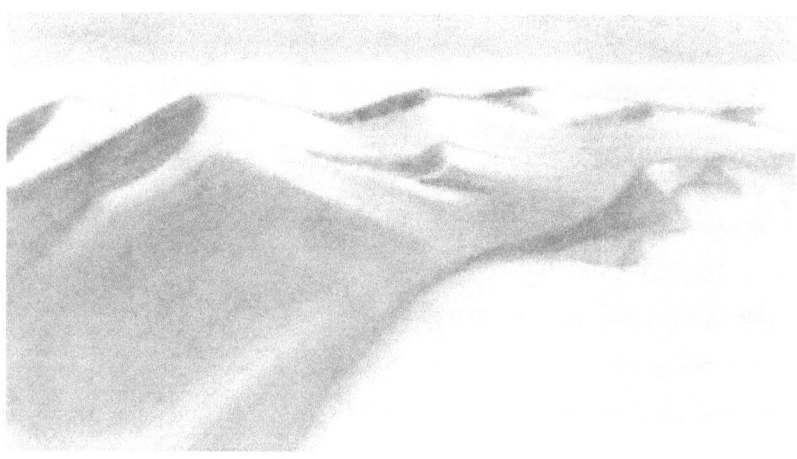

The Chocolate Hills in Charcoal

For this exercise, take all your tools for charcoal: brushes charcoal (you had shaved it and put the dust in the plastic cups) and kneaded eraser. Below is the grid, so transfer it to your working paper.

Note: I used compressed charcoal in all my work: Soft, Medium and Hard -shaved and placed in the plastic container. Also for details, I used Charcoal pencil also with different grades.

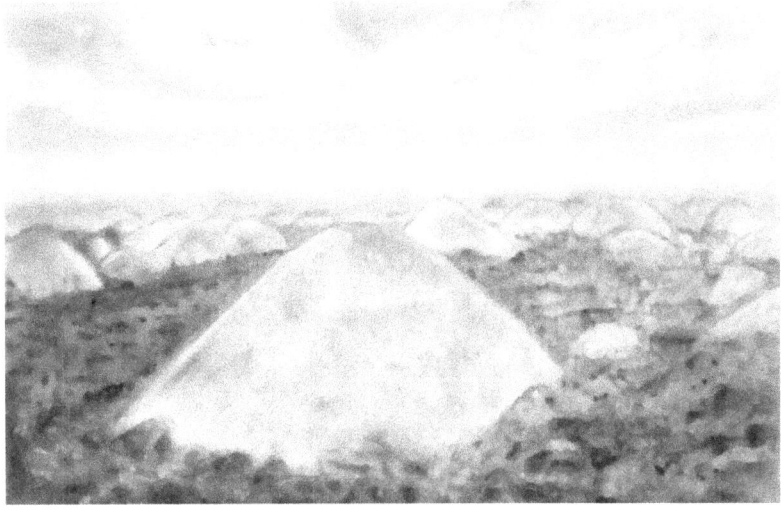

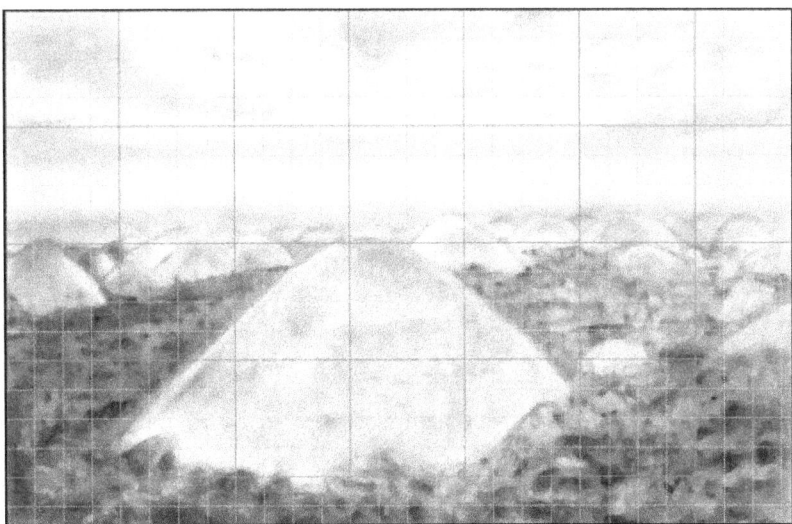

Outline:

Using Soft Charcoal dust or powder (Darkest), shade it to areas indicated, use your small flat brush with control pressure and don't forget to tap it in the container, before you

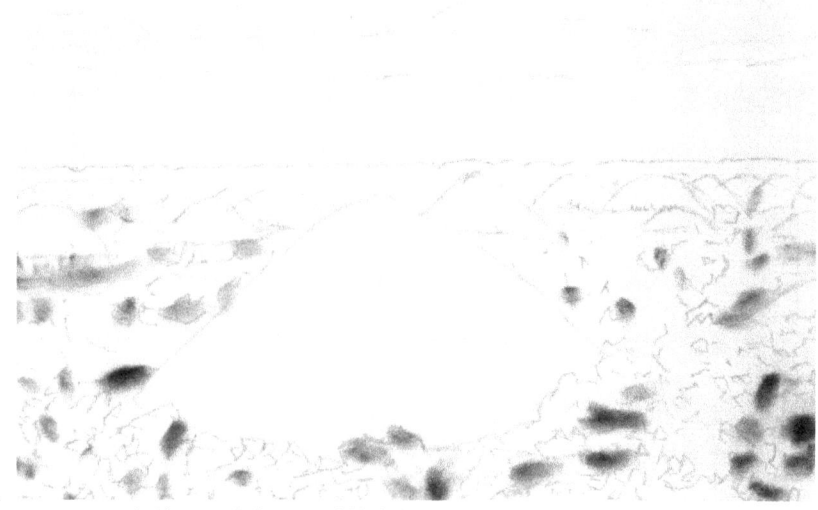

apply.
Next use your Hard Charcoal dust, and lightly apply to areas with the medium round brush, remember to use dabbing strokes.

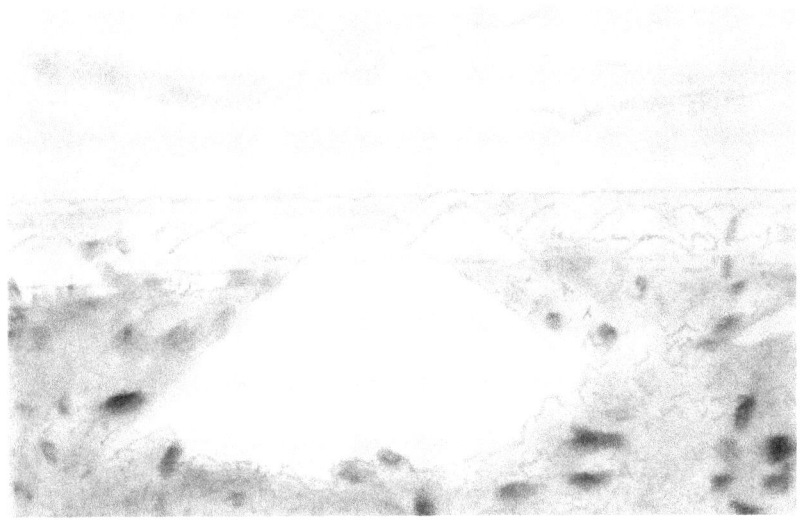

Now let's build up some tones and at the same time work the details on the right side; apply Medium Charcoal by dabbing it with your small round brush, then use your kneaded eraser to erase some dust to create shapes of the foliage carefully, also use your Charcoal pencil to give your work details like fine lines and small dots

For the hills; dab some light tone using small round brush and add highlights.

Render the sky by using your medium tone at the top-middle and hard tone on the sides using round brush. For the clouds use your kneaded eraser lightly erase areas of the sky to create a clouds, be sure to control your hand when creating these, since there areas of the cloud that have a different value, I mean the transition of dark to light are evident.

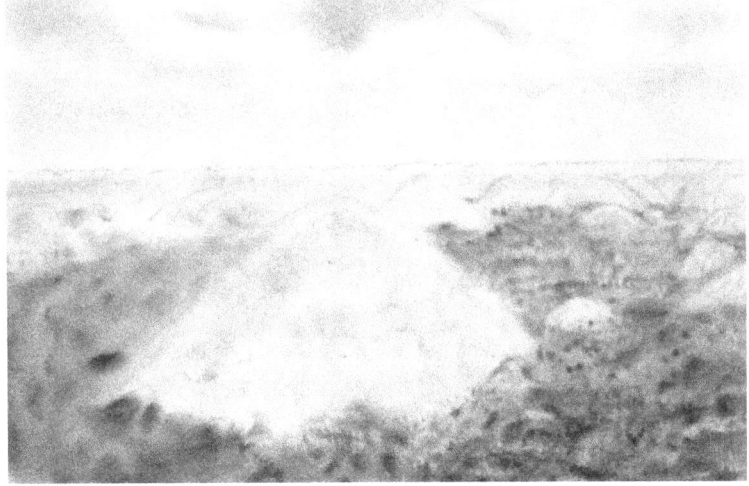

Finish the left side- add tones, use your kneaded eraser and give details using your charcoal pencil.

Also give details on the Hill on the middle, add medium tone on the left side of the slope and a highlight add some light dab dots for texture and a touch of small lines and dots using kneaded eraser and medium charcoal pencil.

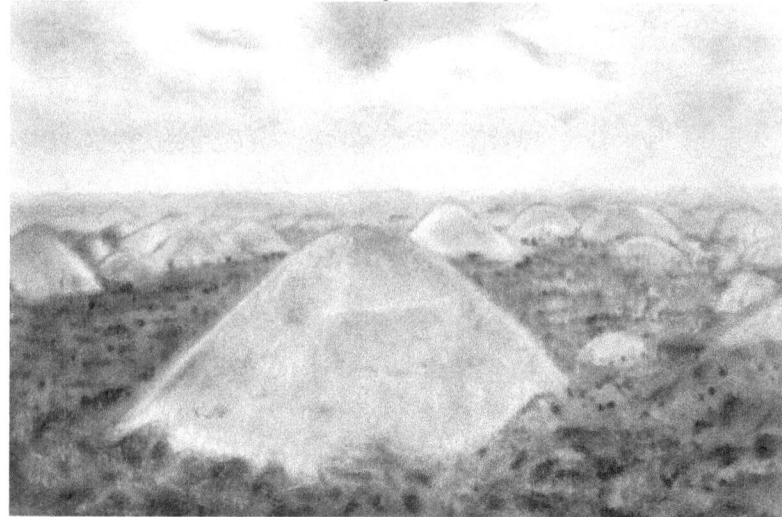

Compare your work below, to see if there is anything needed to add or improve, like the clouds, hills and trees. If you're sure you did not miss anything then spray your work with fixative. And you're done again take a break before working the next exercise.

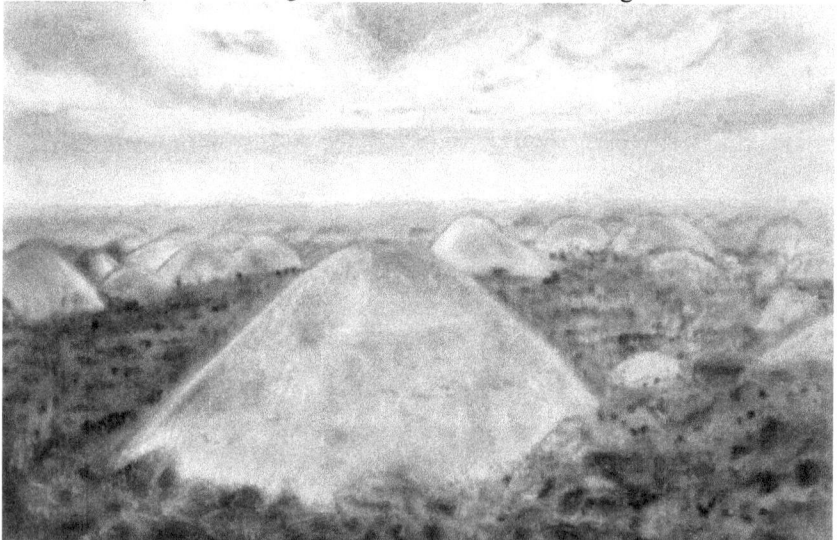

The Lone Tree in Pencil

This next exercise is unique, as it has more details compared to our previous exercises. This is good way to challenge yourself, prepare your Pencils and let's start.

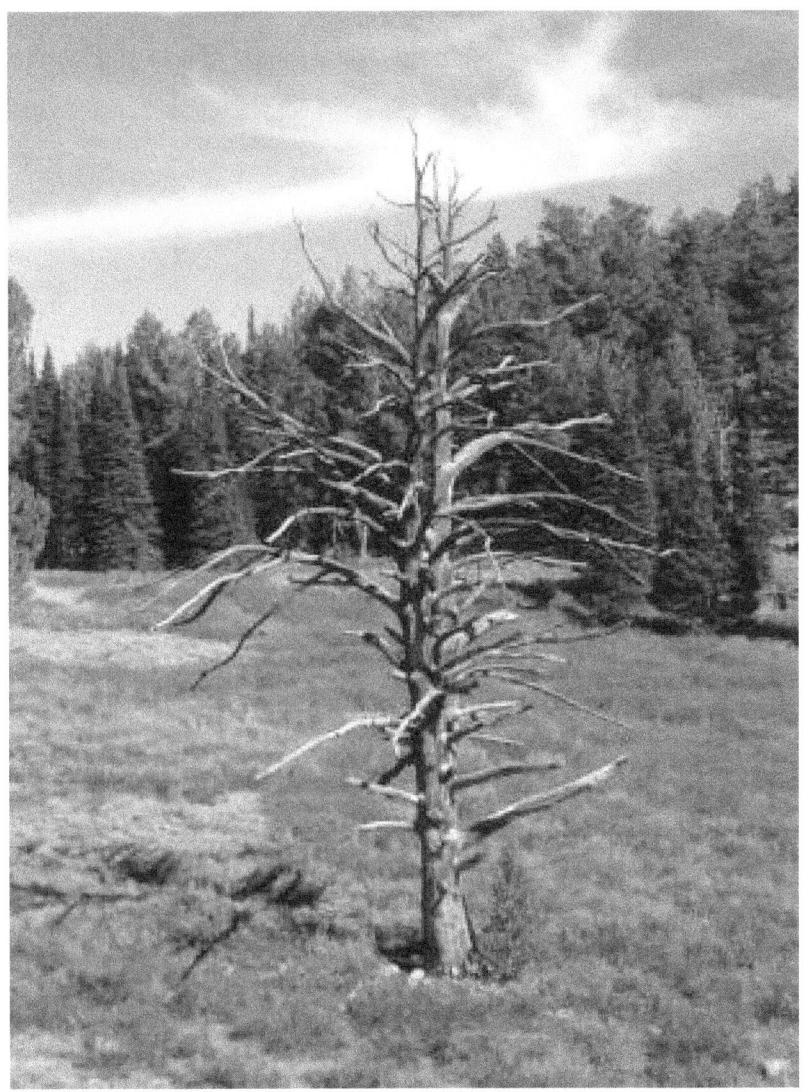

Below is the grid, so transfer this to your drawing paper.

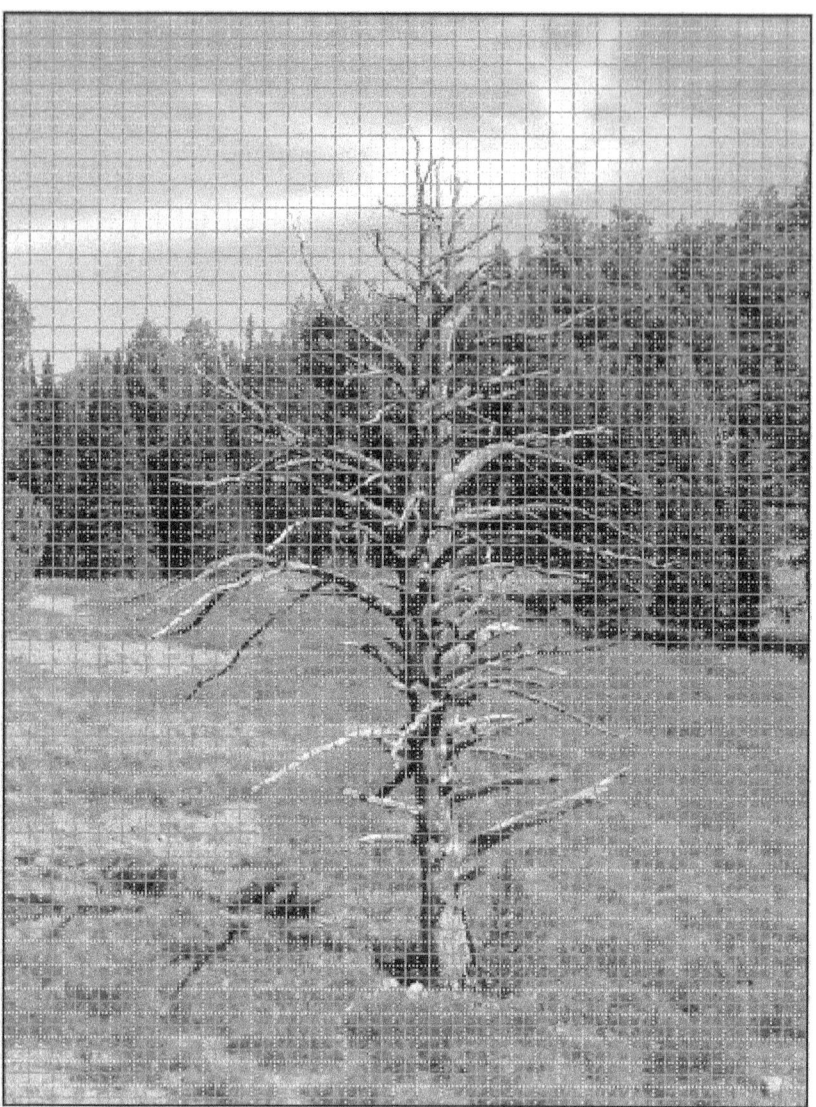

Outline:

Take your 6B pencil and shade the darkest areas.

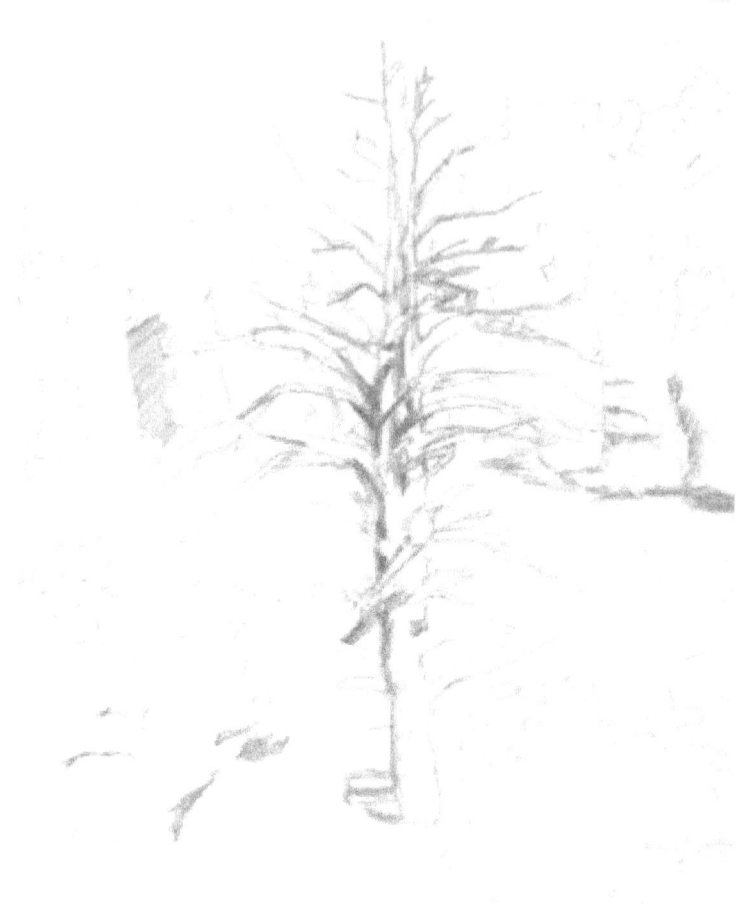

Using your 2B, shade the branches of the tree, add shadows and add details on the tree at the back by shading several line strokes to give the tree a shadow effects.

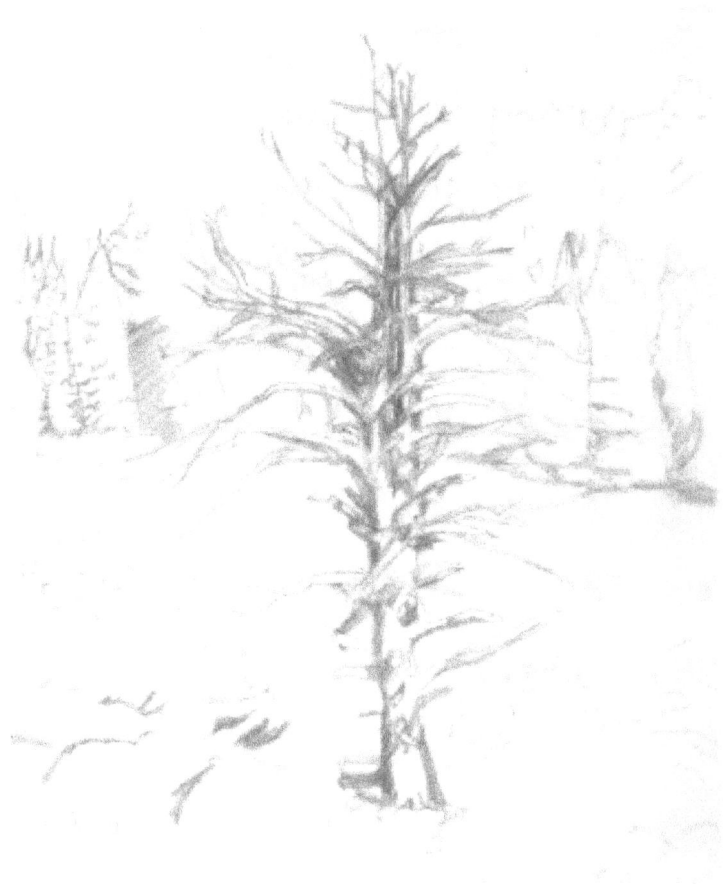

Next is to shade the areas with the HB; the trees on the far back, add more details to the trees on the middle ground (defining it more to render dimensions to it).

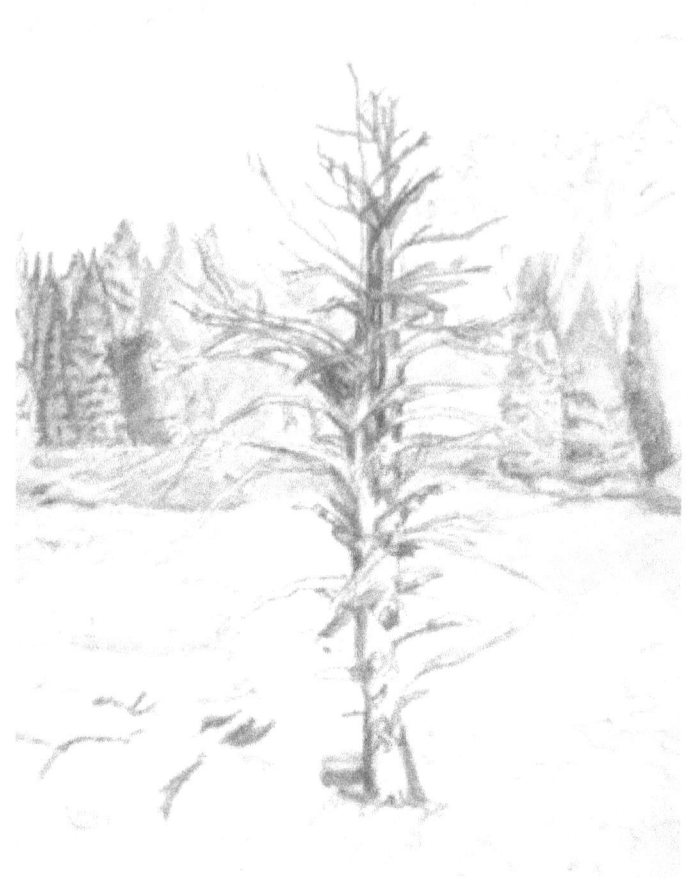

Then Shade the whole area with 4H to tone your work, remember to use a light pressure.

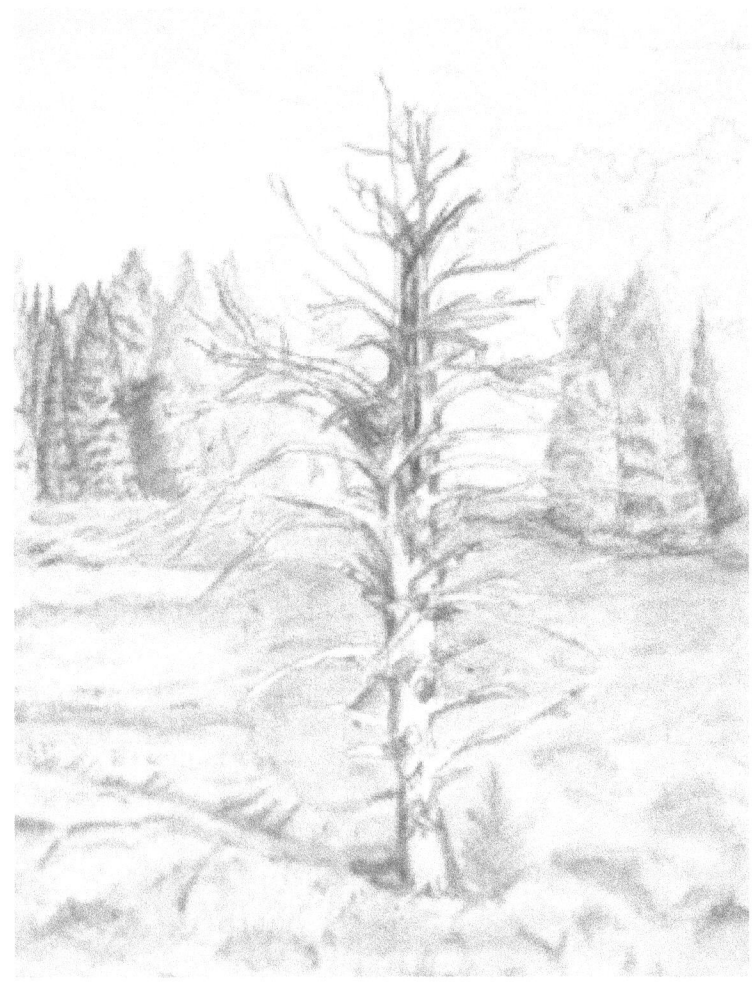

Using 2H shade the dark areas on the ground to represent the grass and also transition of light.

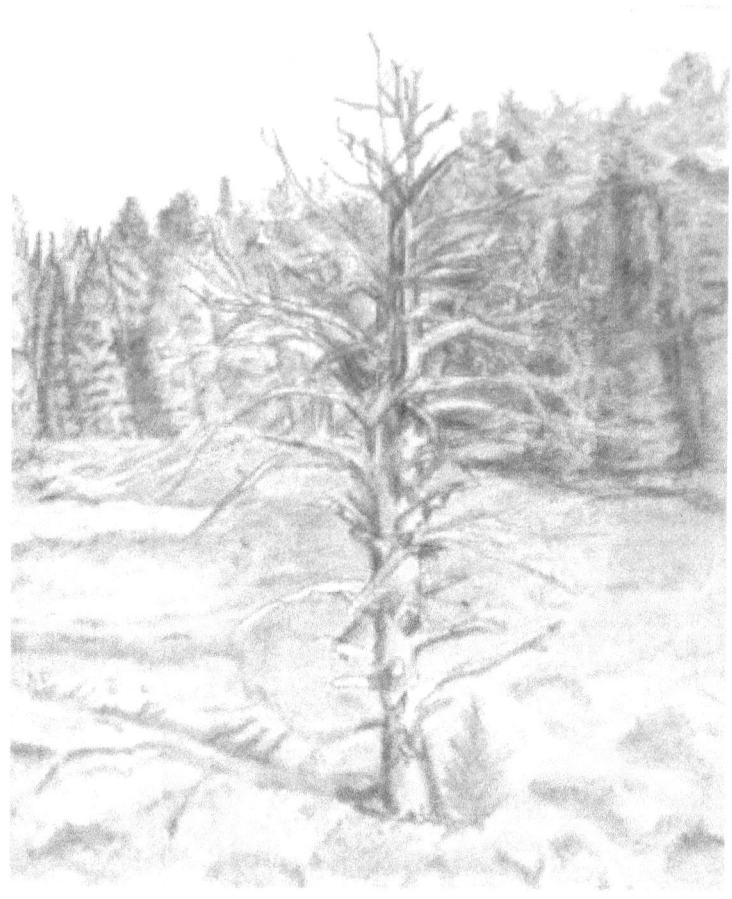

Work the details on the Lone tree using 2B, take note of the branches with highlights (use kneaded eraser), shadows and other darker are, and don't forget to define the small tree beside it using HB. Note: that leaves on twigs are made up of small lines.

Add more details on the trees on the back of the Lone tree, create depth to it, and add also cast shadows to it as well shadows.

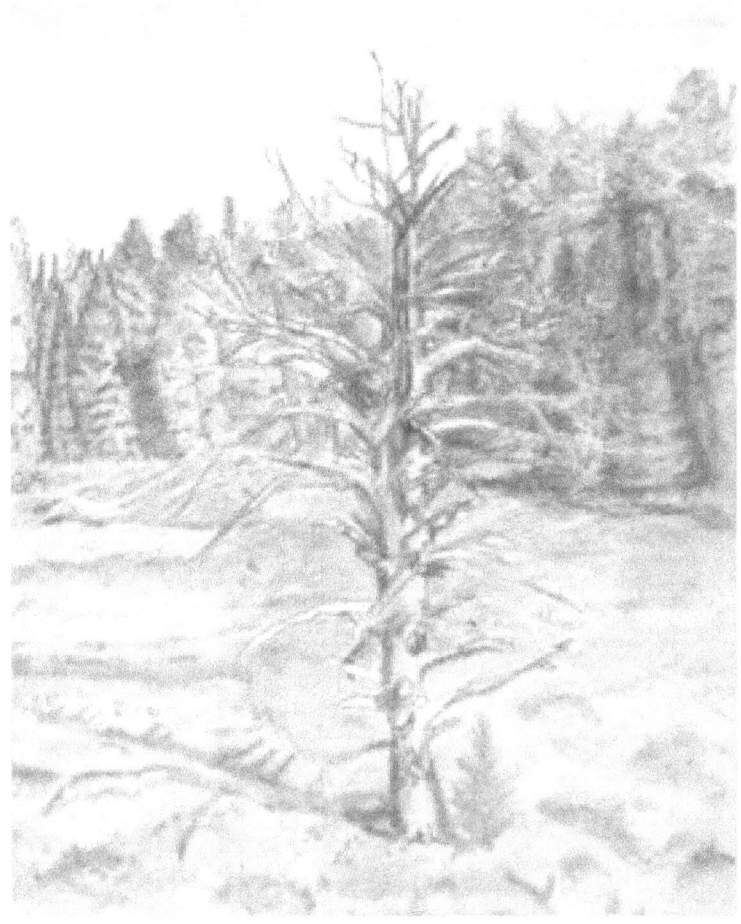

For the sky: shade the area with HB, make it more dark, blend the area with tortillon, after that get your kneaded eraser and create the cloud effects by lifting some tones as if you're drawing a line, but do it lightly with a good hand control making the cloud looks real. If you're sure of your work, spray it with fixative. And be ready for the next exercise.

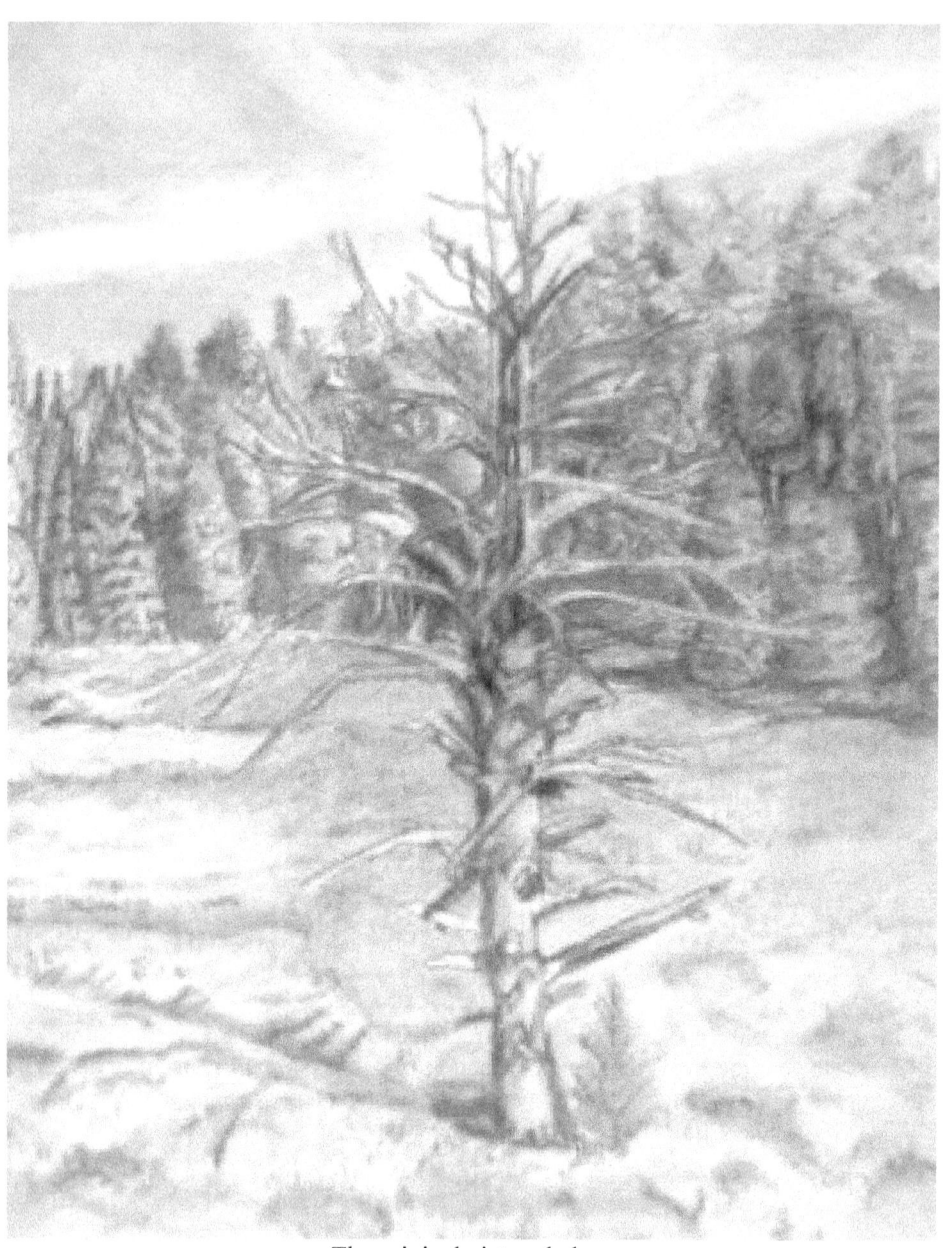

The original picture below

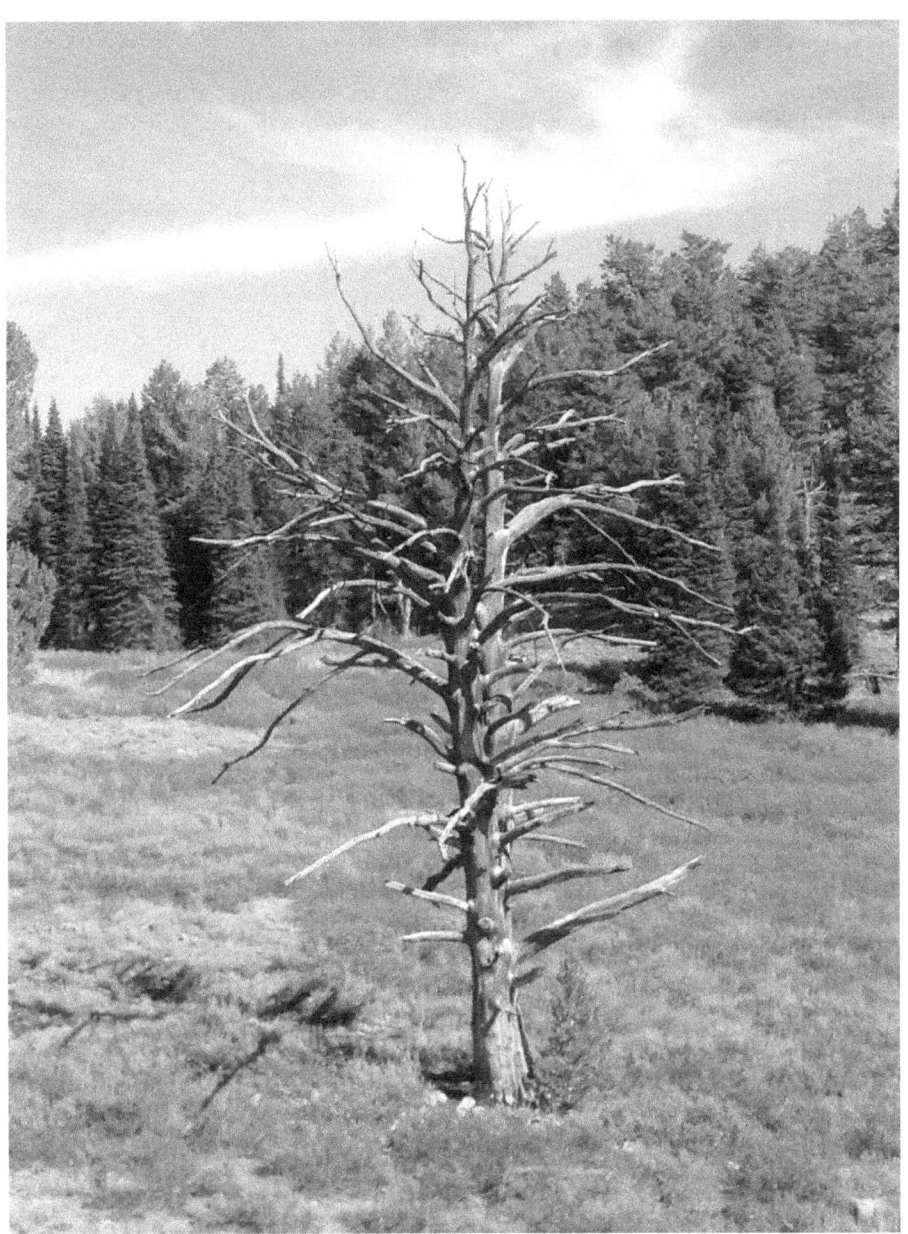

Mountain View in Charcoal

This fourth exercise has more details, also we're going to do it in charcoal, and prepare for this challenge, and you can do it. Below is the grid so transfer this to make an outline.

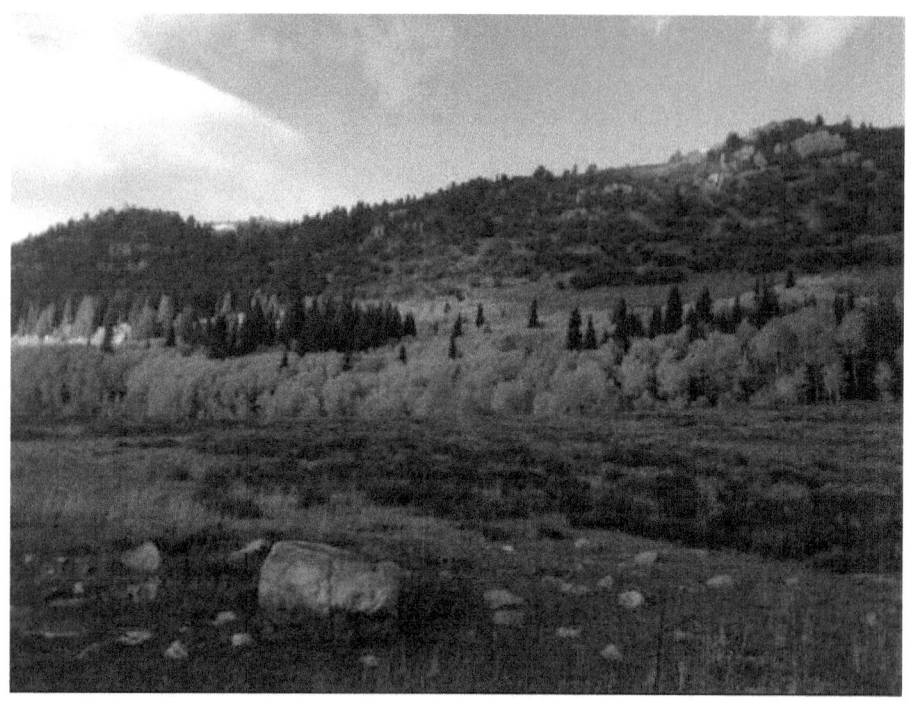

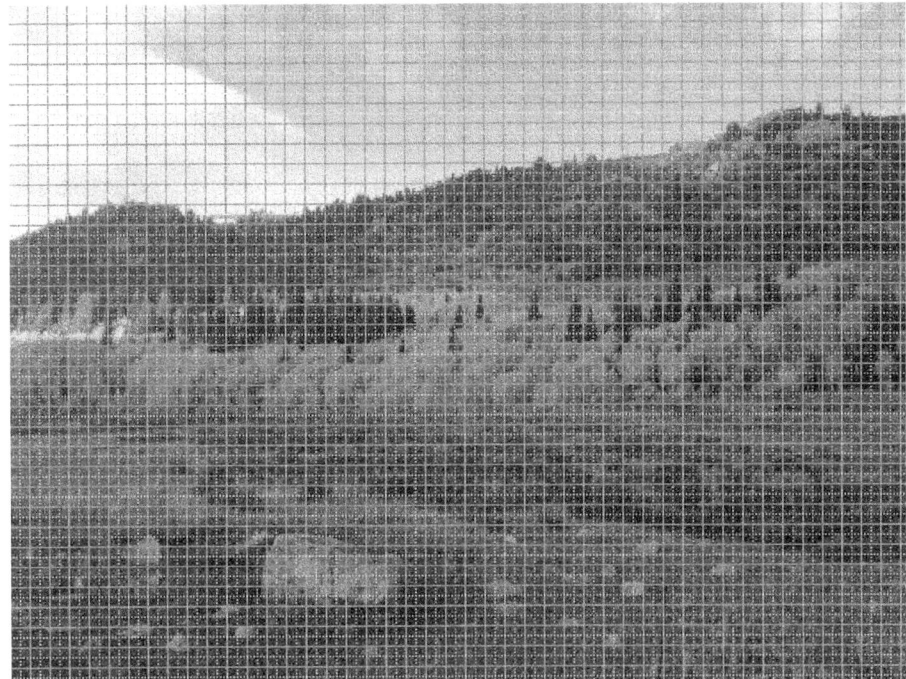

Outline:

Use your Hard Charcoal dust with your flat brush and shade the area on the top of the mountain.

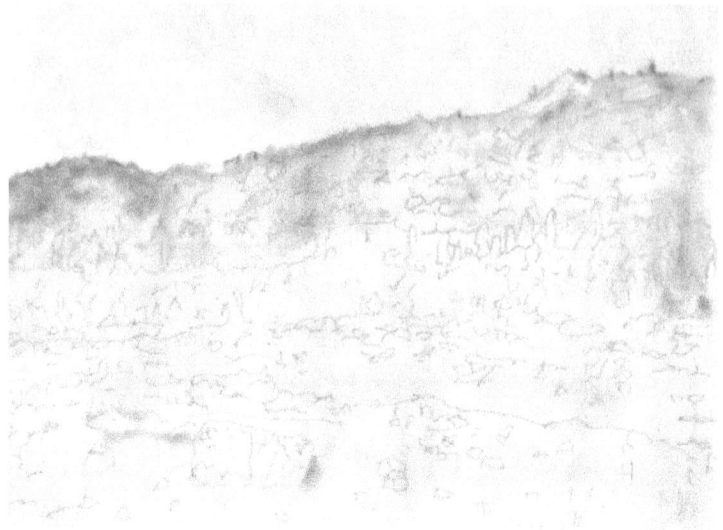

Continue to fill the area with that tone and define the shapes and start rendering the trees on the area by applying the flat brush in vertical stroke.

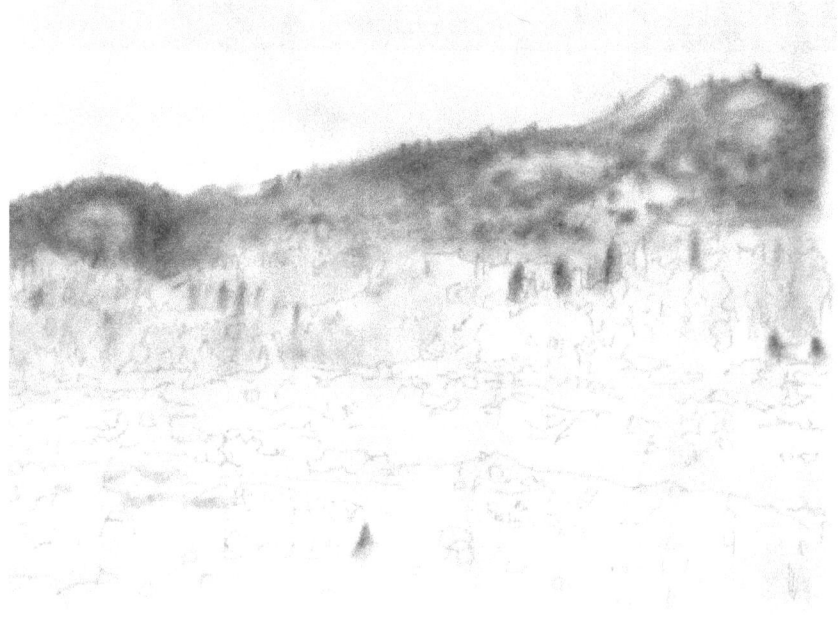

Switch the tone to Medium Charcoal and add the tone to the left side of the area using your round brush, as you are moving to the right direction, the transition will be from dark to light, so moving to the right you will have to switch to light tone which is hard charcoal.

After that add details on the top of the mountain, so use you're Charcoal pencil: Soft Charcoal Pencil to the darkest part like the trees you can see on the far right above the mountain

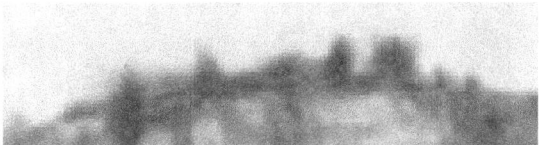

, moving to the top middle define this trees by shading using the light tone so use Hard Charcoal Pencil for this

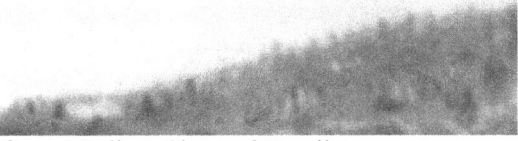

, moving to the top left use Medium Charcoal Pencil.

Note: Use your kneaded eraser to create the irregular shapes and texture of the mountain, you can see that on the white areas on the slope, and also use the charcoal pencil to create the dark areas near that white areas to create depth.

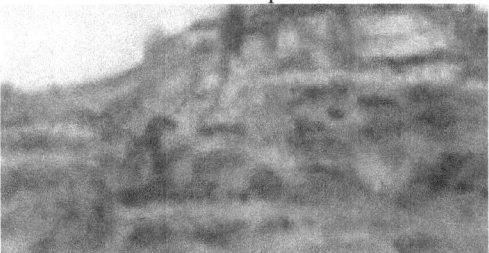

Now let's work on the middle area: starting on the right use your Hard Charcoal Pencil

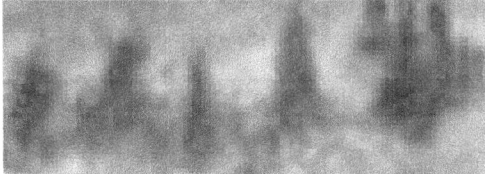

, and draw the Pine trees, do the same on the middle using Medium Charcoal Pencil as the trees there have lighter tone

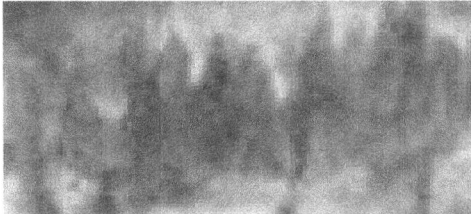

, lift up some tones on the left side using your kneaded eraser to create a strong highlight on the Pine Tree.

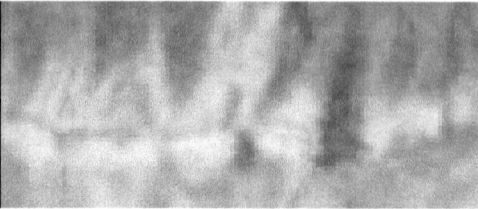

Next work the trees below, they have lighter tone so start defining those trees by applying your Hard Compress Charcoal powder using your round brush, and then lift up some tones to define the shapes and create highlights.

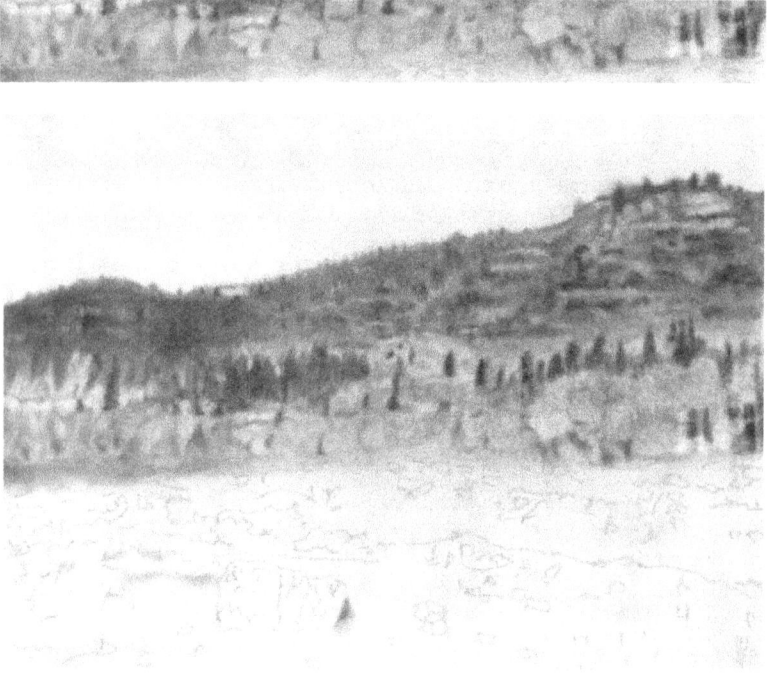

Tone the remaining area below by applying a Hard Charcoal powder using your medium size Round Brush with dabbing motion, and remember to tap it first before applying.

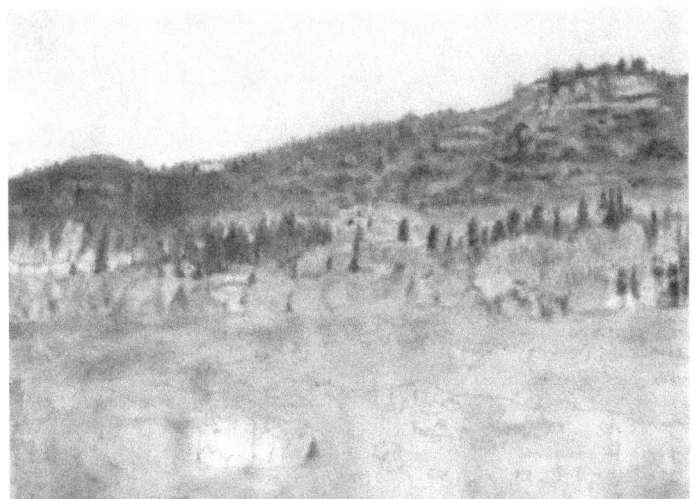

Add a medium charcoal tone on the same area, to create a darker area of the grass and start doing details on the big rock as well on the small ones; create a crack on the big rock by drawing some irregular lines using your Hard Charcoal Pencil.

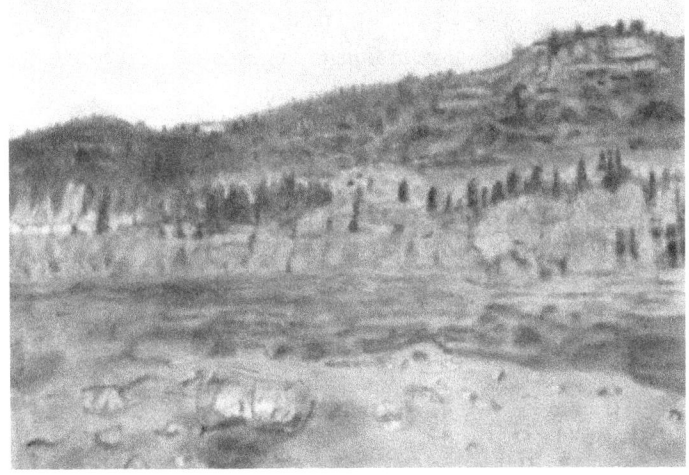

Create some grass, by lifting tones using your kneaded eraser on the area randomly.

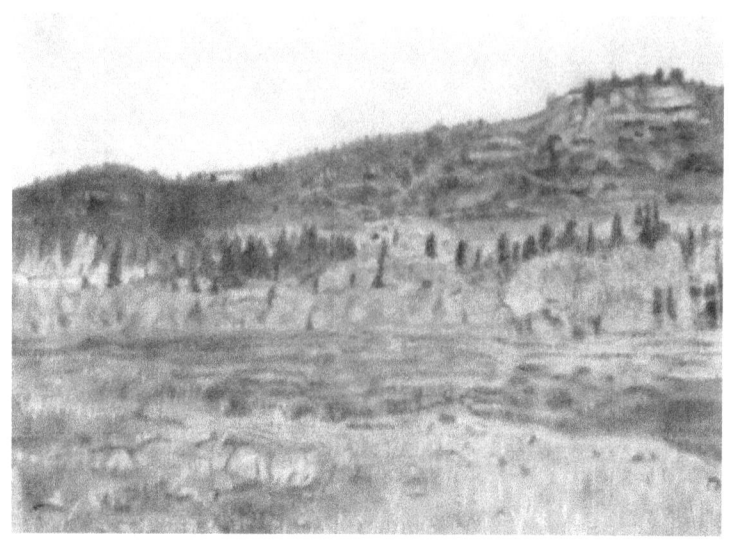

Add more medium tones on the area using Medium Round Brush by dabbing strokes. For the Sky: Apply medium Charcoal tone on the area above, and create clouds using your kneaded eraser, try to imitate the picture below, and take note of the transition. Spray your work with fixative and we're finish. Take a break first before starting the next exercise.

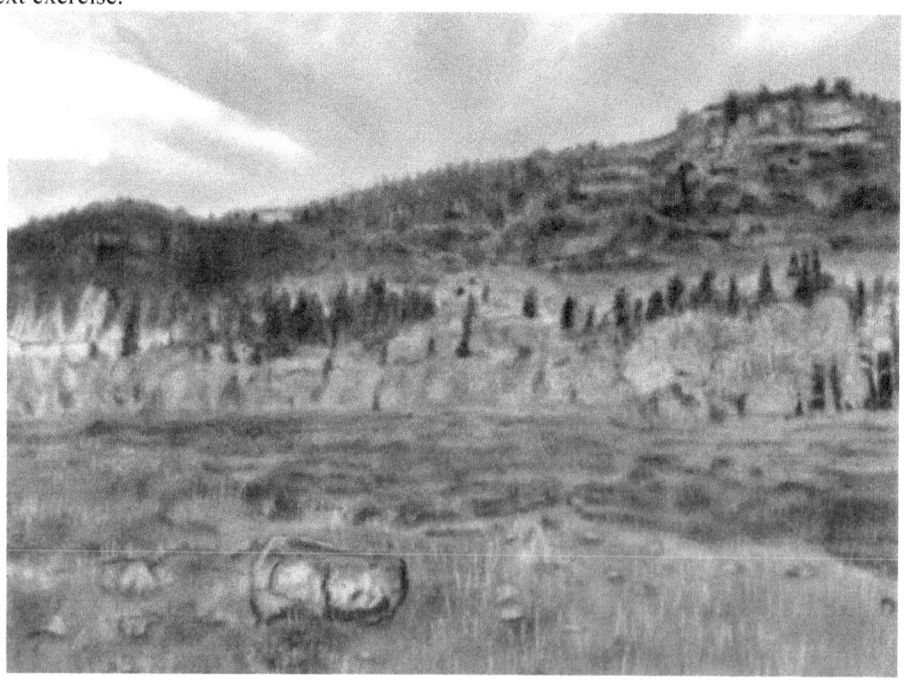

The original picture below

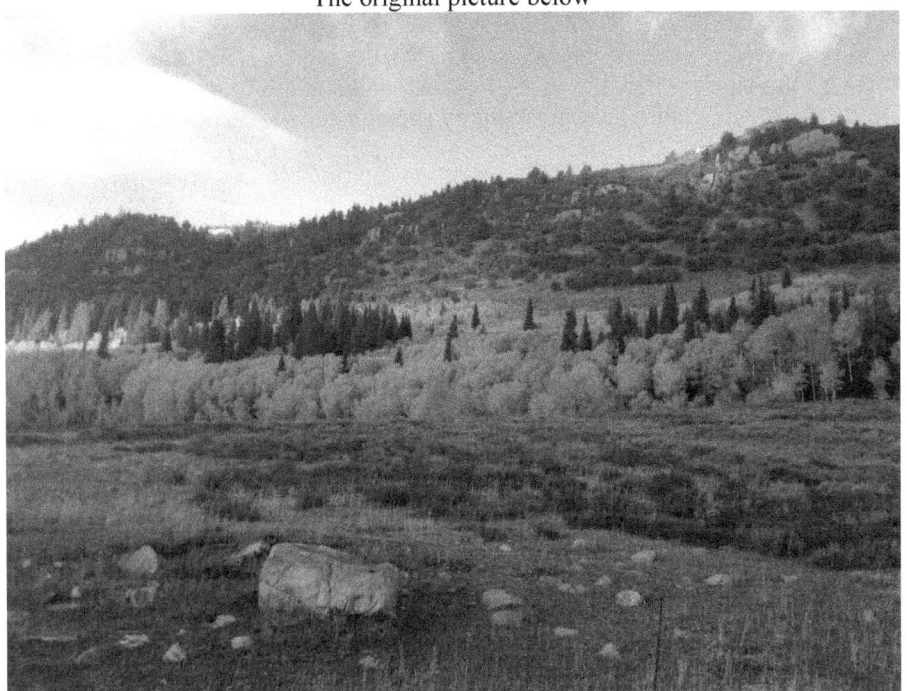

Nature's Path in Pencil

This next exercise have a tight details, so the challenge here is to render it easily, by following this step-by-step, I'm very sure you can do it, Let's draw this exercise using pencil. Make an outline by copying the grid below.

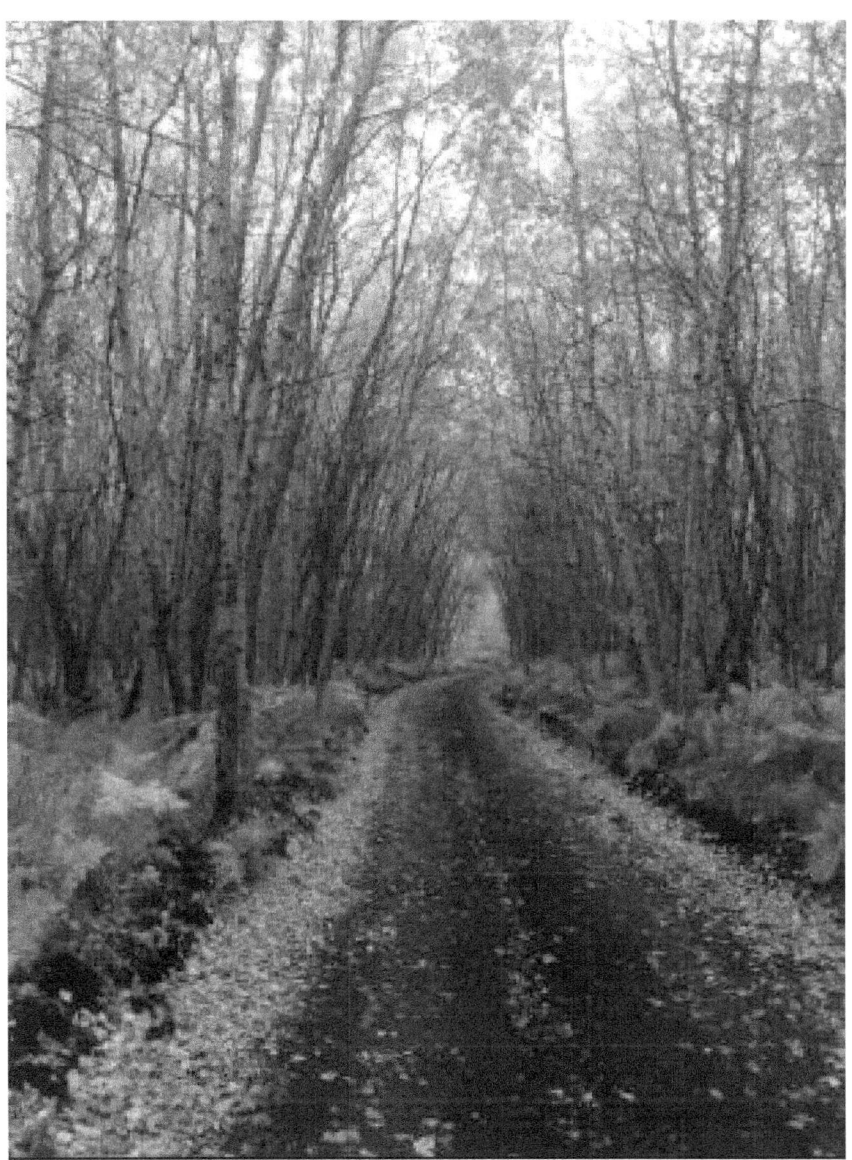

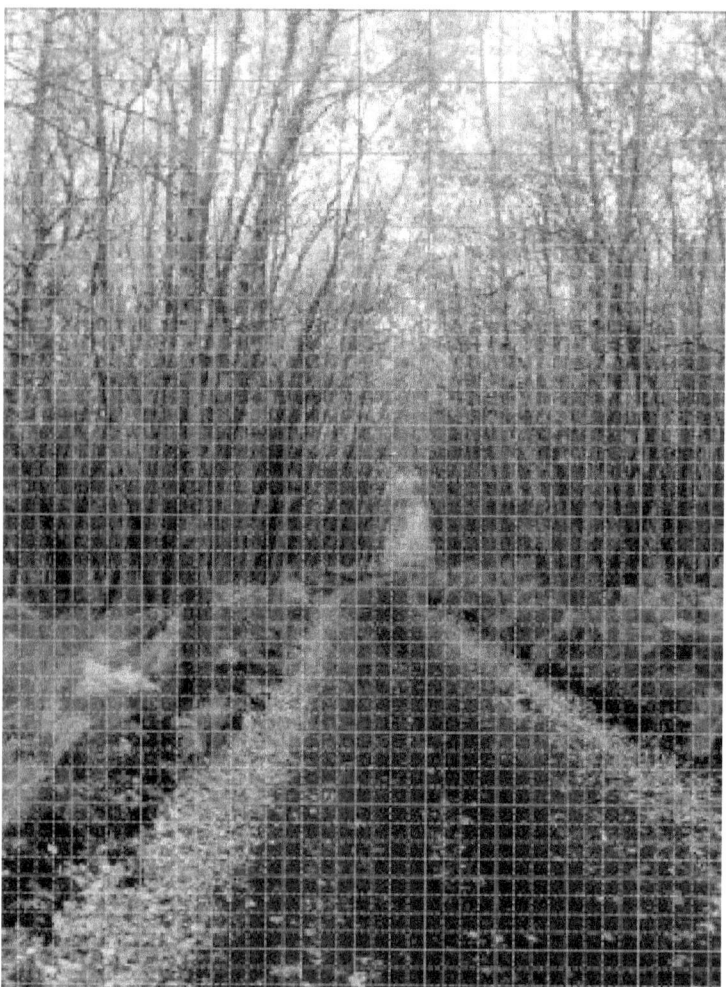

Outline:

Start by shading the darkest area of your drawing using your 6B pencil.

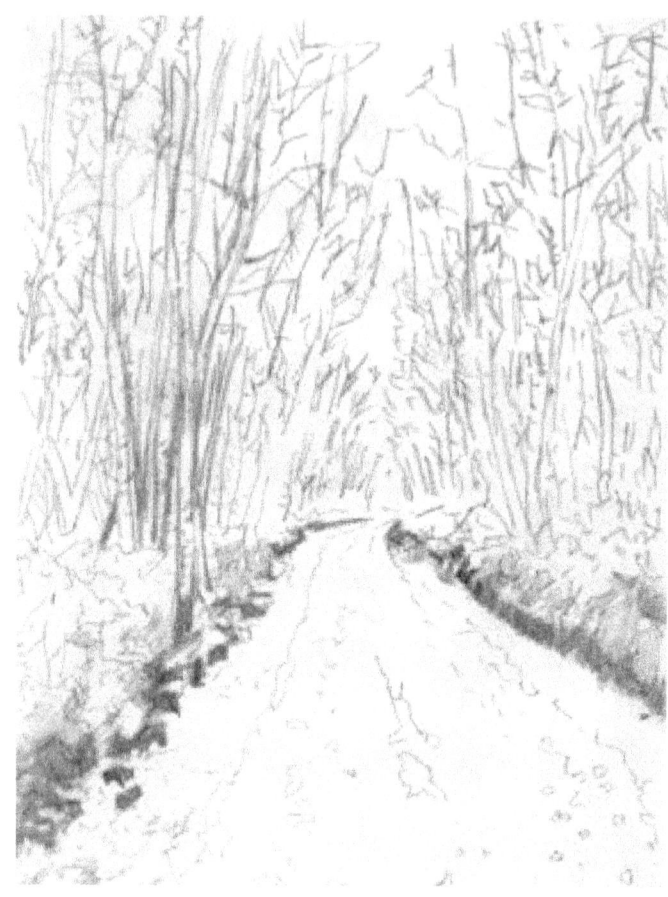

Using your 2B add shadows and other details on the trees, adding shade on the trunks and drawing thin lines for the branches

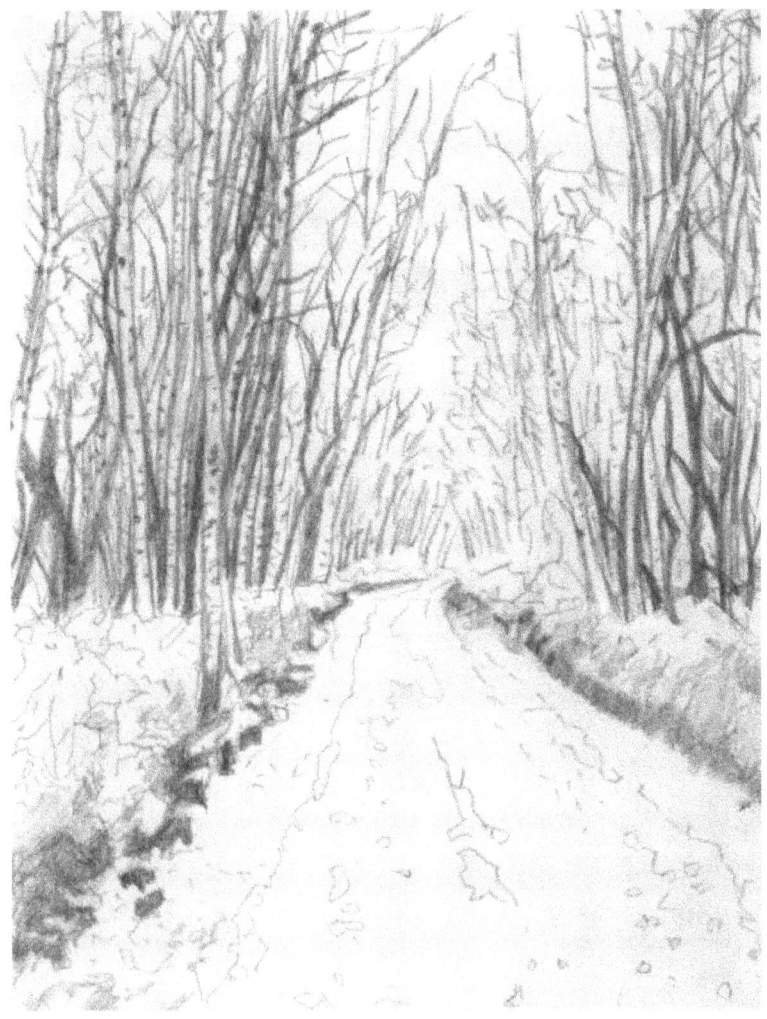

Next is to use your HB, shade the Path and the sides.

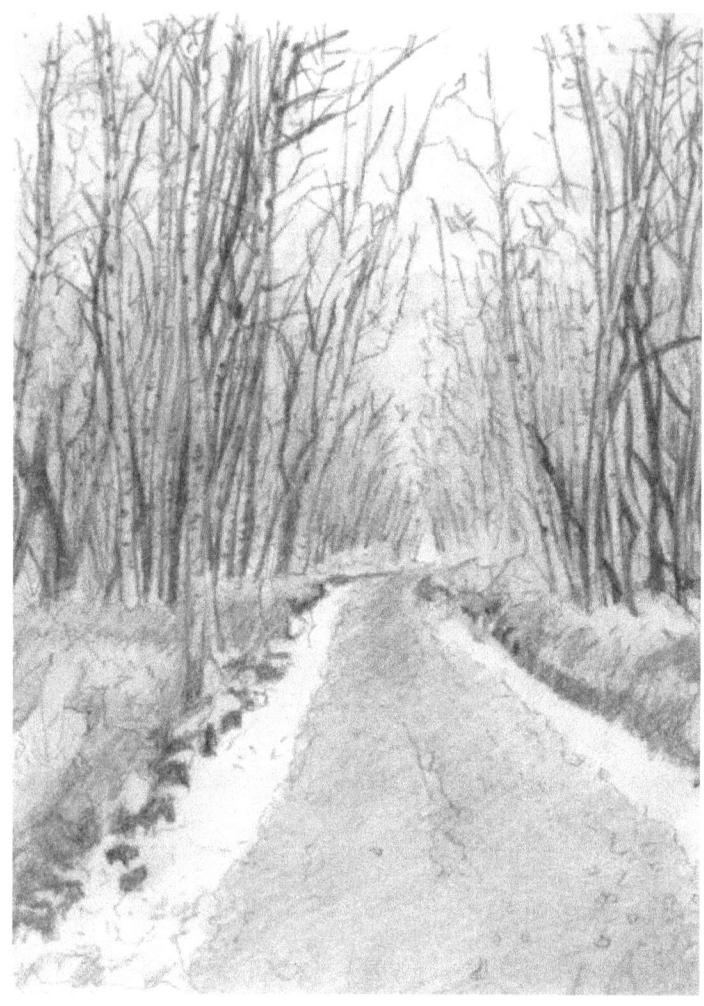

Then shade the whole area with 4H to tone the working area and darken the darker areas with 2H. And work the details below; the leaves on the side as well on the path.

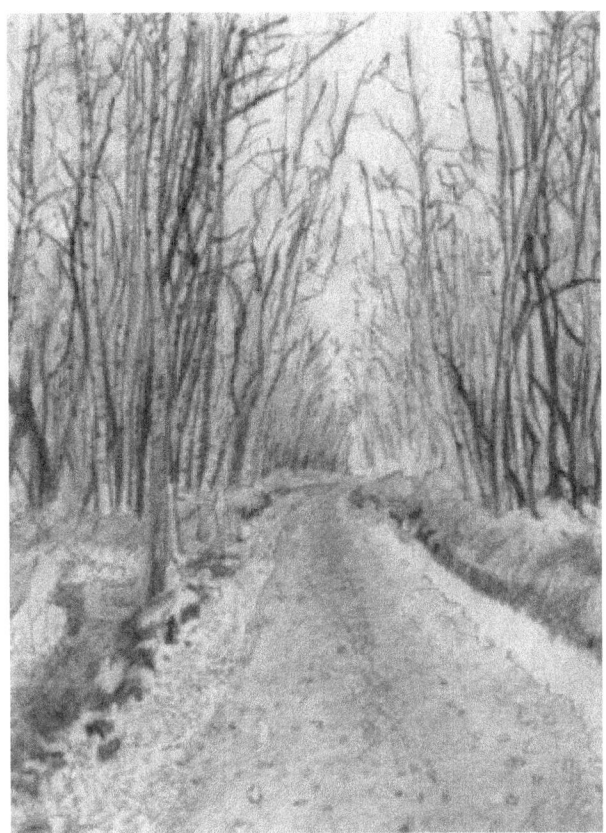

Add details on the Leaves of the tree on the top using your F and 4H pencil to have a variety of light tones, shade it like you're making a dot a.). Shade HB on both sides of the areas to achieve a darker effect and also the path, using your kneaded eraser lift some graphite to make a leaves and bush on the side and also stroke some lines to make twigs effect using your 2B Mechanical Pencil b.), do it also to the other side. Lift some tone to some fallen leaves on the path c.).

Spray your fixative and we're done with all the pencil exercises, at this point I congratulate you, but get ready for the next exercise using Charcoal.

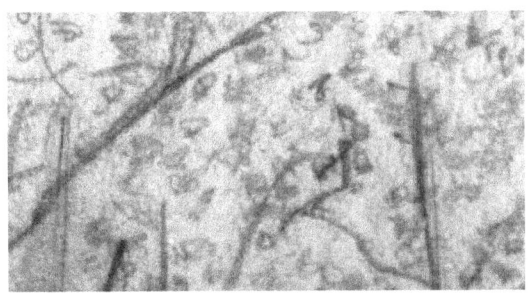

a.

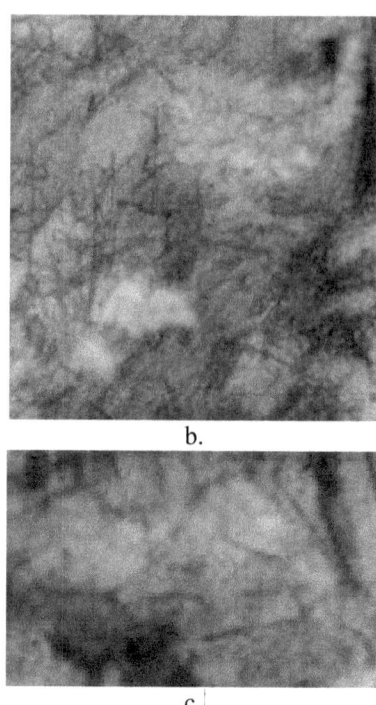

b.

c.

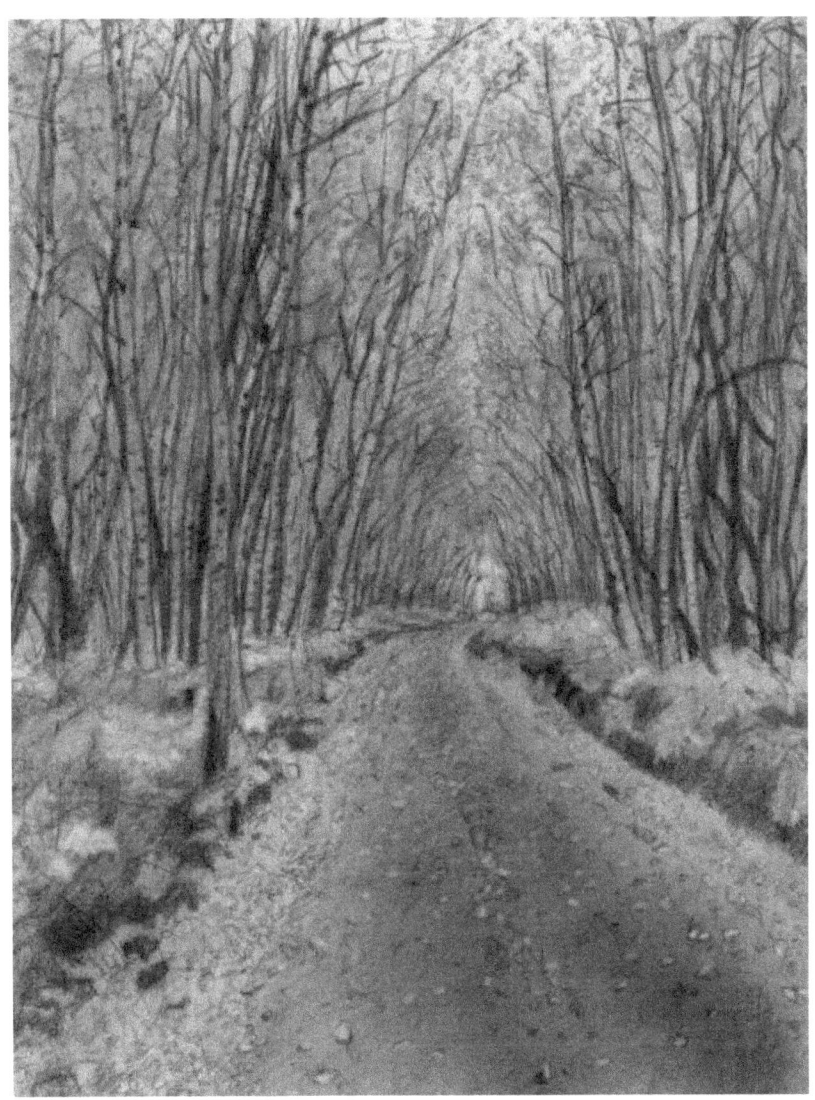

The original picture below

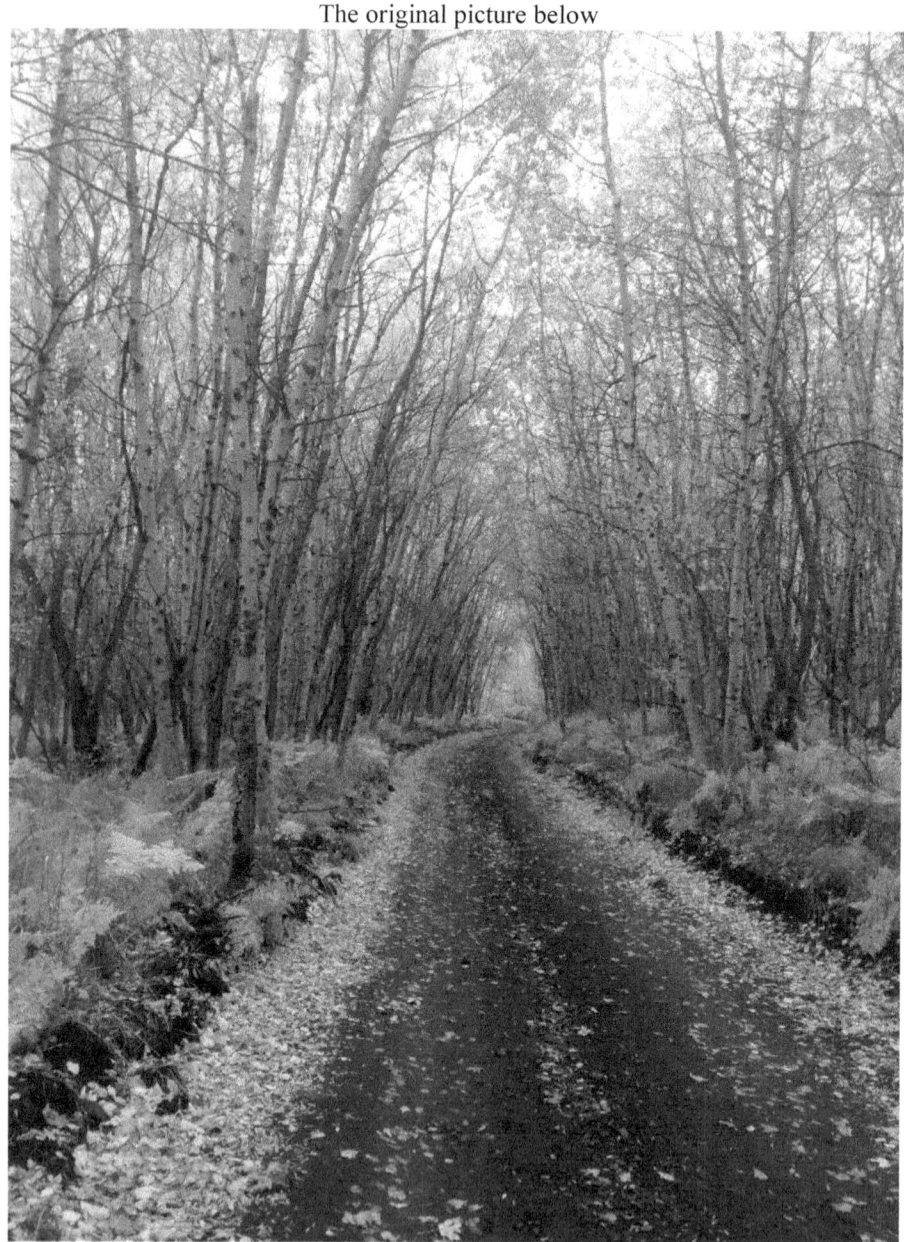

Desert Rock Formation in Charcoal

This Challenge of this Landscape is to train your eye to catch the details and distinguish the textures of the elements of the composition and how we can render it in Charcoal. Below is the outline, copy the grid to your Paper, and let's roll.

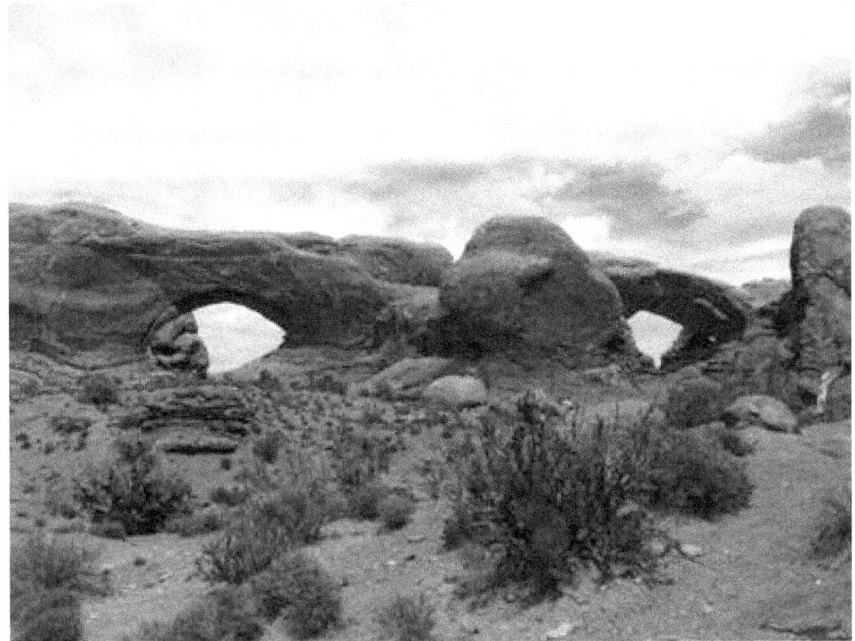

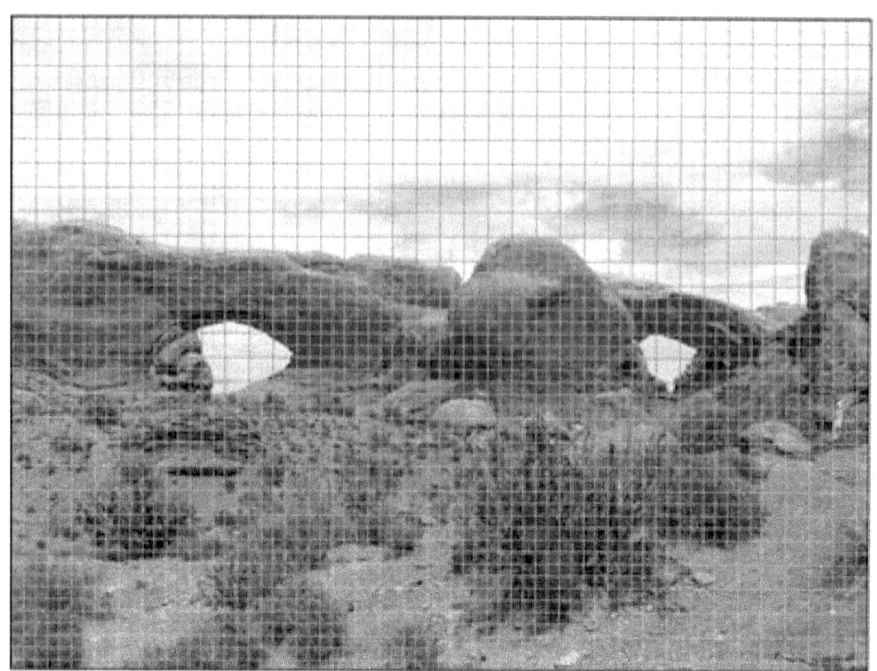

Outline:

Start by blocking the darkest area using your Soft Compress Charcoal powder using your Flat Brush.

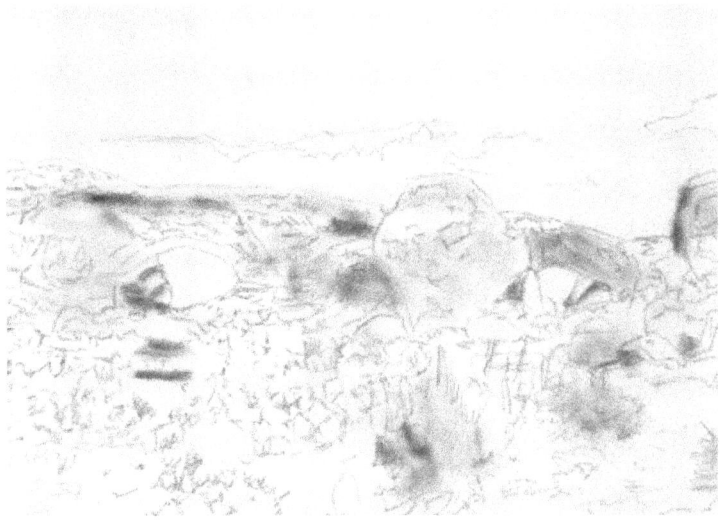

Using your Medium Charcoal apply using Your Round Brush to the darker area and also to tone the area, and also apply some tone for the sky.

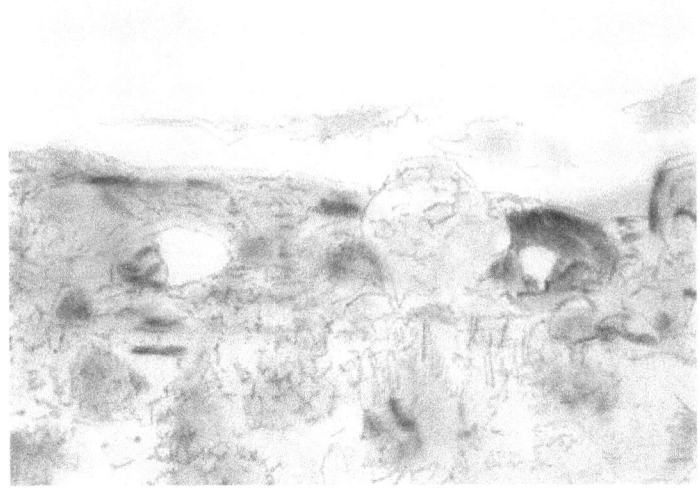

Work the details of the Rock Formation; Match the value of the tone in the picture-Add the Medium Charcoal tone to the darker areas and Hard Charcoal tone to the lighter areas, Add details by using your Hard Charcoal Pencils like cracks and lines, you can soften lines by using tortillon (please use it only for Charcoal and not for Pencil) or use your worn brush to it (you can also use it for blending specially for any transition of light), also use kneaded eraser to lift some highlights and to create texture.

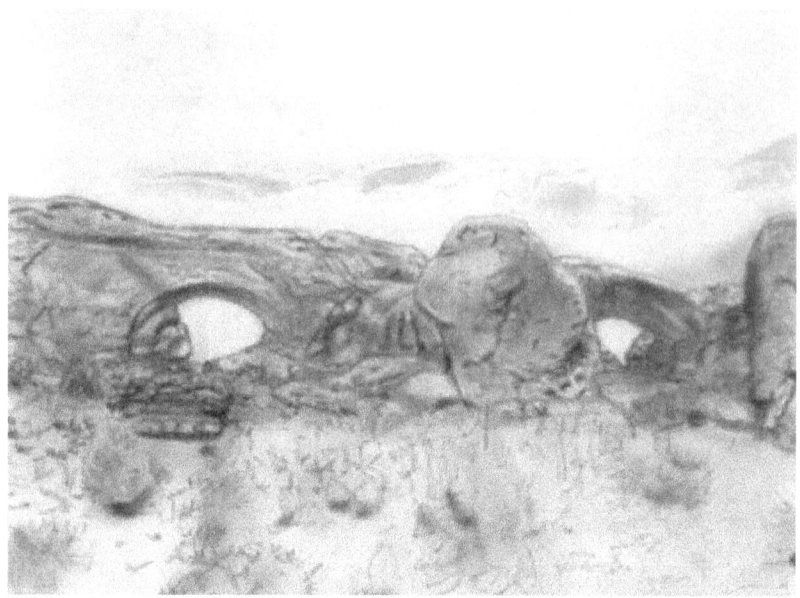

Now let's work on the desert bushes, Apply your Medium Compress Charcoal powder to those bushes.

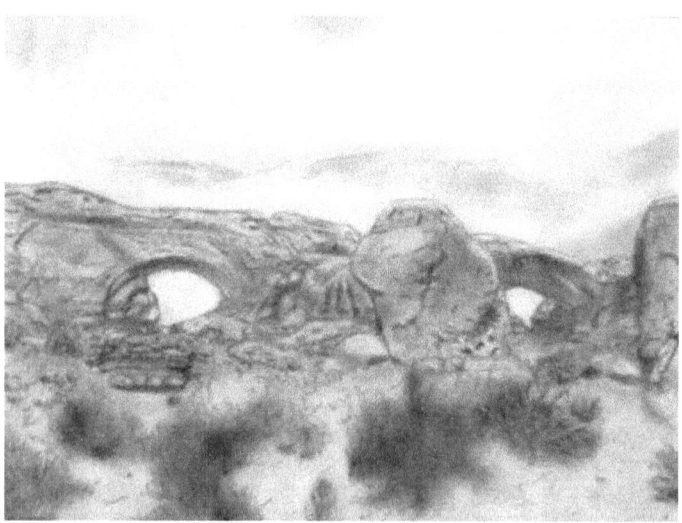

Using your kneaded eraser, mold it to thin blade like shape, lift some tone to create the bush effect, do the same to the other bushes, to create a twigs just draw some quick line strokes using your Hard Charcoal Pencil.

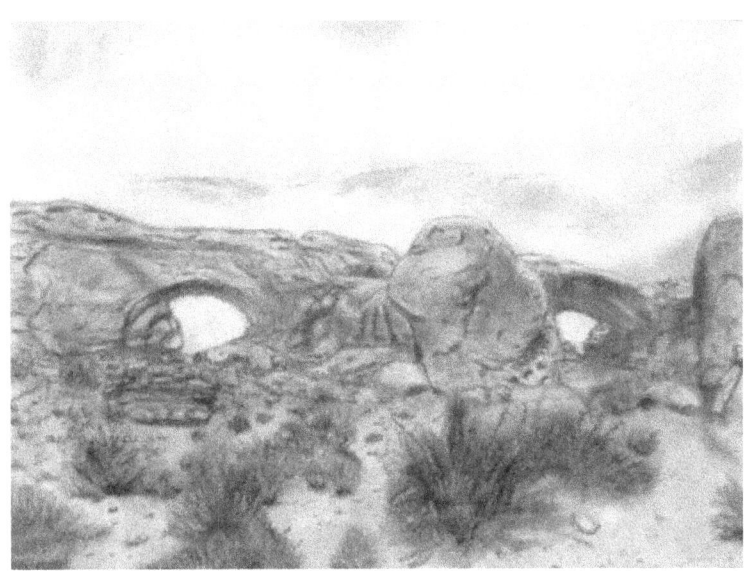

Add some small rocks on the foreground to have a good Landscape. For the clouds, use your kneaded eraser to create the effect, control your strokes to achieve a realistic effect. If you're done spray it with Fixative, Finish- now take a break and prepare for the finale.

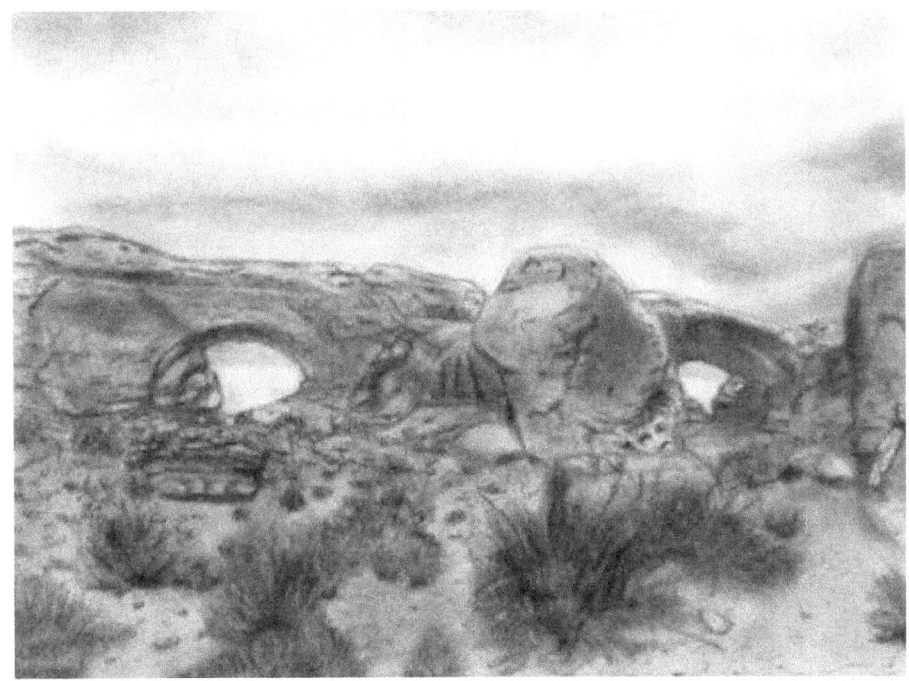

The original picture below

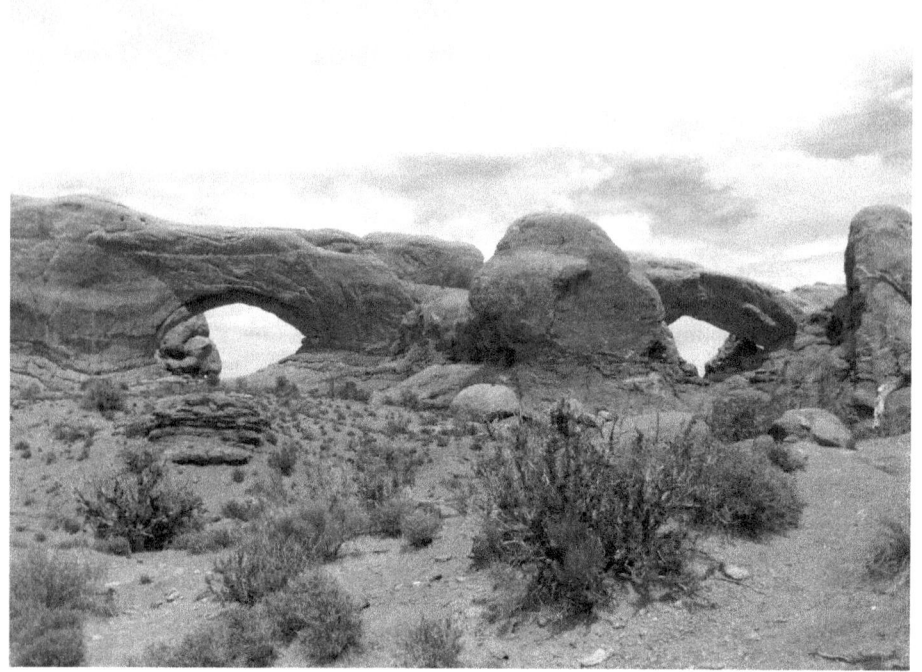

The Bridge in Charcoal

Well this is our last step-by-step exercise, and I'm sure you can finish it. So let's begin, so kindly use your knowledge and skill to make the best of it. Again I included the Grid Just copy it to your drawing paper, Bristol or illustration Board.

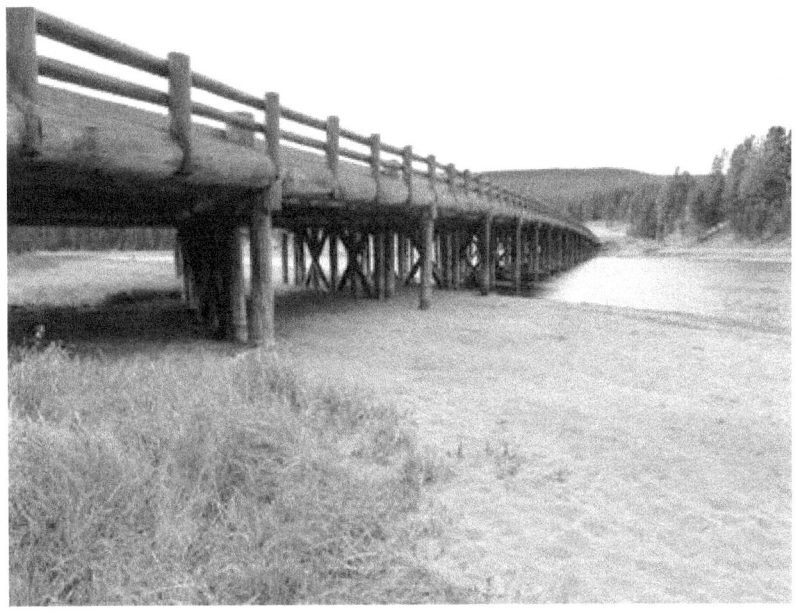

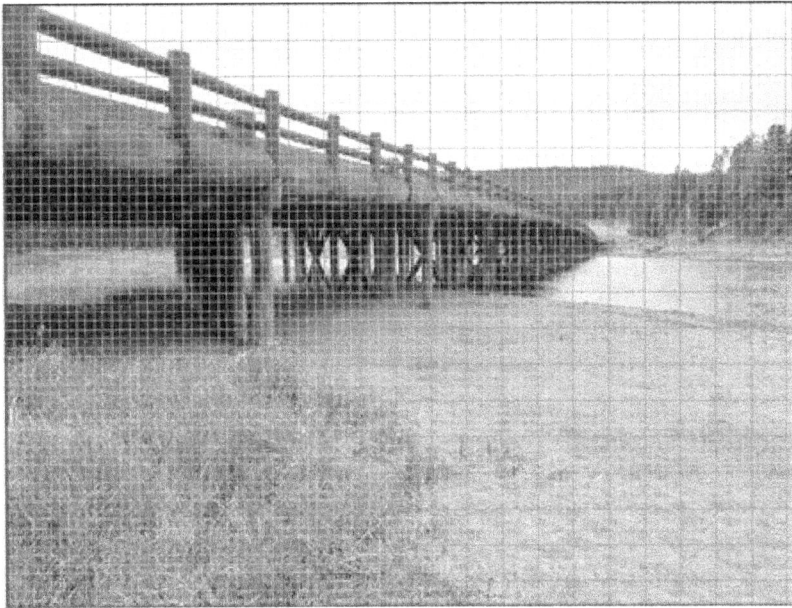

Outline:

Start with the darkest area, using Medium Charcoal powder with your flat brush.

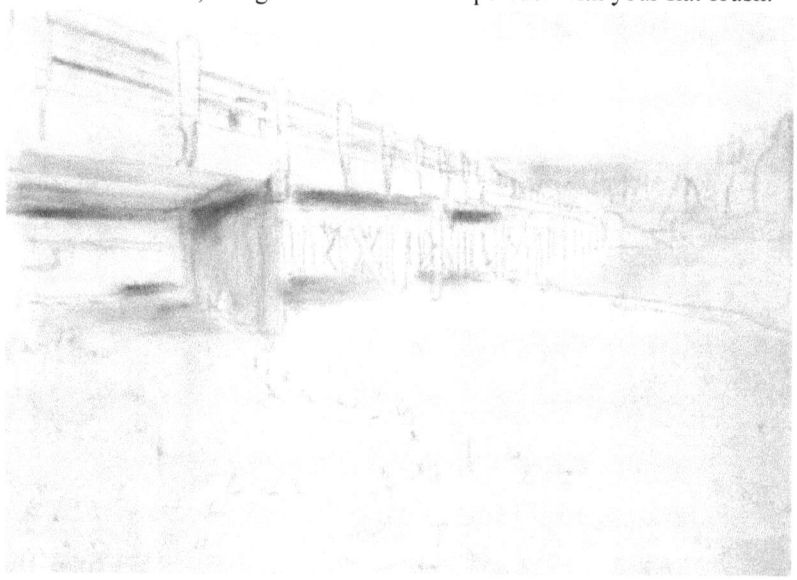

Next work the details of the trees on the right side, using your Hard Charcoal Pencil Also use kneaded eraser to create the foliage and highlights. Add Medium tone on the mountain on the background; include also the trees that you see under the bridge on the left side.

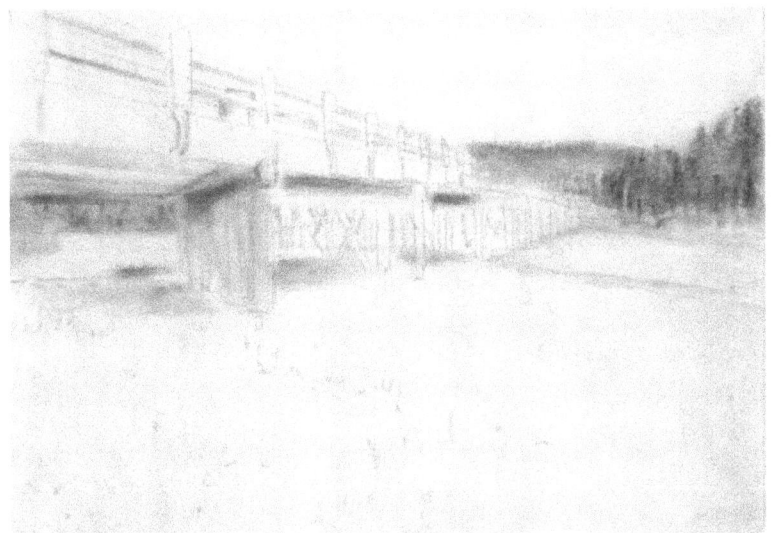

Then add details to our bridge: add Medium tone and also use Hard Charcoal Pencil, also add a Medium tone using Medium Charcoal Pencil on the river below the bridge to create a running water effect.

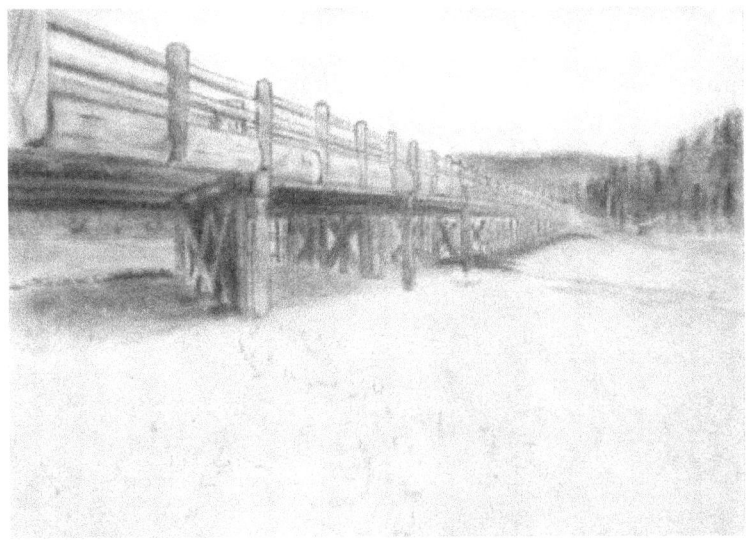

Now Let's Tone our work by dabbing some light tone using Hard Compress Charcoal dust or powder to our work, to have an old picture effect. And let's render the grass on the left side foreground, add a dabbing stroke of Hard Charcoal tone using the Round brush and then using your kneaded eraser molded to blade like edge lift up some tone to make a grass effect.

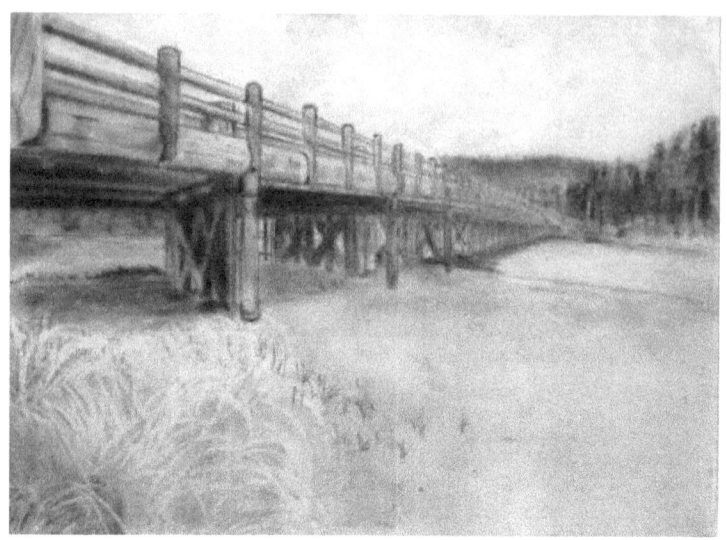

Add some twigs on the grass by drawing some quick line strokes; you can achieve a more realistic effect if you repeat the process of adding and lifting tones on the grass, doing it layer by layer. Don't forget to create the sky scene (adding tone) and clouds (using kneaded eraser).

We are almost done but first, I have to tell you, that you have to sign your signature on the lower part of your work it doesn't matter if it is on the right or left, bottom line feel free, like what I did below. As if I'm claiming it, so do the same Claim your Achievement, having a new Art skills, "CONGRATULATION" you're now considered a True Landscape Artist.

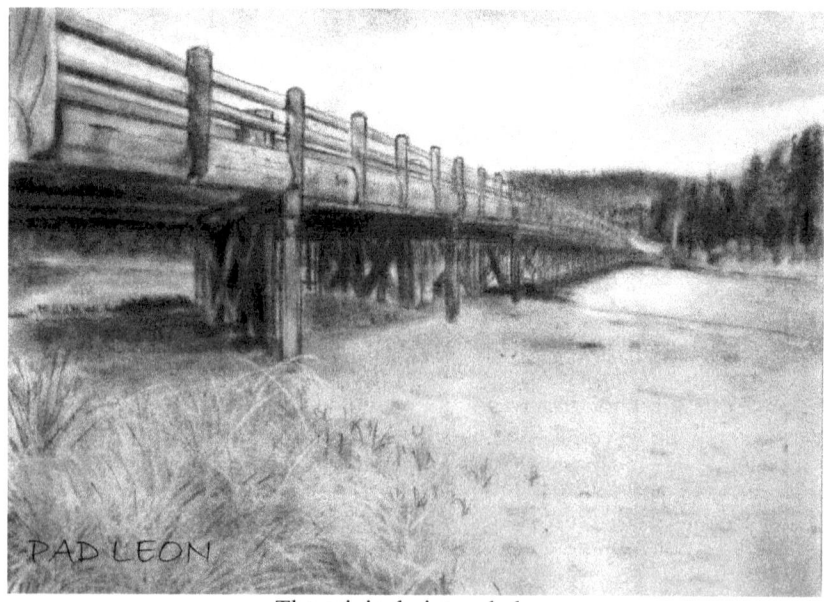

The original picture below

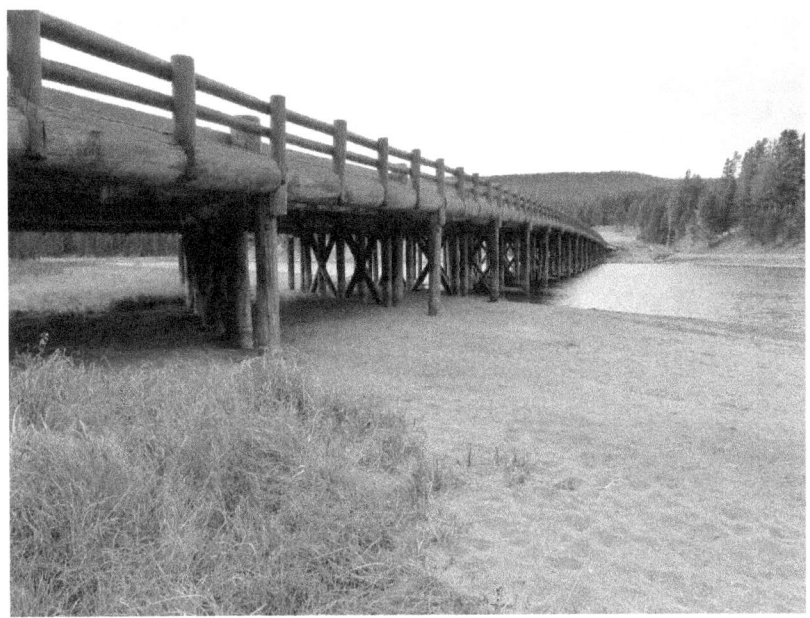

And remember that no one can take away that skill from you. Find ways to enhance it, you are a "Master Artist".

Tips to Remember

- You must have a clear copy or photograph of your subject.
- Sometimes some parts in the photograph are blurred and it's hard to distinguish, in that case, use your imagination.
- It's not bad, to pick up some magazines and newspaper, and find a picture you want to draw and also interest you, since they have good and clear picture.
- Secure yourself a good lighting source when drawing.
- Watch the proportion of shapes with accordance to other shapes.
- Take note of transition of values, especially midtones HB, 2H and 4H
- Remember different textures have different technique or strokes, that you need imitate when drawing.
- If you find some parts of the face, difficult to draw, break it down to smaller components.
- It helps if you have reference in handy or take photograph, so that you will have a guide when drawing and shading, especially if your confuse of the shadows and cast shadow in your drawing.
- If you are already good in drawing and rendering, using the pencils that I mention, try to explore other pencils with different grades, and see what works best for you, also try to explore other kinds of Art, as much as possible.
- If you're having issues with pencil smudges or fingerprints cause by oil from your hand on your work, you can prevent this by placing an extra sheet of paper under your working hand specifically the side of your palm.
- Constant practice drawing and rendering really helps you to succeed.

Portraits of People in Charcoal

Portrait of the Little Girl

For our first exercise let's render my niece Alia, Prepare your materials and follow the steps below.

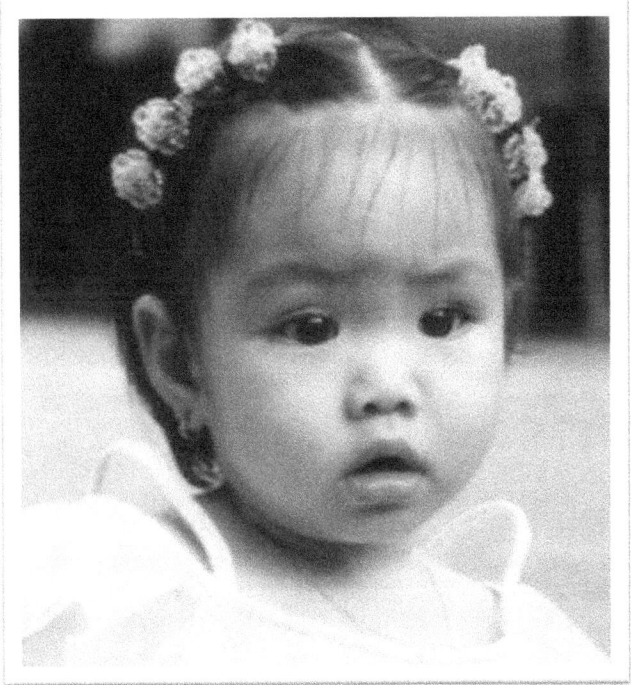

Transfer the outline below to your Bristol board, you may print the outline to your printer and trace it over the Tracing or Light Table as what we discuss in **Tracing Table or Light Table / Flexi-glass with Bendable Lamp.**

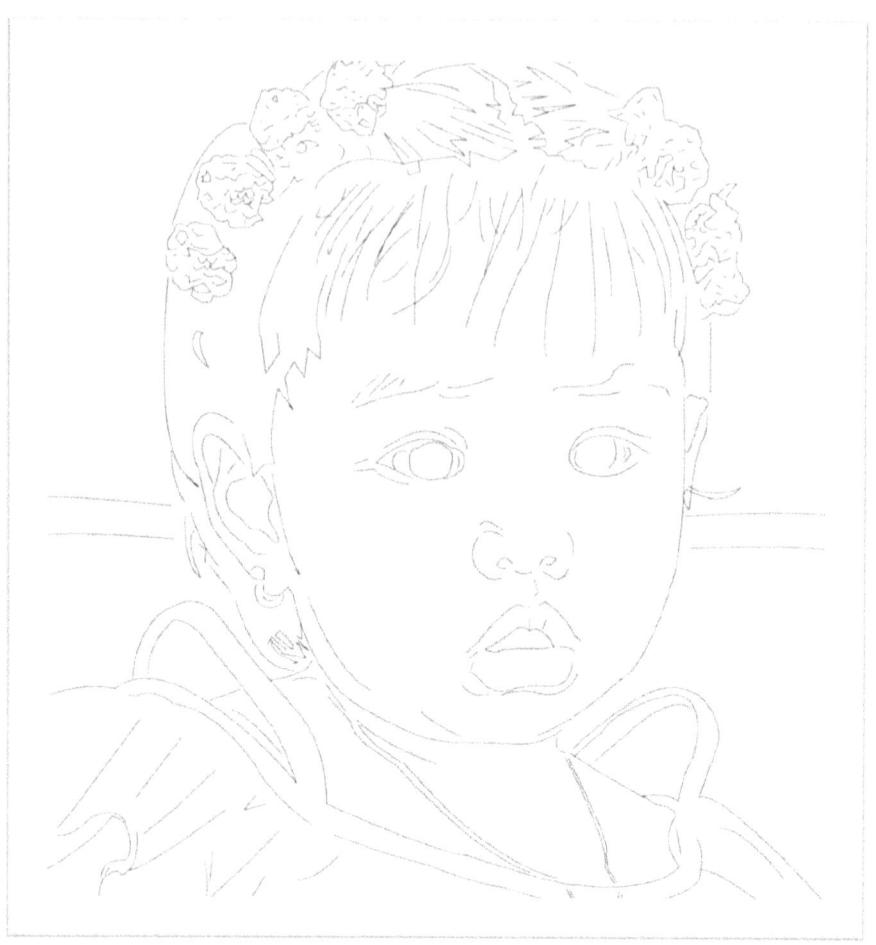

How to render the Eyes

Steps:

1. Apply Medium Charcoal S. (shaved), for the Iris and upper eye lash, using your small nylon flat brush (I used this most of the time), do this on both eyes, also don't forget to use your charcoal pencil medium on the crease and lower eyelash.

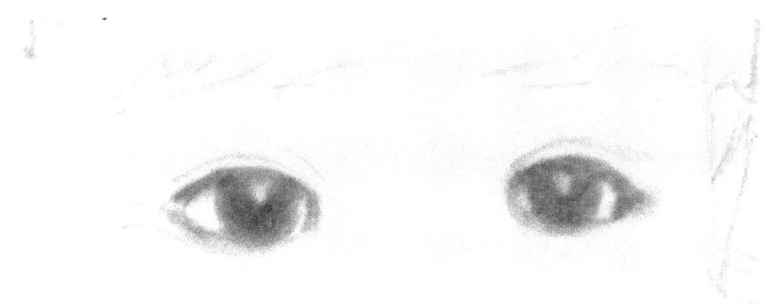

2. Add a tone in the eyebrows with the same charcoal Medium S.; add more pressure to the brush to make a darker tone and lighter pressure to have a lighter tone. As you can see below, also apply some tone on the nasal bridge and area between the eyebrows and eyes with the same range of charcoal.

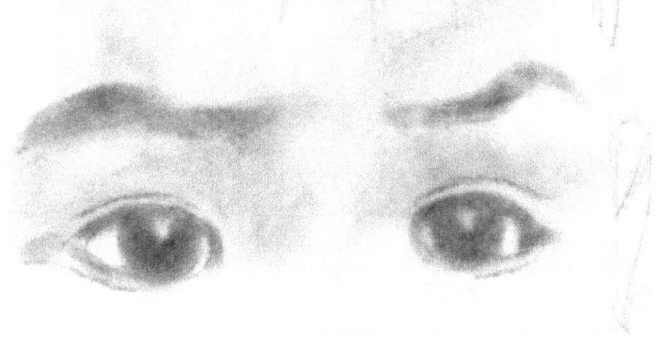

3. Time to add details:
   For the eyes add pupils inside the iris using Soft Charcoal Pencil, you can use your templates to have a small perfect circle, shade(just slide the brush with medium charcoal) slightly below the eye. Use your Hard Charcoal Pencil and make a small curving strokes for the eyelashes of the eye on your right side (start from the bottom and stroke diagonally to the right side upwards), for you the left side do the same starting from the bottom to the left side upwards, also add small detailed hair on the eyebrow, don't try to fill it, since our model is just a toddler. Also don't forget the catchlight (the reflection of light in the eye, you can define or create it by using your Kneaded eraser mold it to a sharp point and lift up by erasing some charcoal above the pupils to make the white of the paper appears to have a catchlight effect.

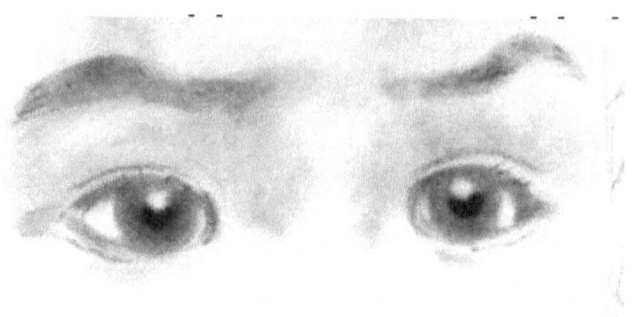

How to render the Nose

Steps:
1. Start by shading the nostril with Soft Charcoal Pencil.

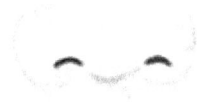

2. Now use your brush and add a tone (dabbing strokes) on the area below the nostril, and the wings or alars of the nose, take note of the area that are more darker, it's on the left side of the top alar and the side, including below the nostril and also shade the left side below the nostril, in that case add another light layer on those areas to make it darker.

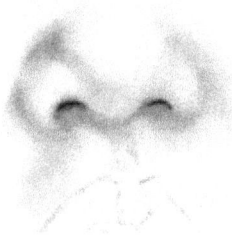

How to Render the Lips

Steps:
1. Apply a Medium Charcoal S. on the upper lip, remember that the upper lip is darker compare to the lower lip as it receive less light, so add pressure when applying charcoal in that area, next apply a tone in the lower lip so you must use less pressure when shading it with your brush, also shade a darker tone on the area between the lips (it's on both sides of the lips).

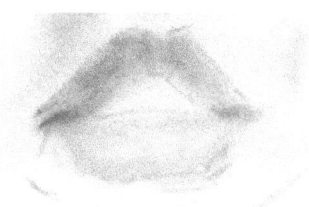

2. Next is to apply a dark value inside the mouth, so use a Soft Charcoal Pencil and shade the area, after that using your small flat brush again, apply a light pressure of strokes to lightly soften the tone (you can also use Tortillon for this). Below the lower lip there's a line (it's surrounded with highlights above it) and also the dark area below the line, so apply some tone on that area too with Medium charcoal S. Add tones to the lower lip and apply highlights in that area and also the highlights on the lower lip.

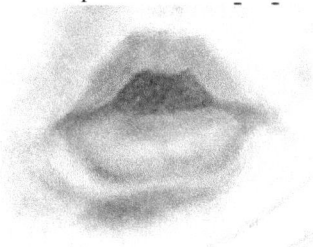

How to Render the Ear
Steps:
1. As you can see in the picture, the areas in the ear received less light, in that case, apply a Medium Charcoal S. using your round brush dab all area of the ear as what seen in the picture below.

2. Now add another layer in the dark areas.

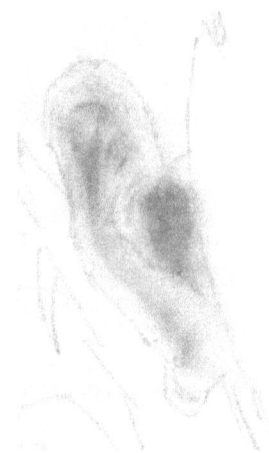

3. Apply highlights to the ear, I also add a dark tone at the back of the ear, just to see how it will looks like, and for me to see the contrast.

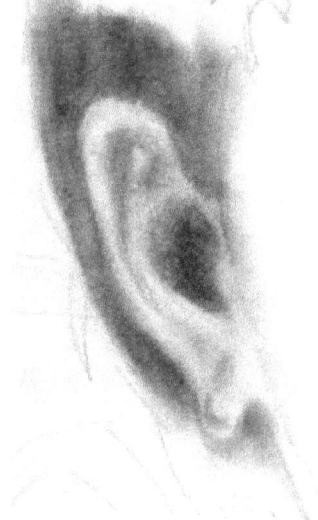

How to render the Face

Steps:

1. Apply the face with a Medium Charcoal S. dabbing lightly with less pressure when using your brush, just to have a tone in the face.

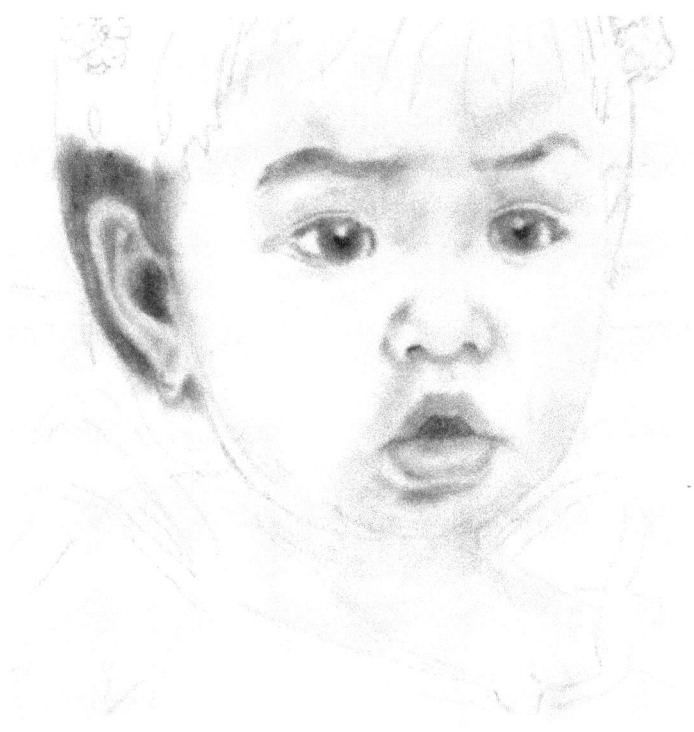

2. Add another layer of the same Charcoal lightly to the darker areas of the face; it's on the left side and neck area.

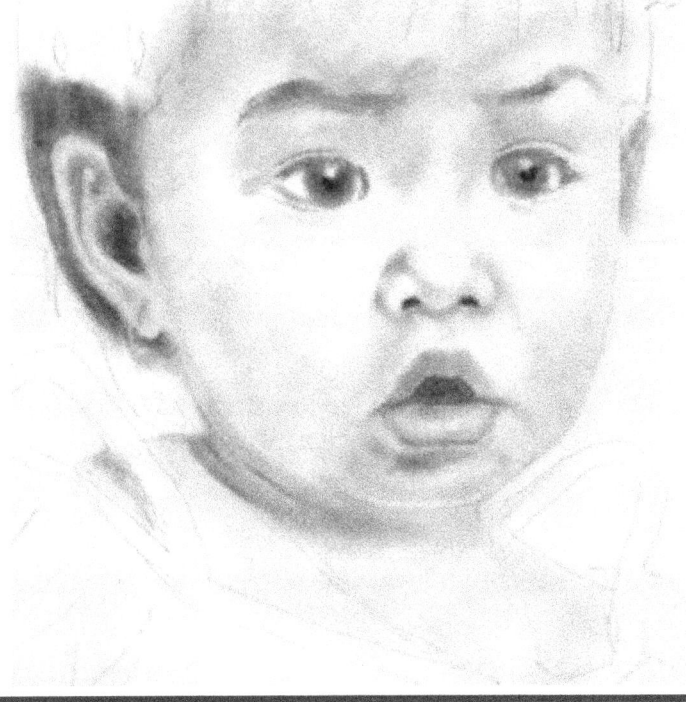

How to render the Hair

Steps:
1. Lightly apply the Medium Charcoal S. with your round medium Brush on the forehead including the bangs of the hair; next apply the same tone on the hair.

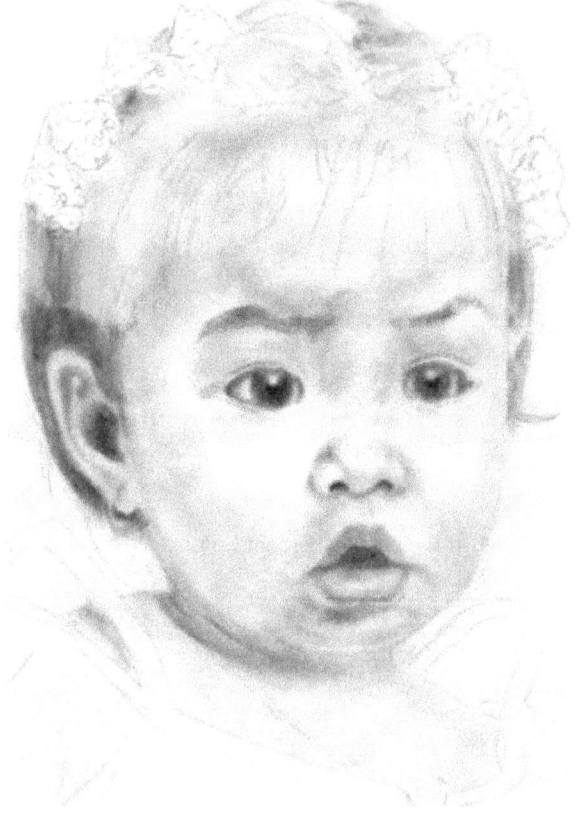

2. Lay more dark tones in the dark area of the hair, filling the area with Charcoal Medium S., take note that some areas of the hairs in the head are less dark due to the source of light, so highlights and slightly dark areas are created.

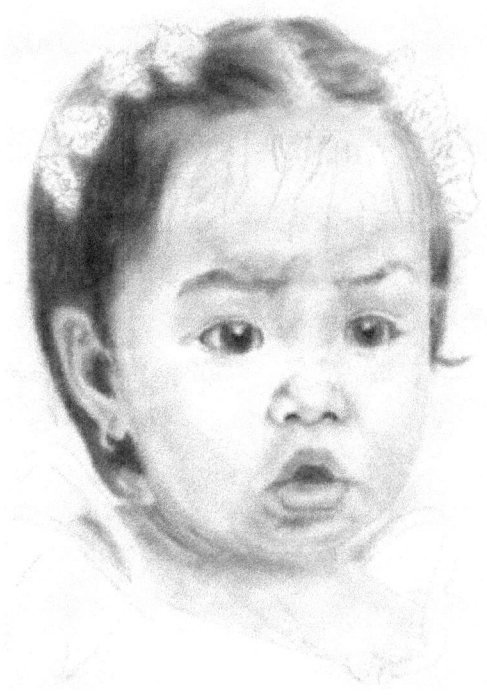

3. Below is the more detailed rendition of the hair, use your Hard Charcoal Pencil when drawing some detailed hair strands, you can see this in the forehead and on the top of the head.

How to render the Gown, Necklace and Earring
Steps:
1. Let's work the Gown of our model:
- Laces –using your brush and Medium Charcoal S., apply the tone on shadow at the bottom of it.
- Sleeves-the right side is simple, you just have to draw a line using your Medium Charcoal Pencil, while the left have more details, take note that the sleeve on the left is translucent, so the skin tone underneath can be somewhat be seen, so add some tone using Medium Charcoal S. and brush in the sleeves as you can see in the picture below.
- Collar- draws a line with Medium Charcoal Pencil for this.

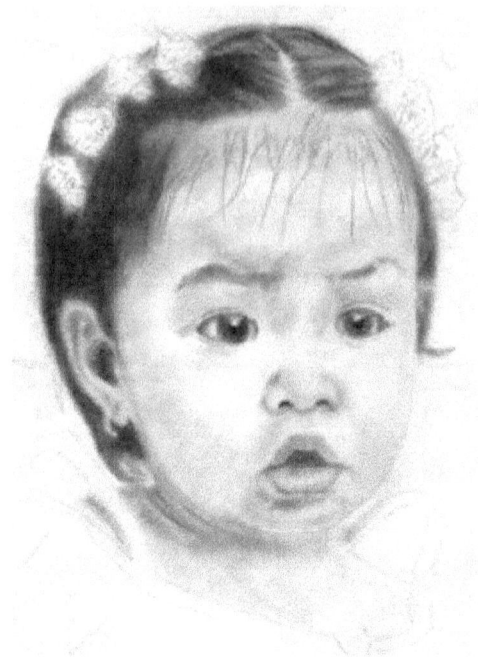

2. Add the details on the earring and necklace use your Medium Charcoal Pencil to add detail line (left and right side) and small round like shapes (left side) on the necklace, most of it is soft edges, so just rub it with your tortillon or brush to make it diffuse(a.). For the earring same as when giving details on the necklace just draw what you see on the details to make it more real on the earrings and use your kneaded eraser to define the shape (b.).

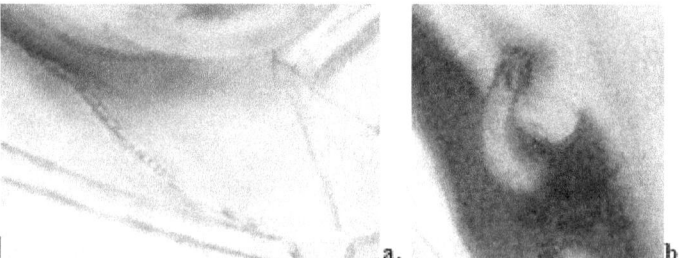

a.   b.

3. Now let's render the Hairclips, use your Medium Charcoal S. and block all the dark areas, using your Medium Charcoal Pencil add enough details that you see, use your kneaded eraser when you want the reduce the tone of the details, also take notes of the highlights and apply it on the flower decoration of the hairclips, remember that later on after the rendition of the background is finish, you have to get back here and check it if there is charcoal dust in this area to be lifted up by kneaded eraser as well as other areas.

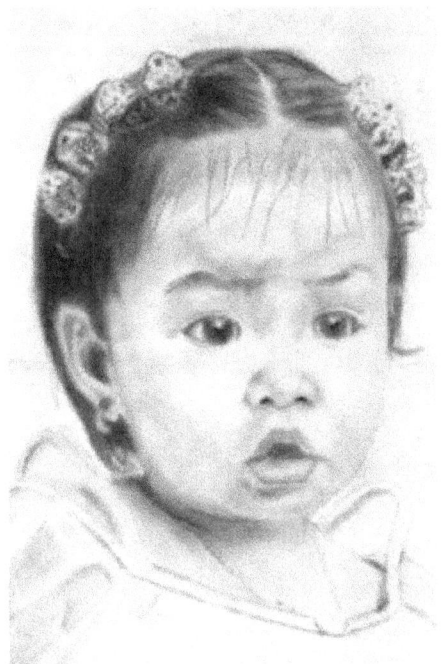

How to render the Background

The background was first applied by Medium Charcoal S. very lightly, from the shoulder level to eye level, and then from eye level to the area at the top fill it with Soft Charcoal S. to have a dark value similar to the picture, take note of the shape that has dark value, as you notice there are areas at the top that has the same value of the shoulder level.

Check your work, if it need more tone or less, if you think you use too much Charcoal then use your kneaded eraser to lift it up and correct that area, and if it has less tone, then apply another layer of Charcoal using your brush. Make necessary adjustment if you find your work out of proportion. The bottom line is you need to polish your work to make it real and to look professional, after that spray your work with fixative.

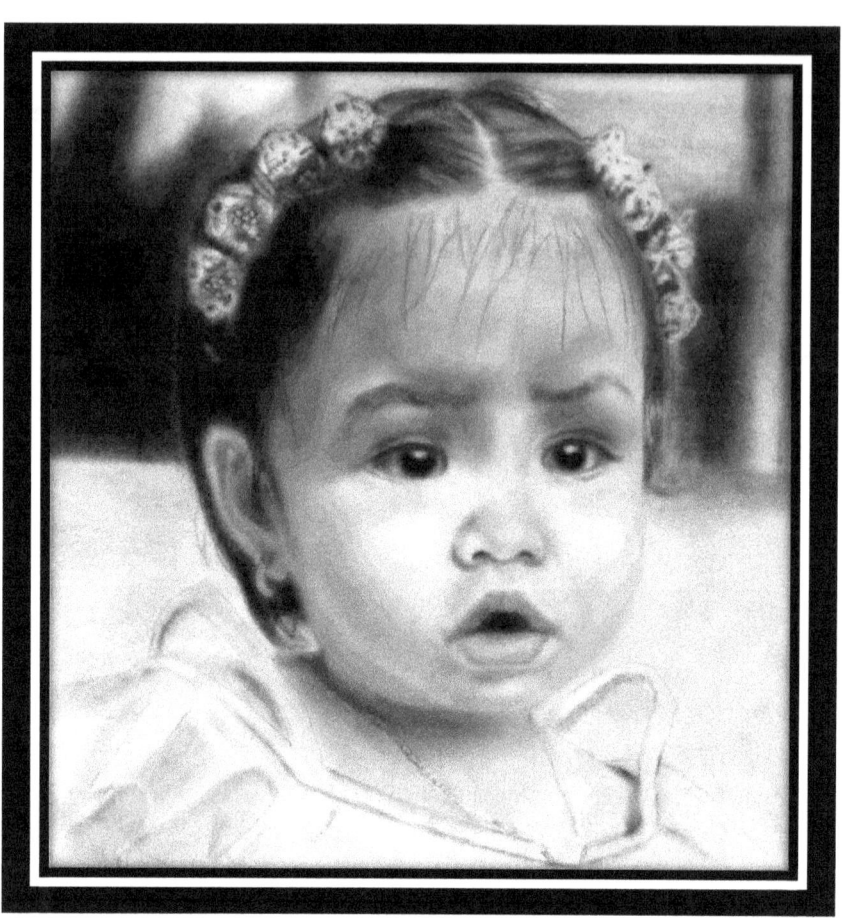

Portrait of a Young Man

For the second exercise, we're going to render Jake son of John our very own Author, here is another close-up shot, the challenge is to render the hair with texture, including clothing and also the granite effect in the background. So let's get star

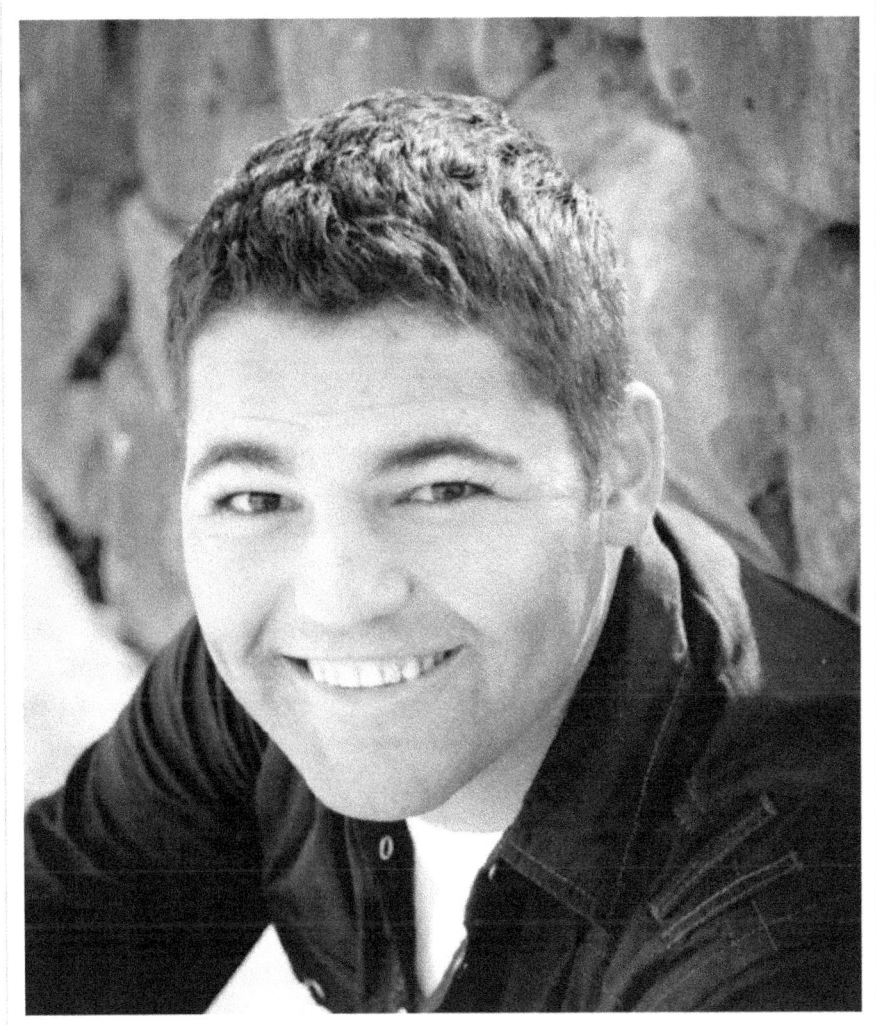

Transfer the outline to your Bristol and begin.

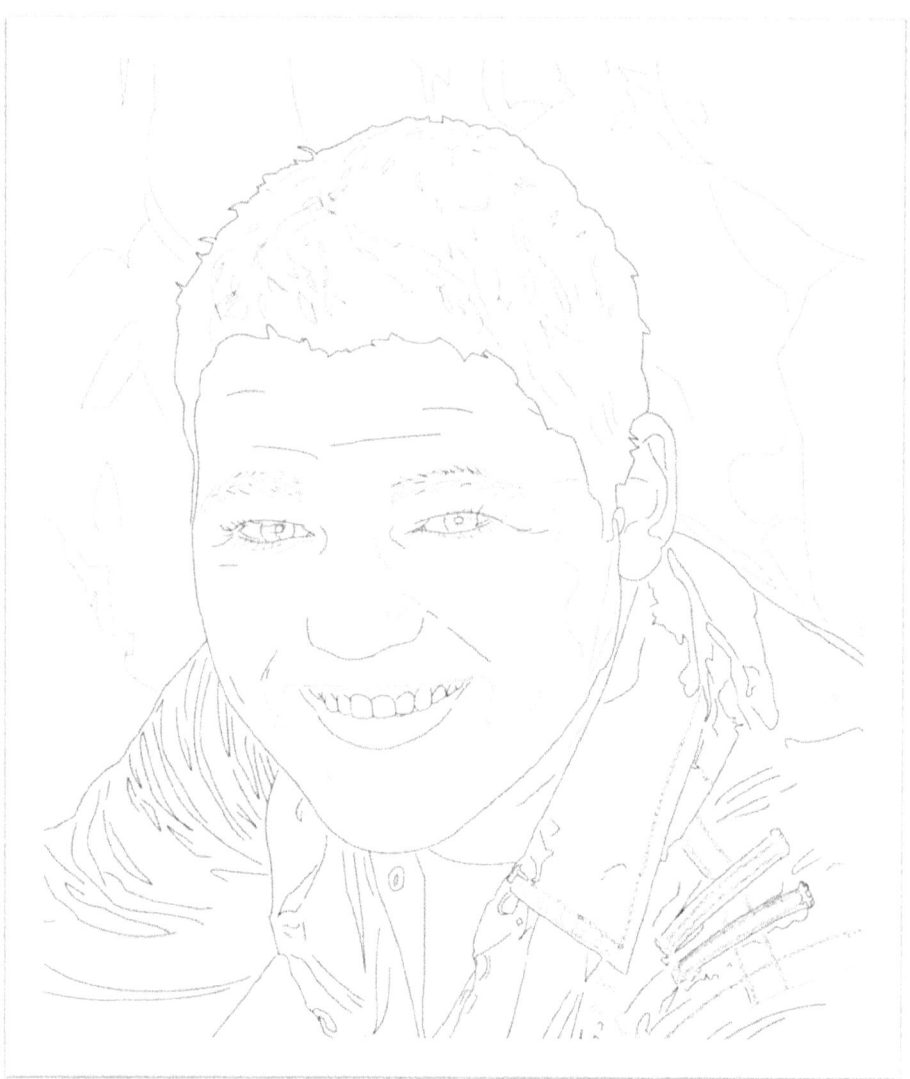

Steps:

1. Start in the eyes by darkening the pupils with Soft Charcoal Pencil, next is to darken the upper eyelid by shading it with Medium Charcoal S. using your small flat brush, apply Soft Charcoal Pencil to the accents on the side of the mouth.

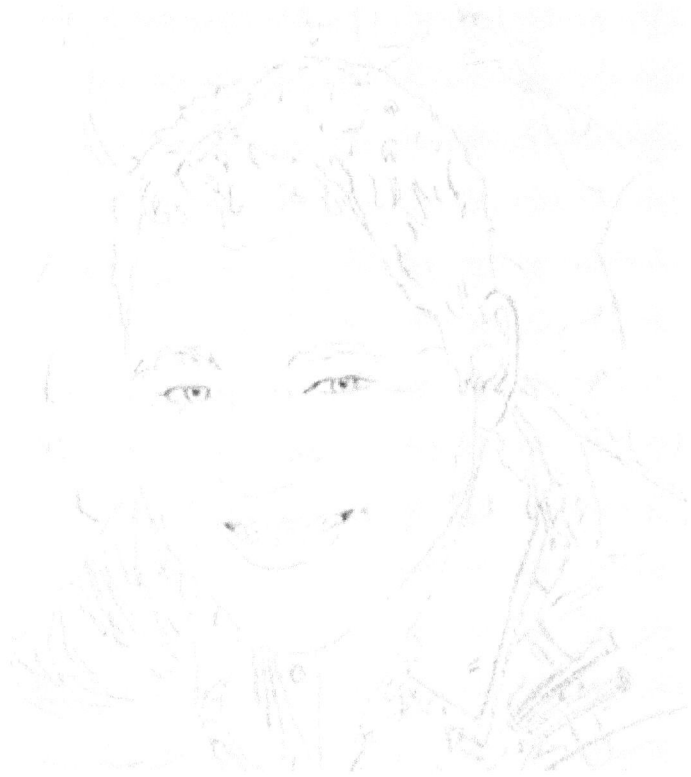

2. Apply Medium Charcoal S. to the both Iris using your small or medium brush; also apply some to the eyebrows.

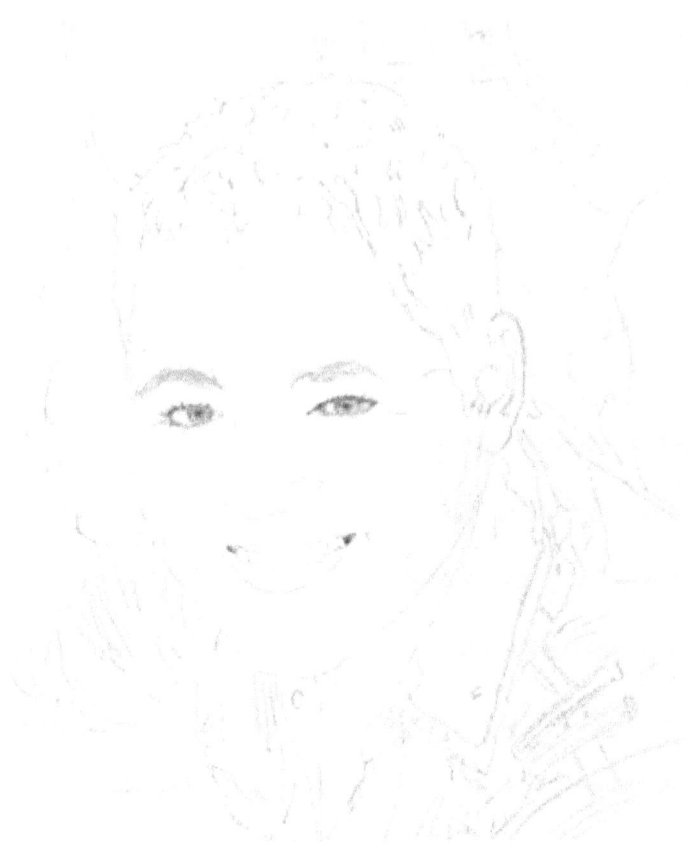

3. Shade the Nostril, the wing of the nose and Nasogenian folds using Medium Charcoal Pencil. For the Lips apply Medium Charcoal S. using your brush to the upper lip, again take note that the Upper Lip is always darker compared to Lower Lip, so just apply that area lightly with your brush. For the gums you can use your medium used tortillon to add a tone and detail the teeth by using a Hard Charcoal Pencil but with light pressure to control the value (you may use pencil first with shading and use Hard Charcoal Pencil lightly for darker or shadow areas).

Tip:
A man lips are lighter compare to a woman lips.

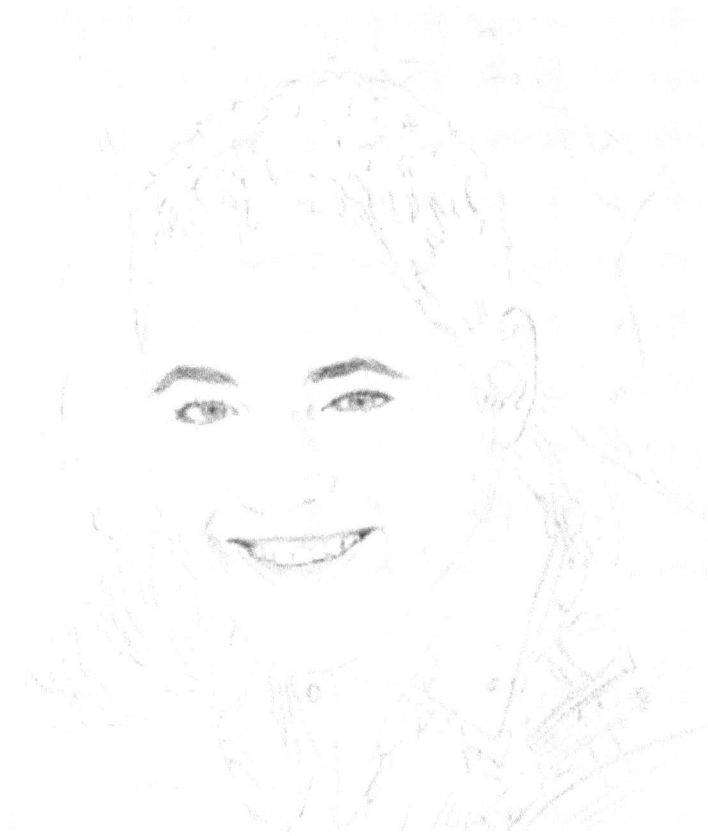

4. For the ear add tones using your Medium Charcoal S. on the dark part of the ear located in the hollow area.

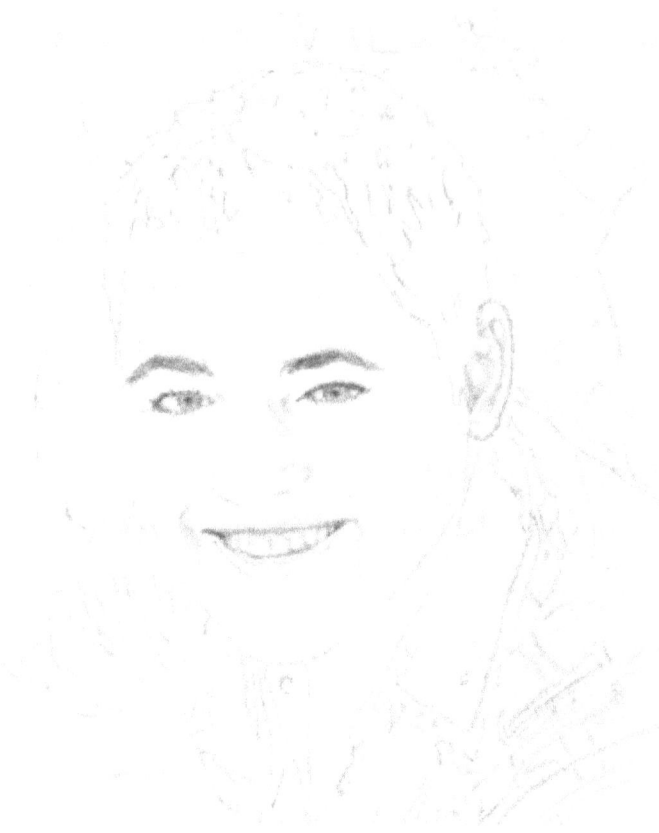

5. Now let's render the face starting from dark to light, begin dabbing some Medium Charcoal S. lightly to the right side of the face, also add same tone lightly for the temple and cheek, and also for the area on the side of the mouth to the chin, take note that the tones defines the feature of the smiling face of the subject, as you know the head is composed of planes, as the planes gives dimension of our portrait, so here is the list of planes- front planes: forehead and face, side planes: ears, cheek and temples, top plane: Hair and scalp, and bottom planes: chin and neck area. Start dabbing some Medium Charcoal S. on the dark side of the head (left side).

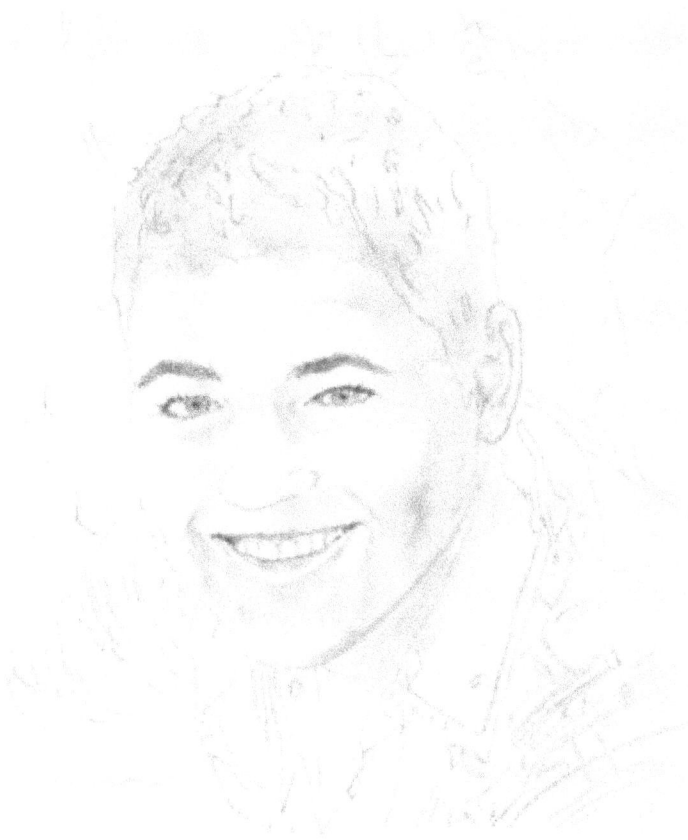

6. Darken the dark area of the hair using your Medium Charcoal Pencil then soften it with tortillon or brush.

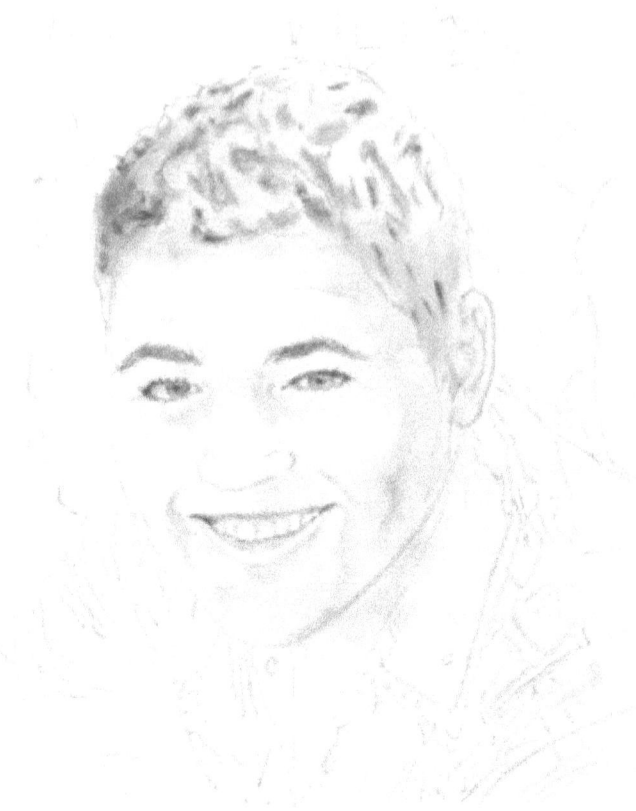

7. Now add details to the hair, using your Hard Charcoal Pencil by drawing small thin lines on the right side(where there are many highlights is visible on the hair), the top middle area if you observe has also highlights but the front has a dark value, that's because the light source is on the top right corner at the back, because of this the left side receives less light of all the areas of the hair, so render the left side of the hair by dabbing some Medium Charcoal S. and also Medium Charcoal Pencil for dark details. When adding details on the hair, take note of the irregular bands of light aside from highlights, so work closely and add it to hair to make it real.

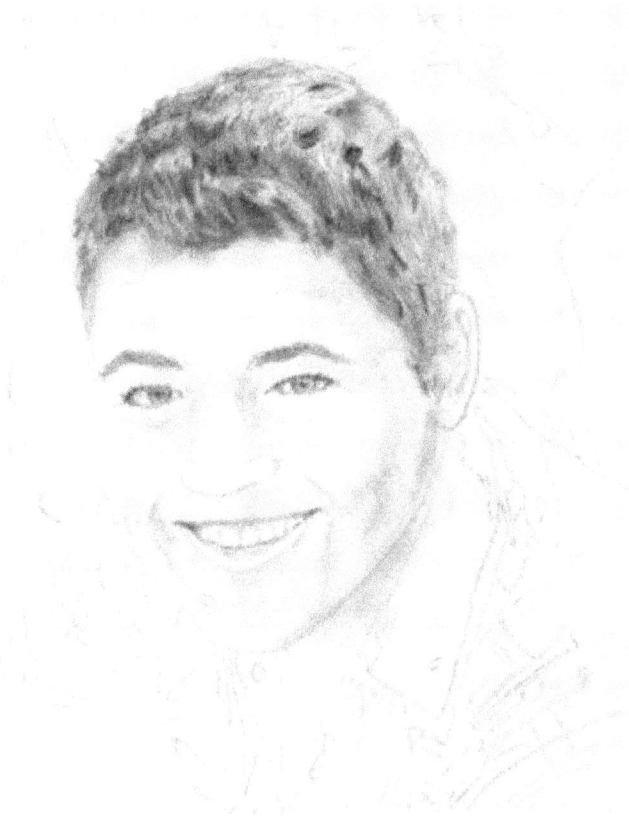

8. Time to render the clothing, so from Dark to light, let's dab a Medium Charcoal S. to all the areas of the clothing and darken a little bit the dark areas in the folds and other dark areas.

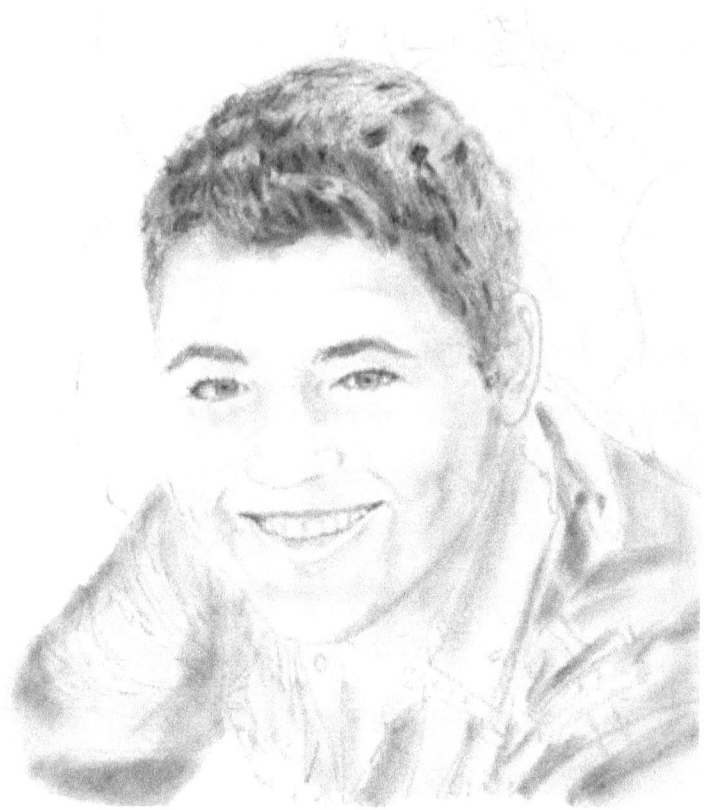

9. Now add another coat using Soft Charcoal S. with your round and flat brush; use flat for darkest areas with shading strokes while the round for light for dark areas with dabbing strokes, and add details like the buttons and thin dark areas using Medium and Hard Charcoal pencils, and kneaded eraser for giving texture and highlights to the clothing as well as stitches.

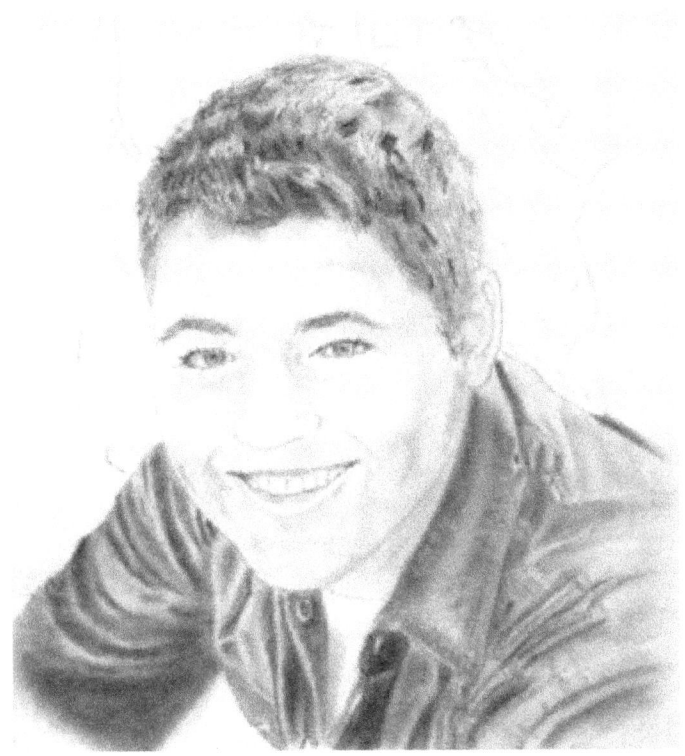

10. For the Background start shading the Dark Values with Soft Charcoal S. with your Flat Brush.

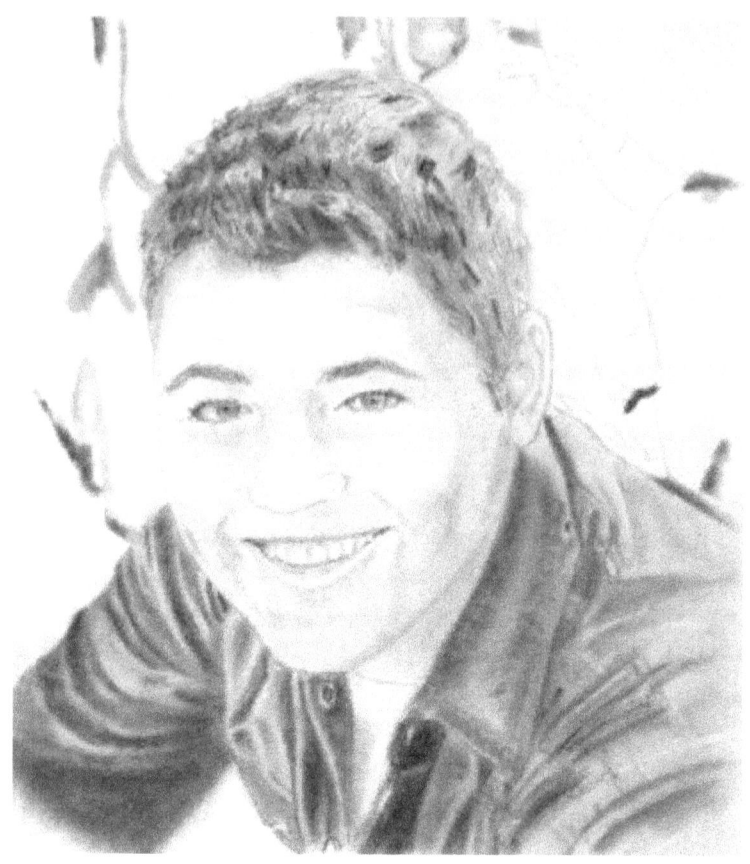

11. Finish the background by shading Soft Charcoal S. to darken the parts of the

rocks   , for the darkest part of the rocks, you may use Soft Charcoal Pencil

   , and add details such as lines and textures using same Charcoal Pencil. At this stage you can add value by shading another layer of Medium Charcoal Pencil to the face if you think it need more tone, and don't forget to polish your work after, after that sprays it with fixative.

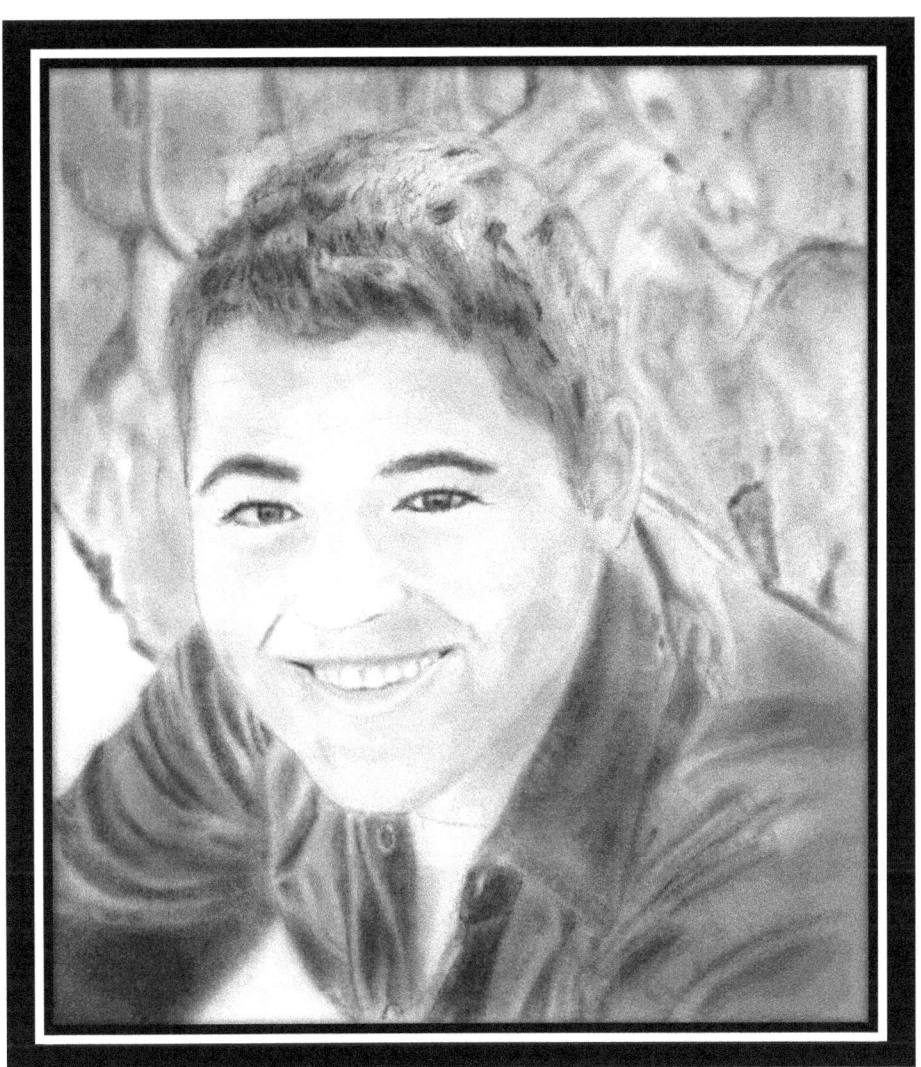

Couples Portrait

For our third exercise, we have 2 subjects to render, and it's a medium shot of an adorable and sweet couple: Jake and his wife Taunie, unlike the exercise 1 and 2 which is close-up shots, you will notice that my method will be slightly different from the previous exercise.

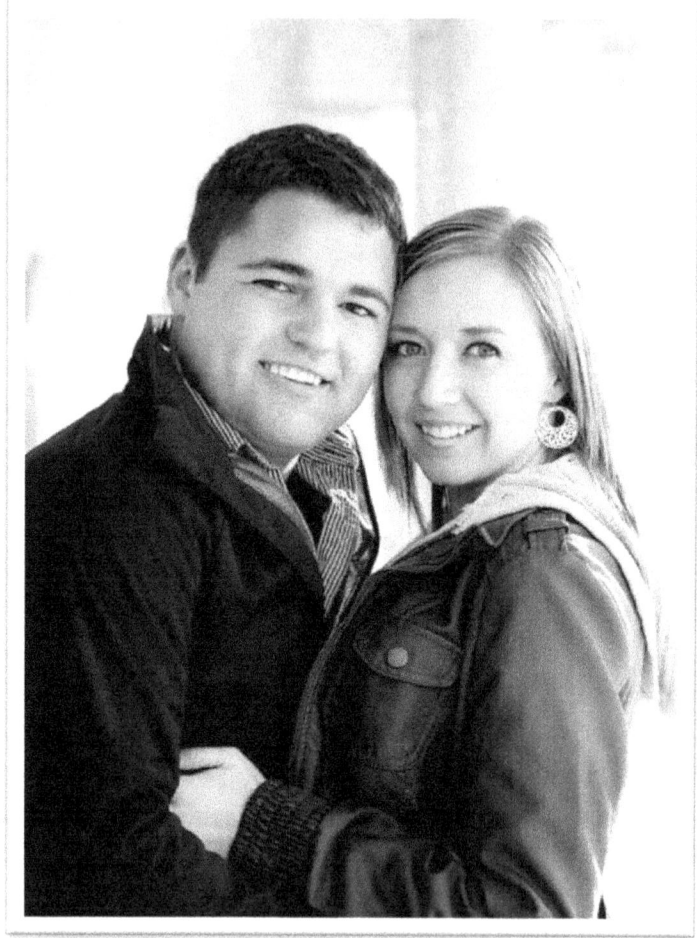

So for the outline below you know what to do.

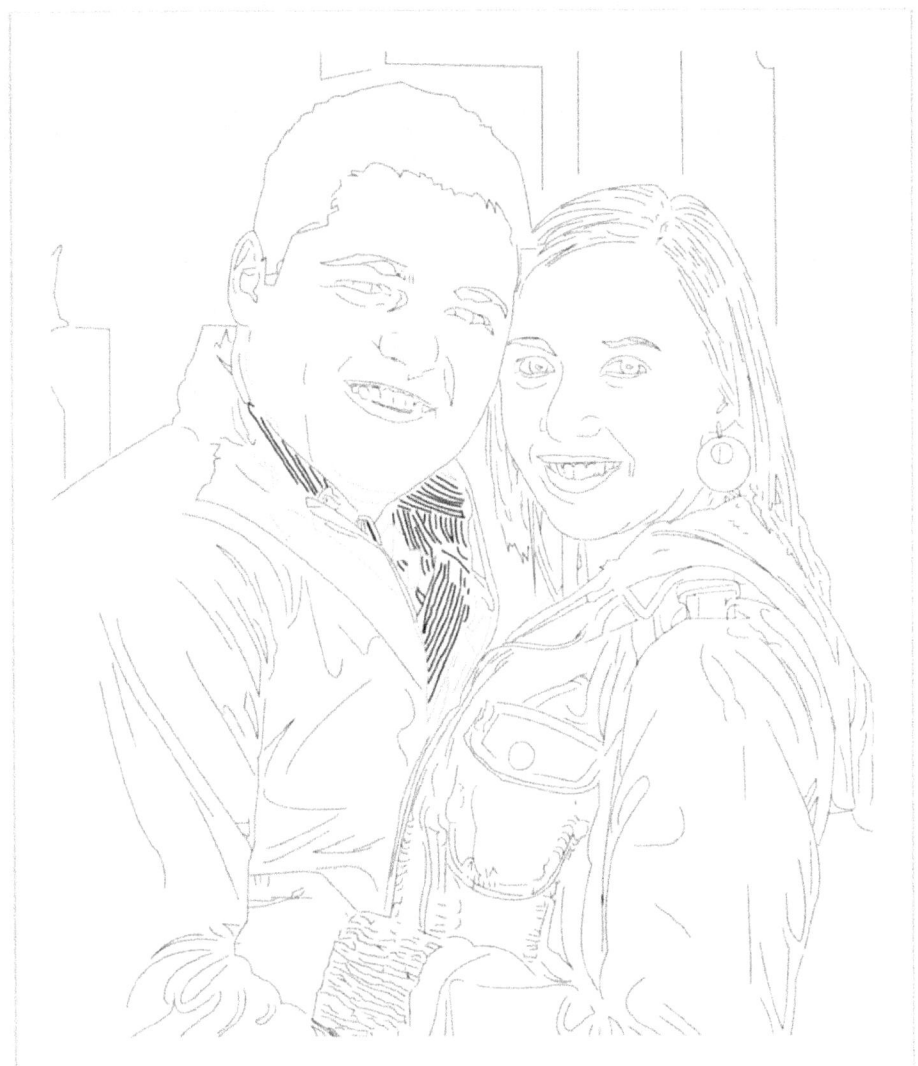

Steps:

1. Starting on the faces, shade some Medium Charcoal S. to the darkest area, the purpose is to see the depth before applying more tones.

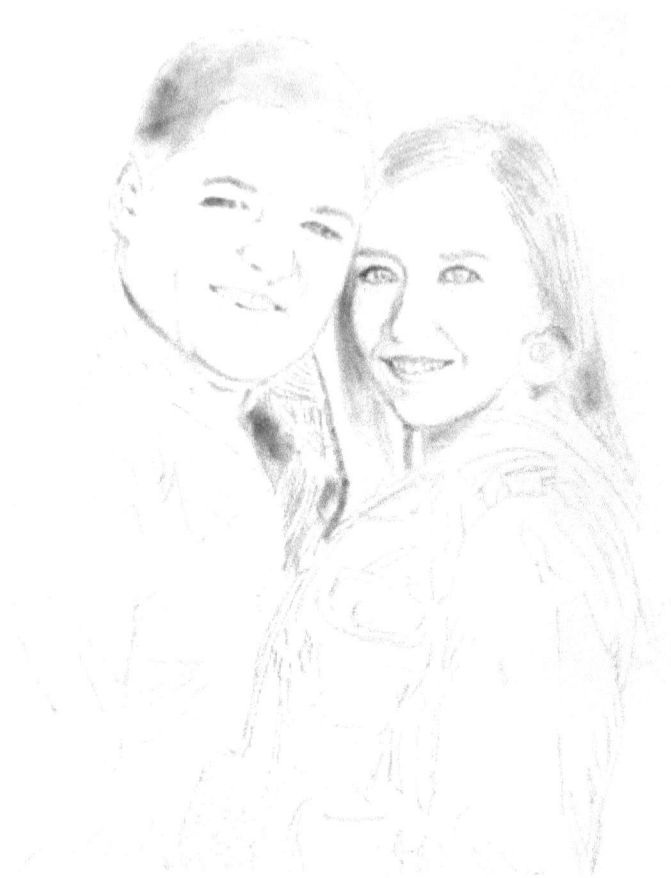

2. Now darken areas all dark areas with Soft Charcoal S. and Hard Charcoal Pencil for details, this steps is similar to molding clay, adding something to create and define shapes: on the hair and coat of both subjects.

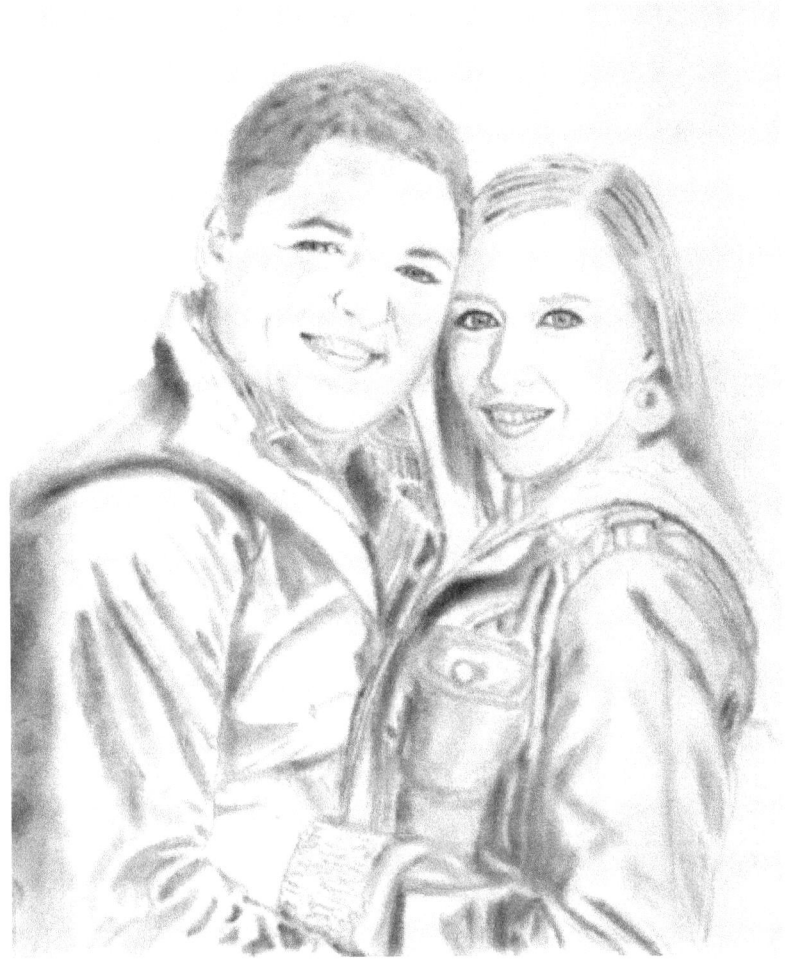

3. Continue to darken especially tight areas using the same Charcoal from Step 2. add details to the Hair of Jake using your Hard Charcoal Pencils draw some hair lines, Blend it using your Tortillon or flat Brush, and then add again draw some hair lines again for a nice hair effect, don't forget the highlights. For his wife Taunie since she have a blonde hair, to render just add the details for the visible dark strands of hair, let me remind you that the left side of the hair is darker compared to the right side, again the Light source is in the right side at the top, so highlights can be seen in the right side of the hair. At this point I made adjustment to the subject's faces and clothing for corrections, if there is irregularity of the shapes and tones.

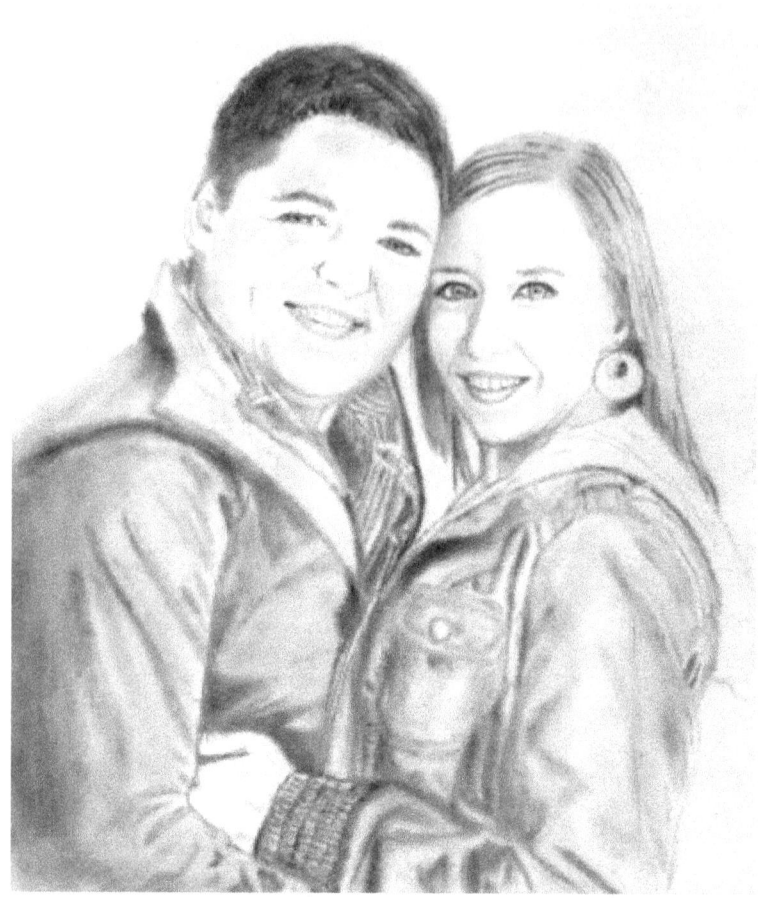

4. Continue darken areas, checking the contrast; add more necessary details in the following including highlights: sweater, coats, shirt, earring, button and collars using your Hard Charcoal Pencil.

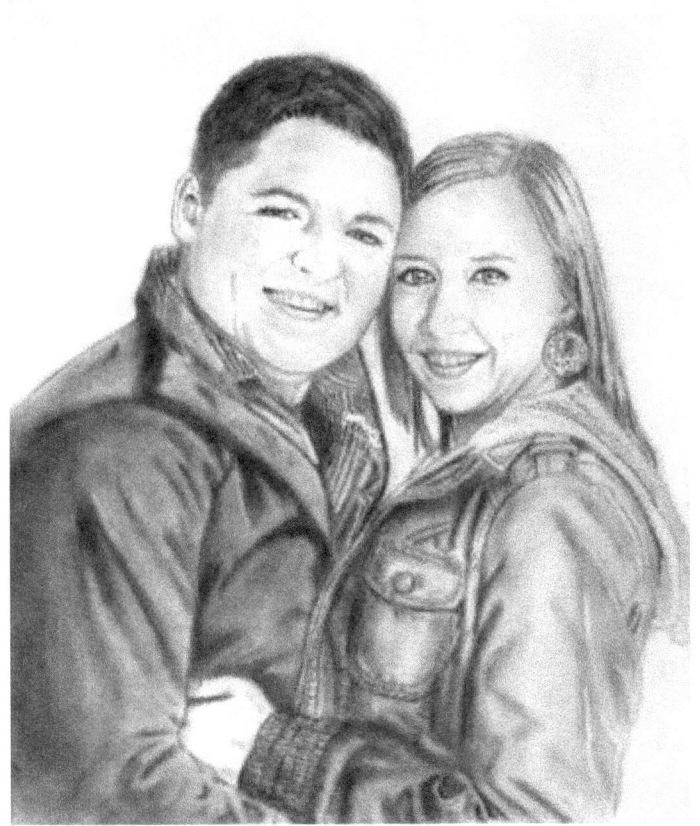

5. Render the Background, on the left side use your Soft Charcoal S. as it has a dark Value, and for the Middle and right side pillar use your Medium Charcoal S., use your ruler as a guide when rendering the pillars, after that polish your work and check if there is anything that need to be corrected, and spray it with fixative, and we're done. Take a break and get ready for the next exercise.

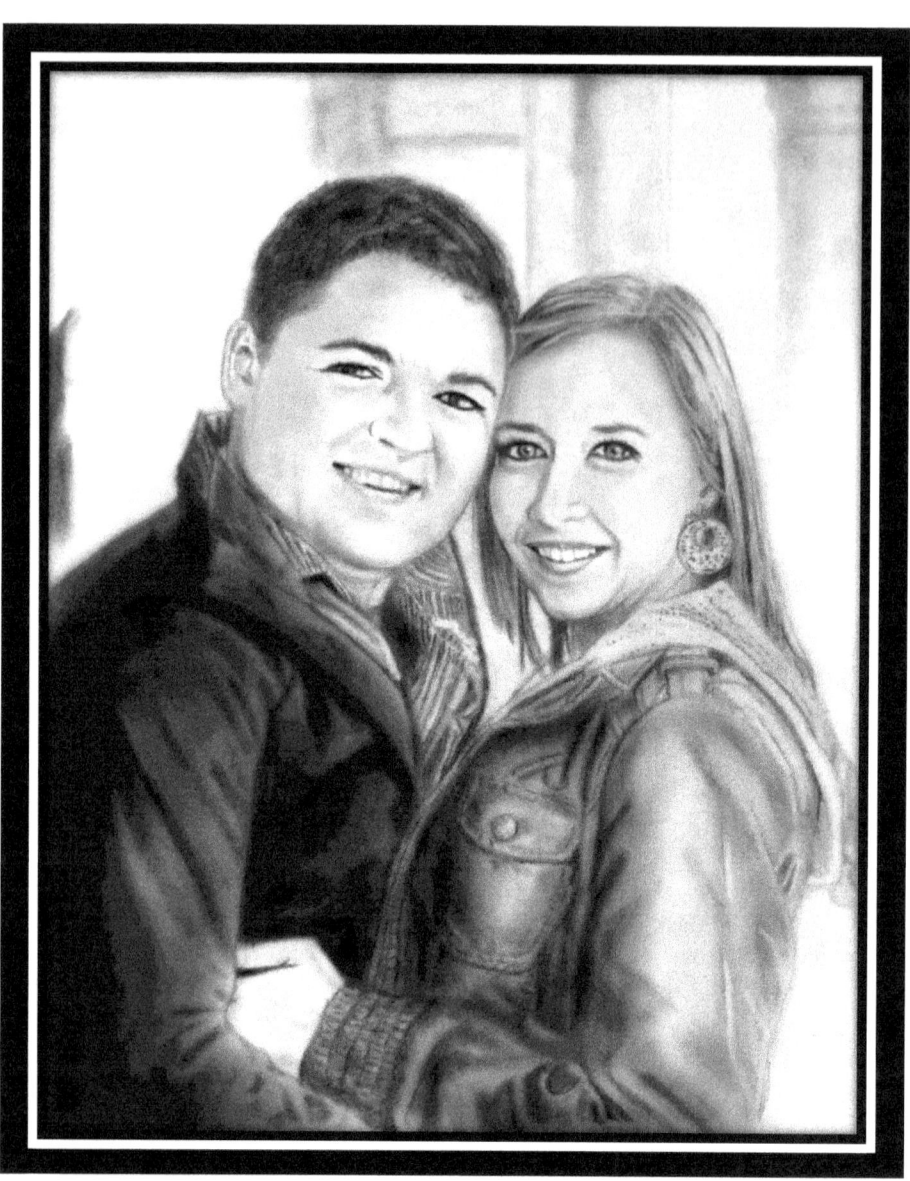

Couples Portrait 2

For our fourth exercise, we will be rendering our author John and with his wife Karla, The challenge aside from rendering the faces is the texture of the background, so let's start.

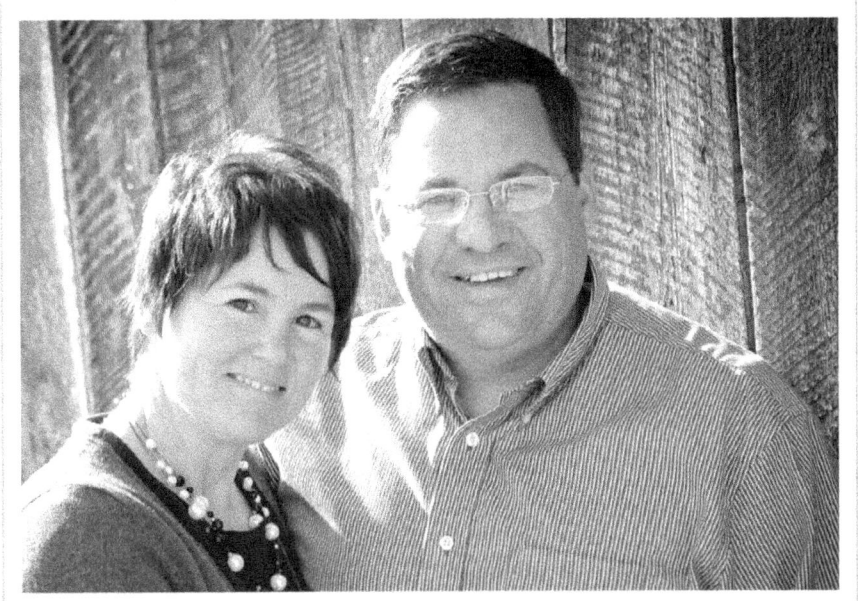

Transfer the outline to your paper.

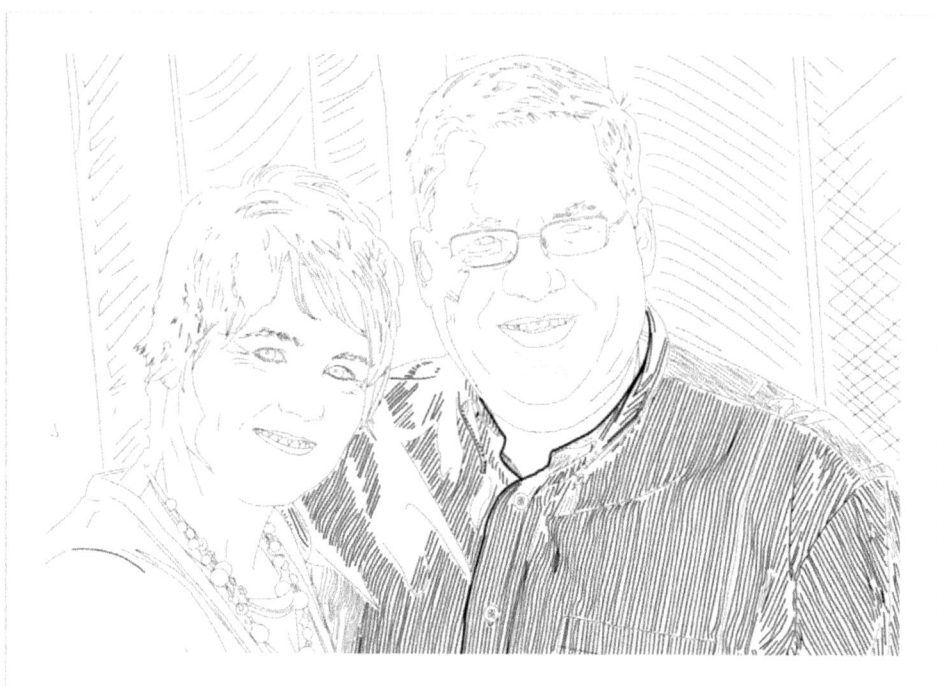

Steps:

1. Shade the darkest areas using Soft Charcoal S. with your Flat Brush:
   John's Hair on the right side and also for Karla, accent of mouth for both, right side of neck for John, and also for shirt of Karla.

   For the background: lay some lines for the textures at the back using the same charcoal with the Flat Brush, in case you're wondering "Why are we rendering the background in this early stage?", well aside from we're rendering a medium shot picture, I want to see the contrast of the background compared to foreground, so that I will have an idea of what Value of Charcoal I will be using next.

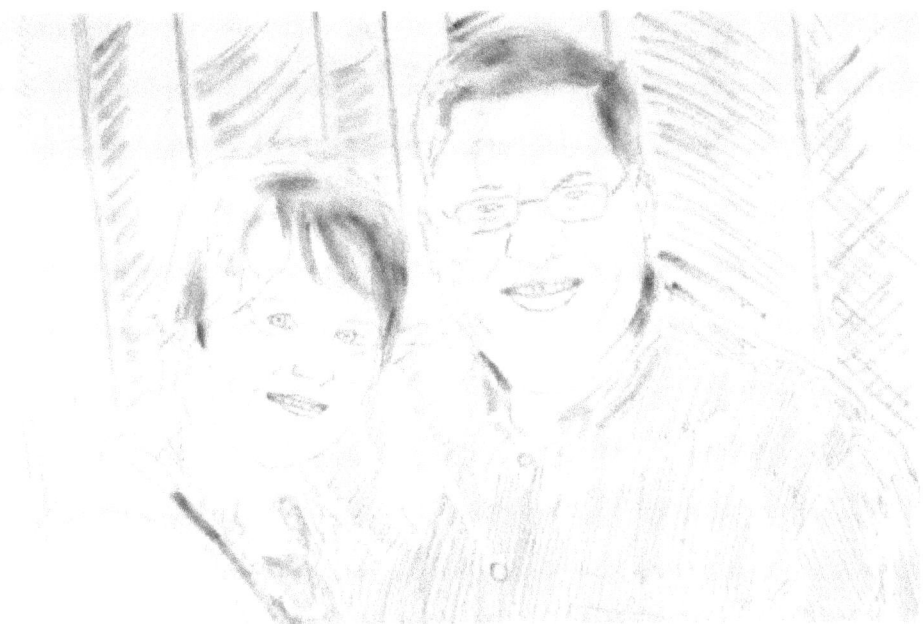

2. Add a light tone on the faces first and next apply to the other areas with Hard Charcoal S. (this is the safe application of tone as if later we need a darker tone we can add another coat of Charcoal to it) using your Flat brush, a tip when rendering is, first think that this is the only Charcoal Value you will be using for the rest of the painting.

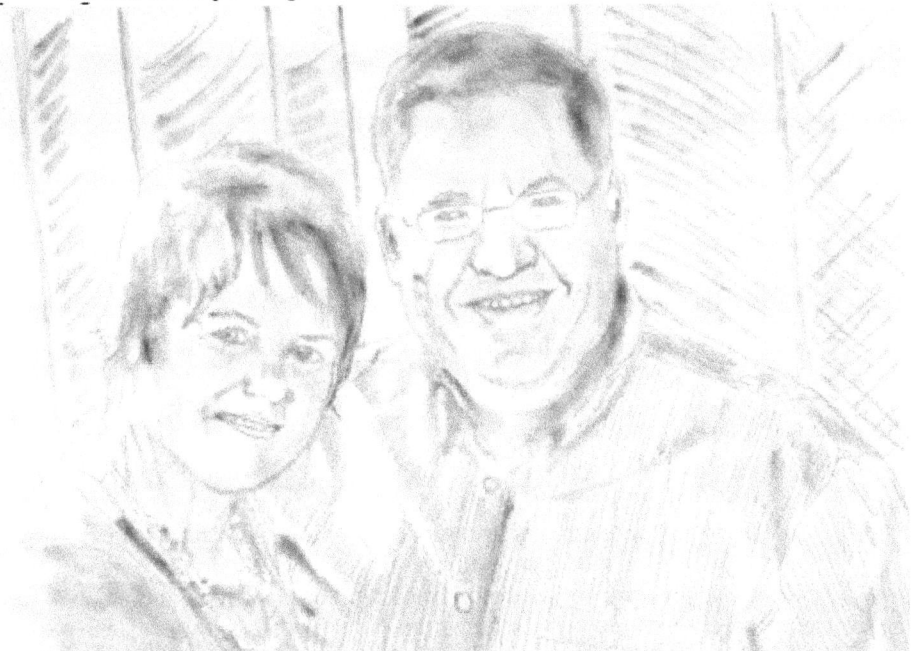

3. Next apply Medium tone using Medium Charcoal S. with your flat brush to darken the value, you don't need to fill all the areas of faces with this tone, just apply it to the areas that you need to define the shapes like in the side of the face, forehead, ears, nose and under it, and also the neck. Add details to the eyes, nose, mouth, ears, chin and neck, don't forget to apply Highlights using your kneaded eraser by molding it to a sharp edge and use a quick stroke to pull the highlight.

Now use Soft Charcoal S. to the darkest part of the hair for both of them, including eyeballs and eyebrows (apply light pressure).

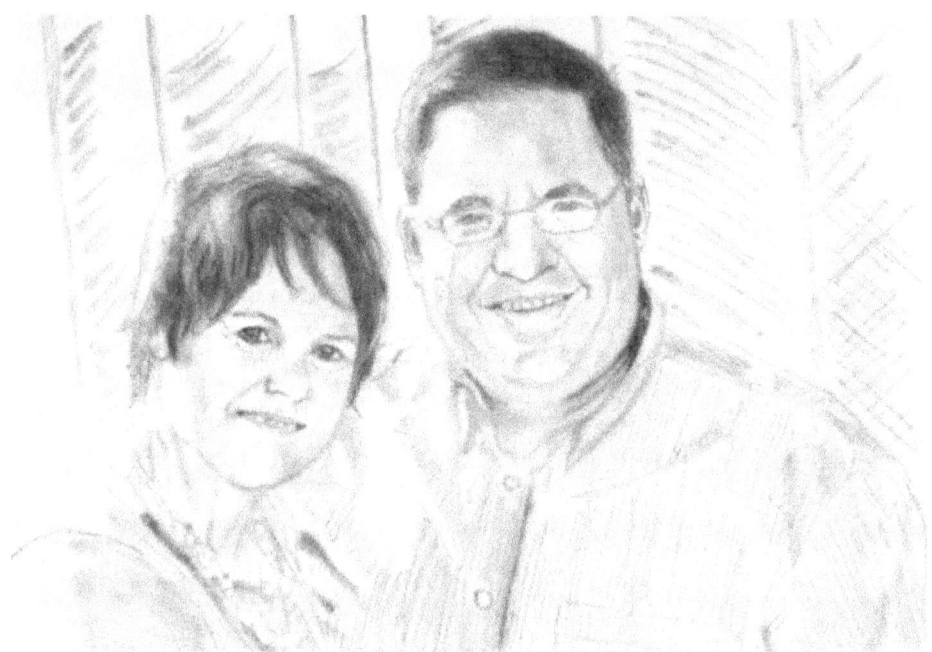

4. Render the clothing:
- For John- Shade the Dark areas of the collar and folds using Medium Charcoal S. and Medium Charcoal Pencil for details like the thin lines of the shirt, and buttons. And apply highlights on the shirt.
  Also notice that I didn't render any glare on John's eyeglasses, I want the viewer to see John's eyes.
- For Karla- Use the Soft Charcoal S. again for the shirt including the area at the back of neck and add details on the necklace of Karla, remember that it have white and Black round pearls and beads decoration on it, shade the pearls with hard Charcoal S. around it and add highlights in the center to have a shiny effect. Also take note that some of the dark beads have highlights so don't forget to apply it. To have a good texture of the sweater dab a Medium Charcoal S. on the shoulder area using your Round Brush.

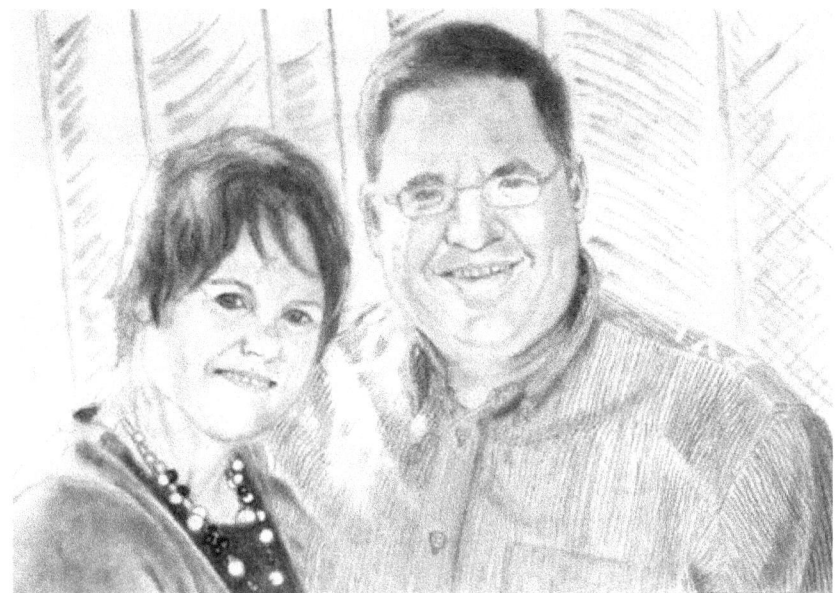

5. Rendering the Background:

The background is not hard to render, here how to do it: starting from left to right-

The first board is easy- just give thin random lines for details using your Hard and Medium Charcoal pencil, and after that apply dabbing strokes of Hard Charcoal S. with your round large brush vertically lightly. Then draw a long vertical line on the side with Hard Charcoal Pencil.

For the second board- darken the left edge of the diagonal lines with Medium Charcoal S. using your Flat Brush and apply the dabbing strokes like what you did in the first board and again draw a vertical line but use flat brush to have a soft edge.

For third to sixth boards- Third board was added with a layer of dabbing strokes of Hard Charcoal S. with Round brush only, same as the fourth to sixth board, the only difference is the diagonal lines third board have a thick diagonal lines, while fourth and fifth have thin diagonal lines. The sixth board (just above John's head) has thick diagonal lines like the third board. Also some thin vertical lines were added.

The Seventh Board- has vertical thin lines, and dab some strokes of Hard Charcoal S.

The Eighth board- has a combination of thin and thick Diagonal lines starting from the upper left to lower right. Small vertical lines and thick vertical lines on the side were also added with Hard Charcoal Pencil.

The Ninth board-has diagonal random thick and thin diagonal lines starting for the lower left to upper right and vice-versa like board eighth including thin vertical lines also it has a detailed patch on the upper right side.

Now check your work for any correction, and when your finishes spray it with fixative.

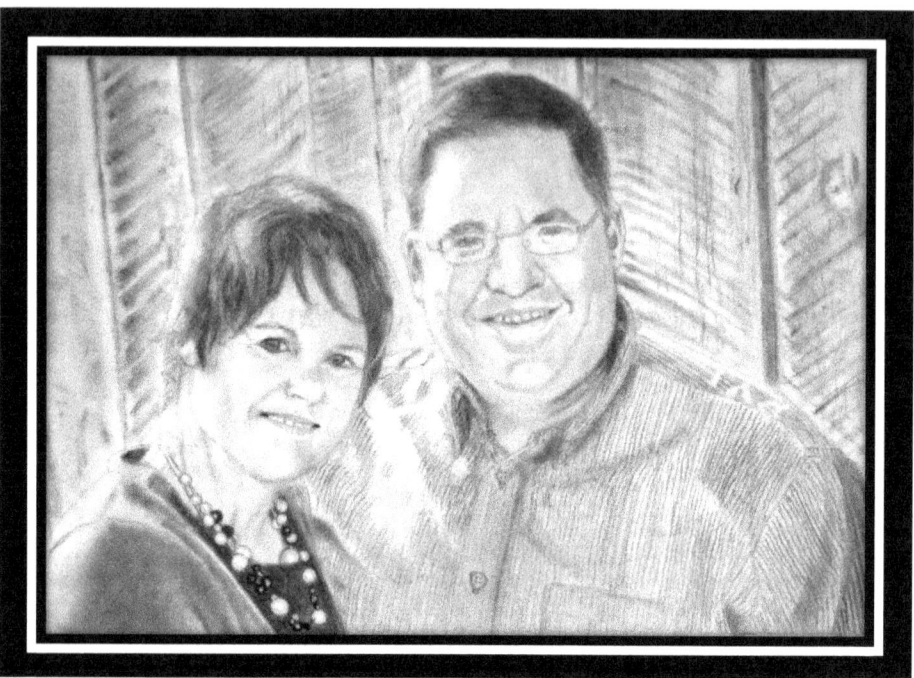

The Portrait of Grandfather Grant

For our last exercise, let's draw a half body Portrait, it's a picture of Grant the Father- in-law of John. So do your best, I know you can do it.

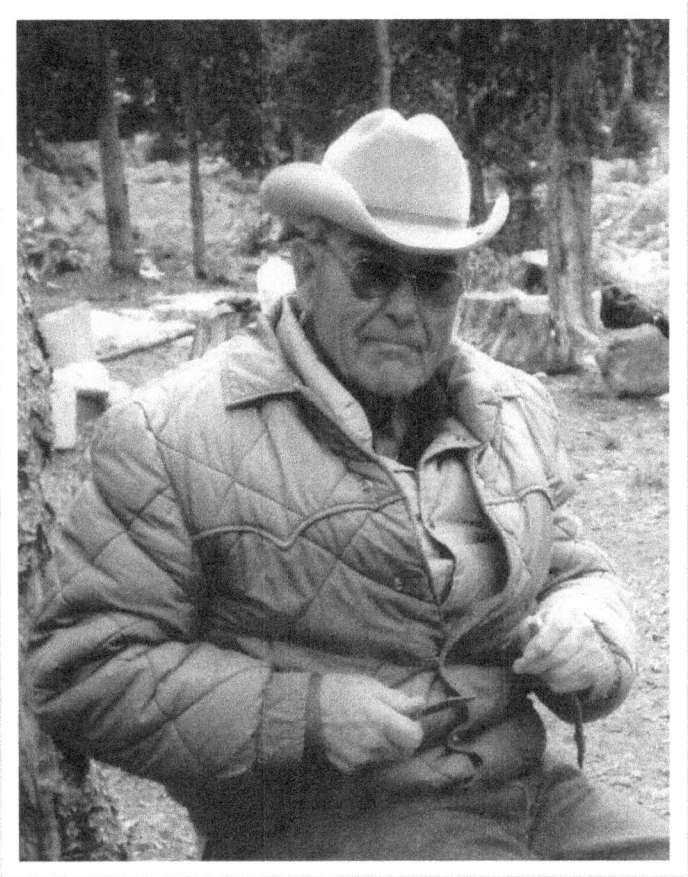

Again transfer this outline to your working paper, and let's start.

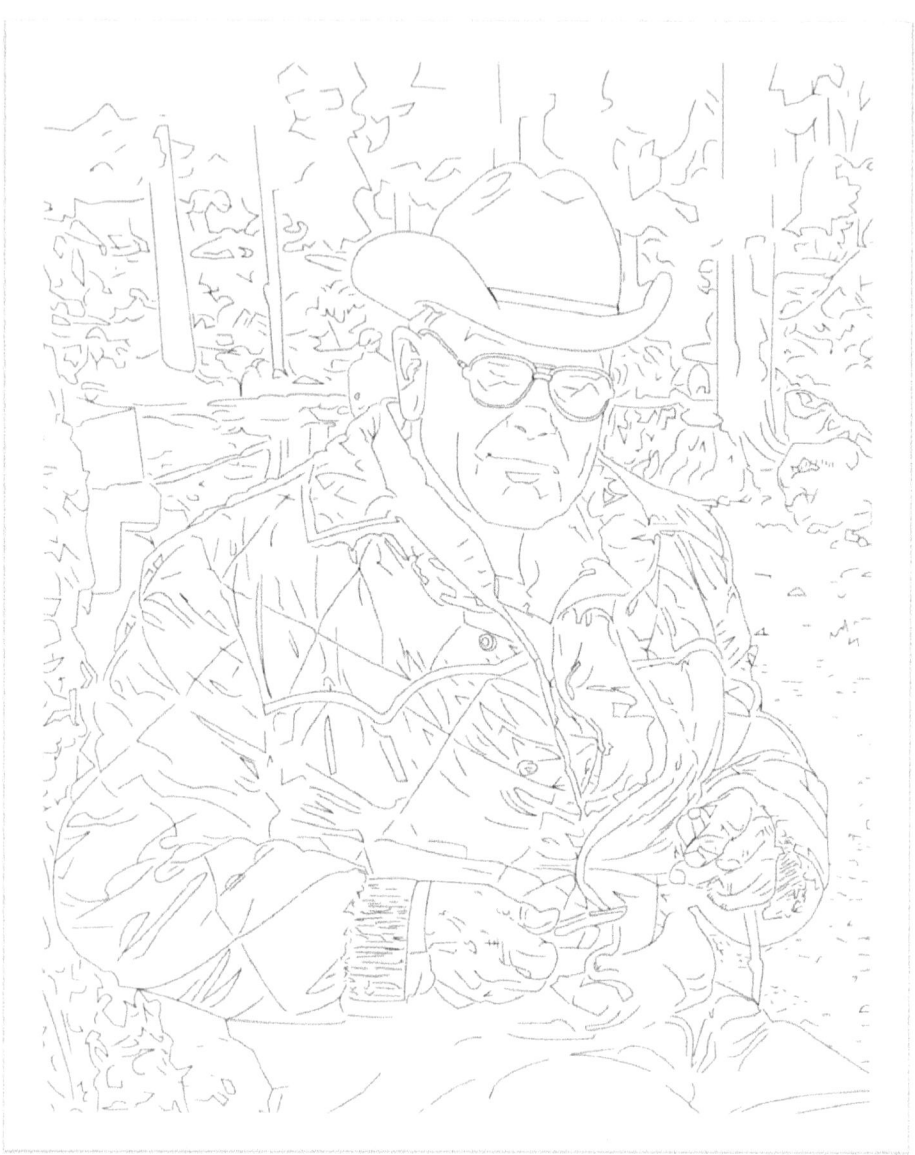

Steps:

1. Like what we did in Exercise D. We Block all the dark areas first, with Soft Charcoal S. (use light pressure).

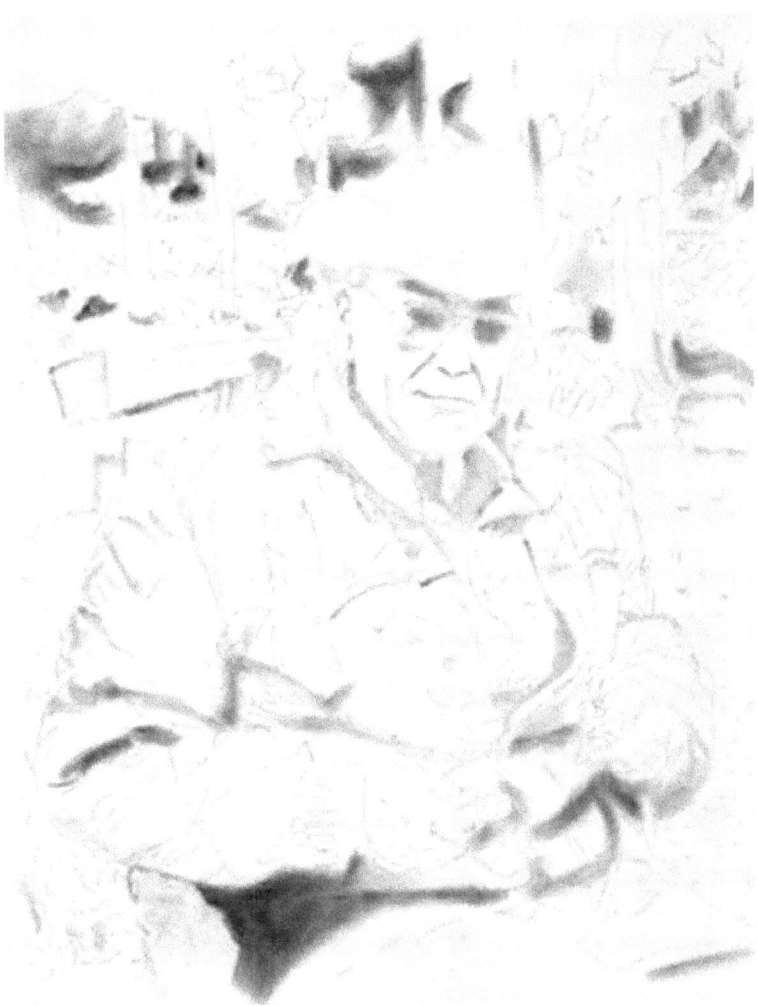

2. Let's move to the facial feature, add the details: sunglasses, eyebrows, nose, nasogenian folds (side of the nose and mouth), mouth, ears and chin using your Medium Charcoal Pencil, Then Apply a Dabbing strokes of Hard Charcoal S. with your round brush on the face including the ears.

Add another layer of Soft Charcoal S. on the neck area. Add the highlights on the face.

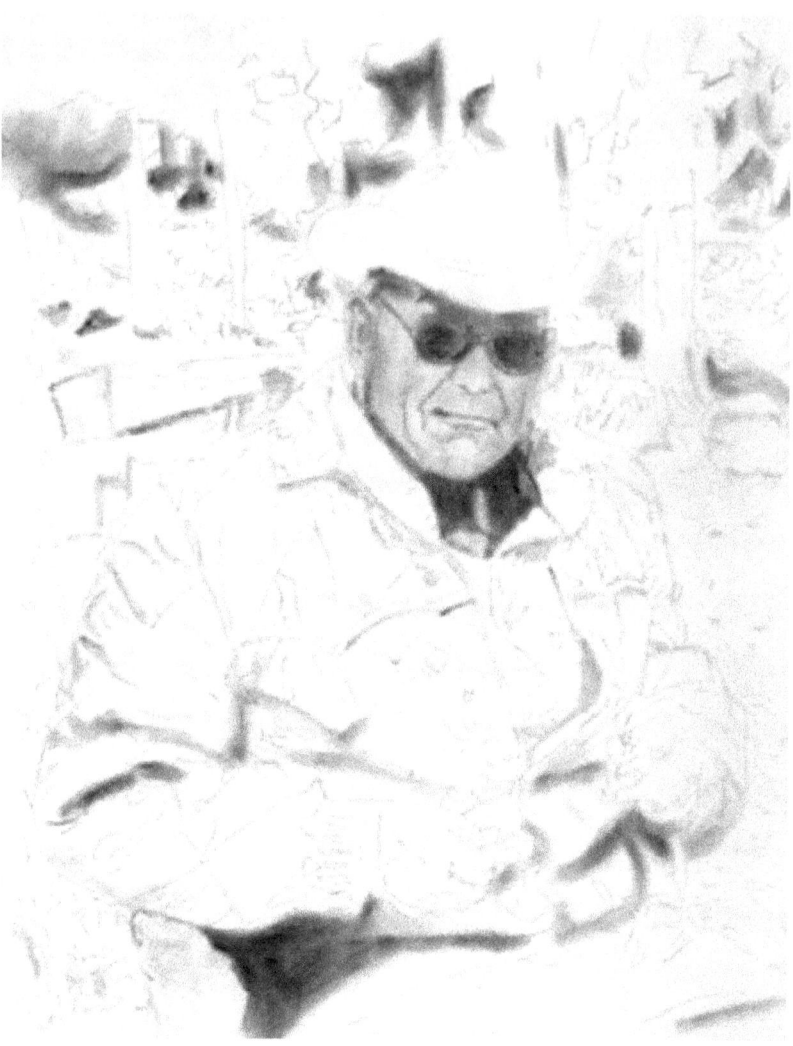

3. Using your Medium Charcoal S. apply the tone to the Hat including the band with your Round Brush, add details using your Medium Charcoal Pencil on the top of the hat , side of the hat for shadows and for the line in the band on the hat. Apply the same value to the hands and same Charcoal Pencil for details. For the knife just shade it with Charcoal pencil you used before.

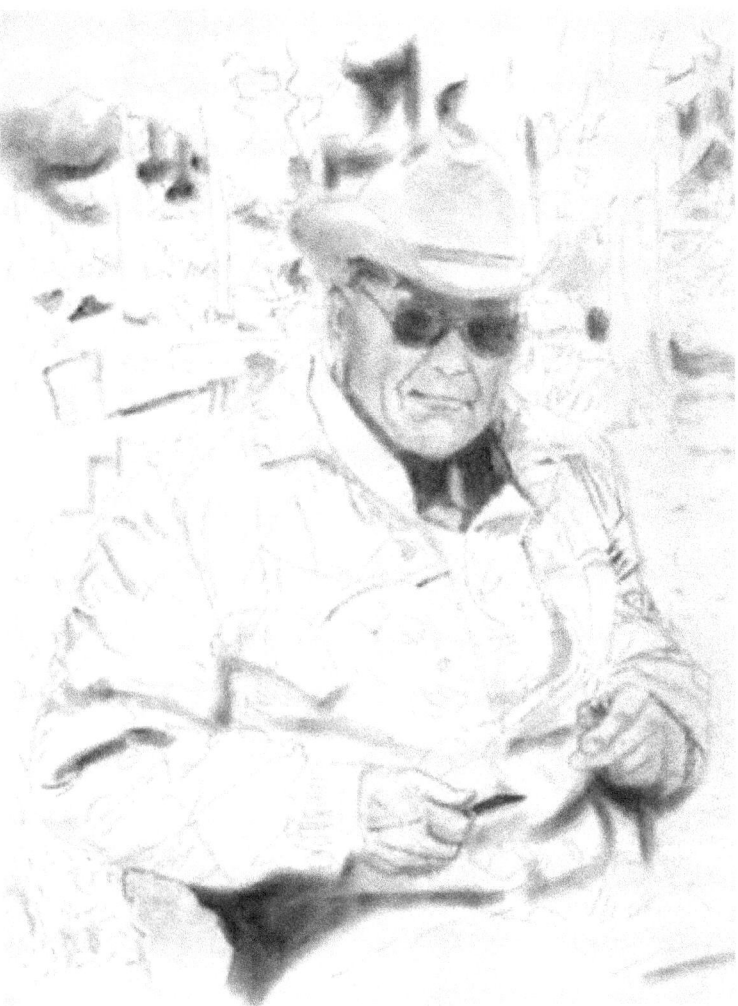

4. Let's work the Jacket and Pants:
- Jacket- adds the details by drawing lines using Hard Charcoal Pencil(buttons and thin lines) and shade it to the dark areas like shadows and apply Flat brush over soften it. For the folds I suggest shading a Medium Charcoal S. with light pressure on the areas to lightly darken it, and apply highlights to the jacket, especially to the elbow areas and side of the body.
- Pants- shade the shadow areas of the pants with Medium Charcoal S. using the flat brush and Hard Charcoal pencil for the details.

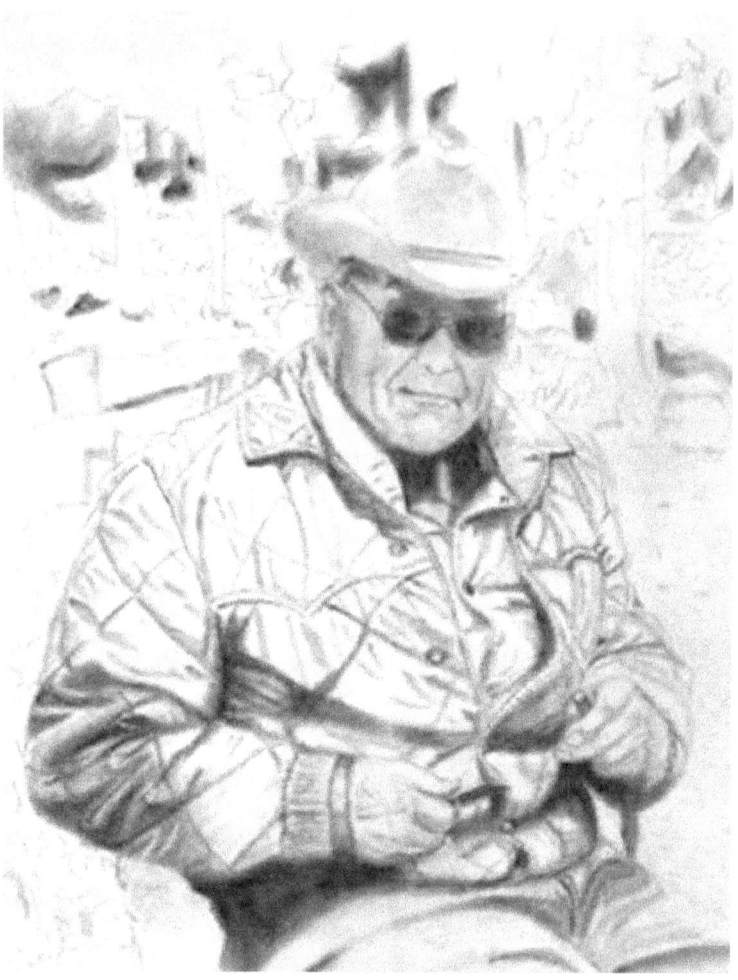

5. Finish the background, work the background by adding dark values using Soft Charcoal S. with your flat brush top areas(foliages of the trees), add small dots for a light areas of foliages on the trees using your kneaded eraser, add details to the trunk of the trees using Hard Charcoal Pencil, add tones to the trees by dabbing Medium Charcoal S. with round brush, make sure that the tones are consistent, also add highlights to the tree on the right side, when rendering the view at the back, create it by just dabbing tones and adding details, same process when rendering the tree beside Grandpa Grant, finish giving details to the other objects in the painting like the rocks and short grass, again it was done by dabbing and adding details.

Checking the foreground again, I add another layer of our previous tone which is Medium Charcoal S. to skin, I see to it that it's not too dark and not too light just enough Gray tone.

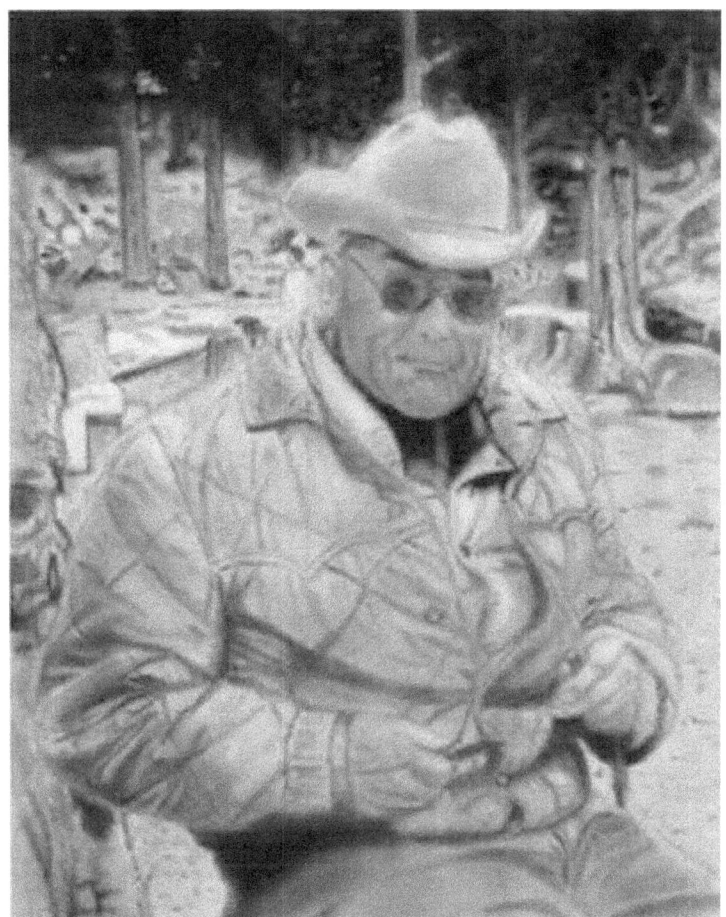

Before spraying your work with fixative, from now on every time you finished your Charcoal painting sign your name at the bottom, so that people who view your work will know that you made it, and also as a sign that you finished all the exercises in this eBook - "Congratulations" and I'm very proud of you. Don't stop here continue to draw and harness your new skill.

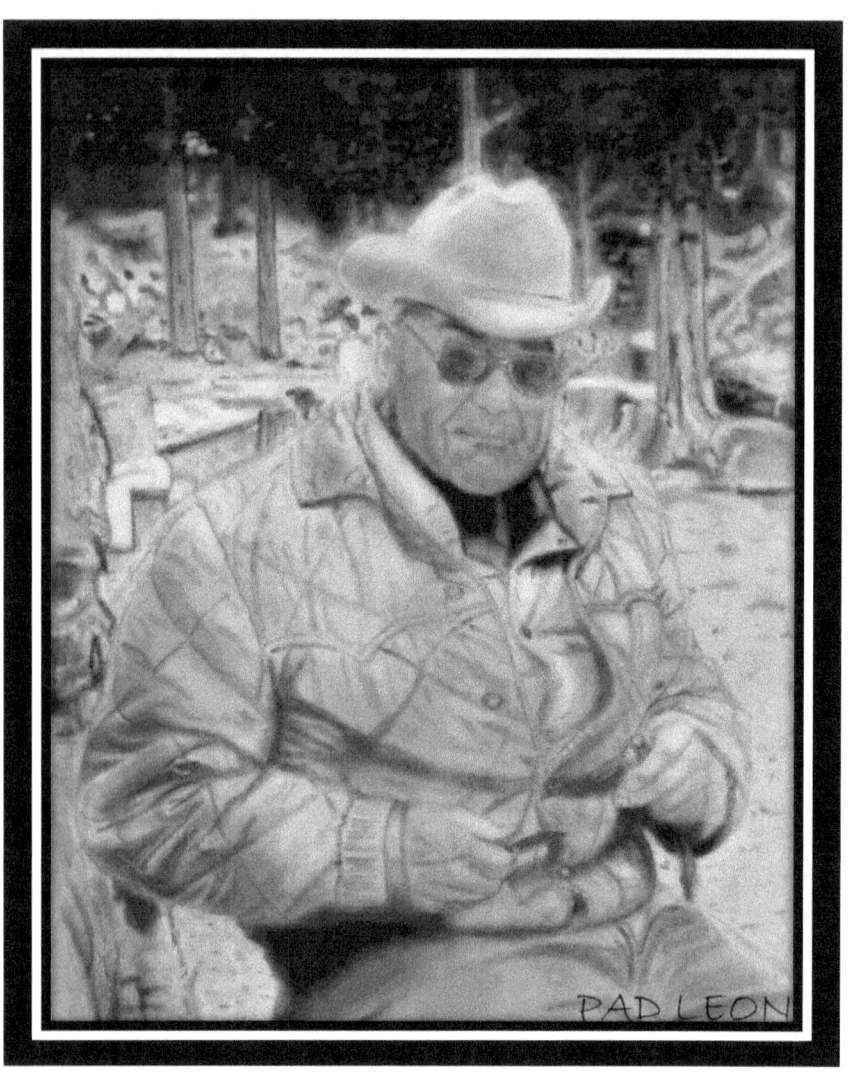

Animals in Charcoal

Zebra

As this is our first exercise, take a look of the picture of the zebra below; take note of the shapes, tones of the body, the light source as well the transition of tones, and the contents in the background, middle-ground and foreground (subject). I assure you this is easy, so let's start.

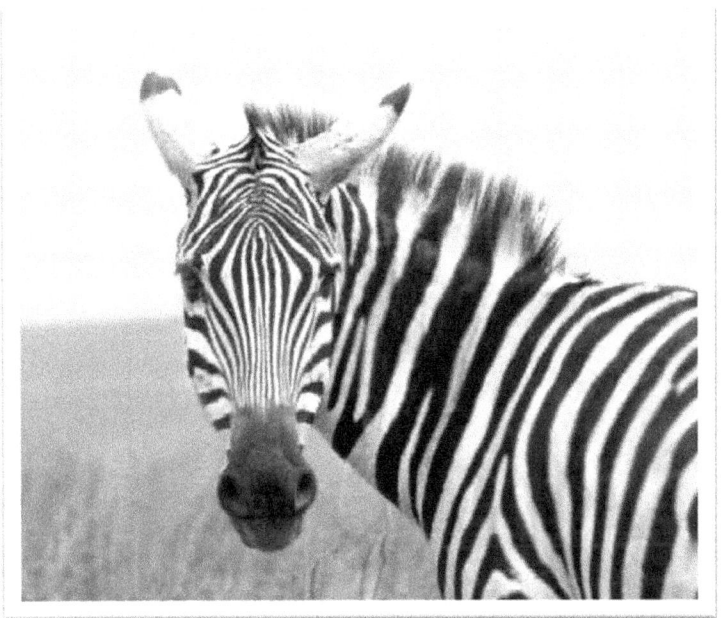

Copy the outline below to your Bristol Pad or Illustration board, or you may scan it using your scanner and enlarge it, after mount it to the Tracing Table or Light Table / Flexiglass with Bendable Lamp and place your Working paper (Bristol Pad or Illustration board) over it and trace the outline. That's it very simple.

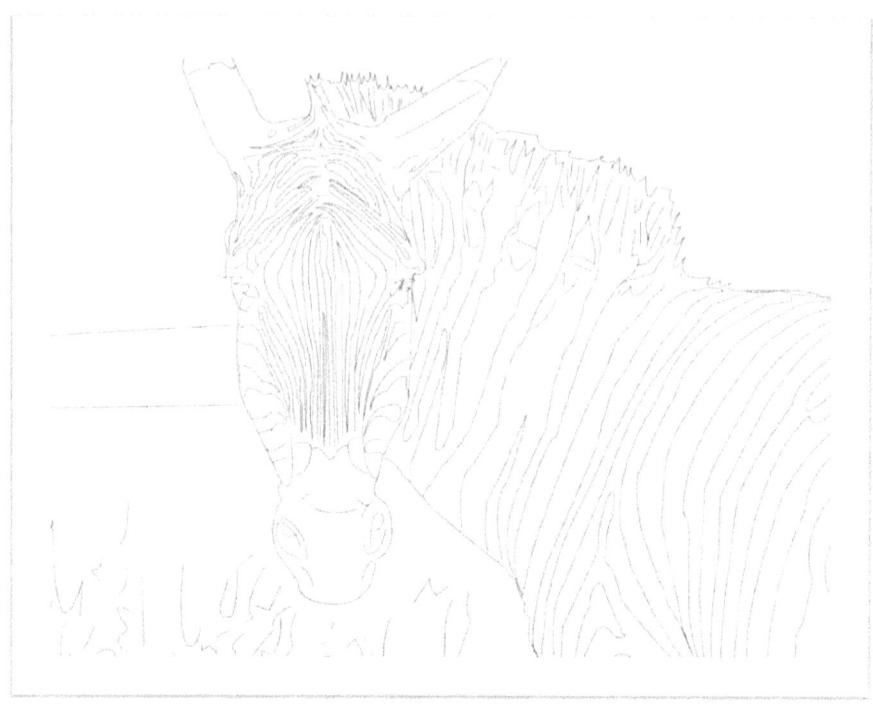

Steps:

1.   Using Soft Charcoal S. with Flat Brush, apply it to the stripes on the body of the Zebra; use the method we used in <u>rendering Sphere.</u> And also apply it to dark areas: hairs, dark tone above the ears, eyes, and nostrils.

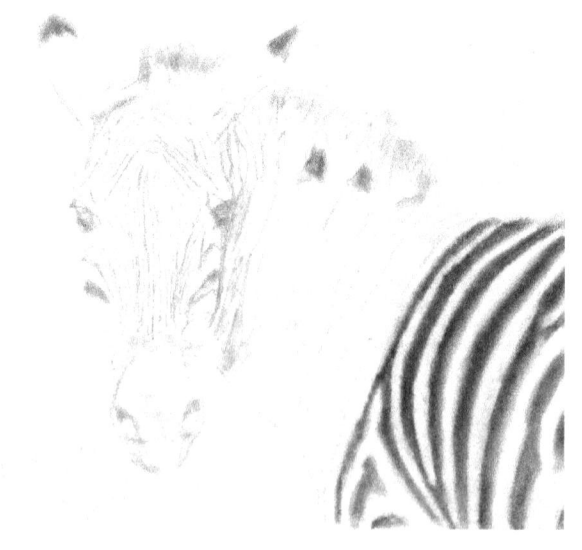

2.	Continue applying the tone to the rest of the Stripes, take note of how the value varies there are dark and light tones, dark tone requires a heavy pressure and light tones use light pressure, a heavy pressure- the brush is almost close to the paper while for the light- only tip of the brush is touching the paper.

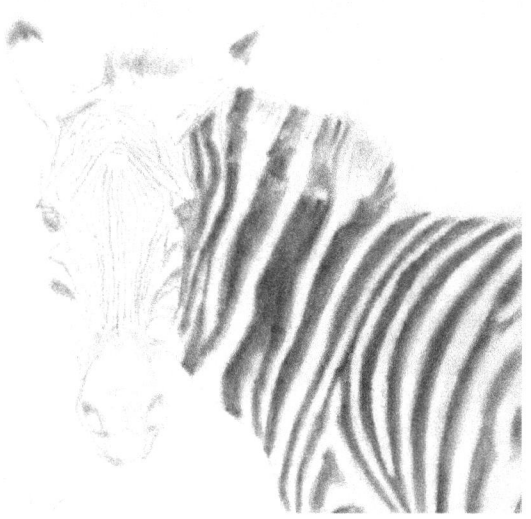

3.	Next apply Medium Charcoal S. with Flat brush, in the stripes on the face

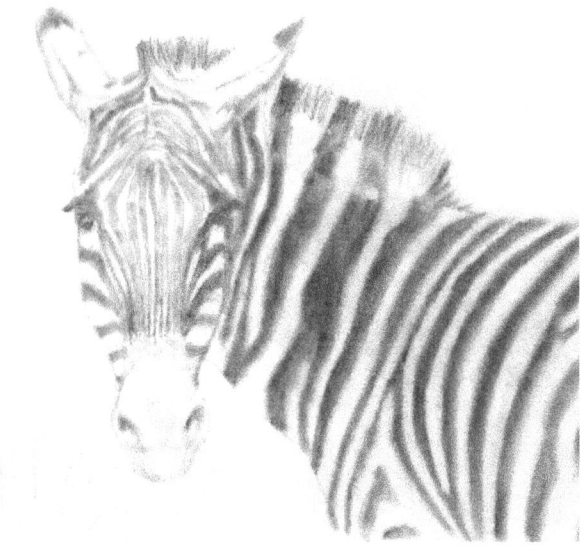

4.	Finish the snout by shading it the same charcoal we used in Step 3. take note of the transition or how the light appears in the snout shape, so render it with light pressure.

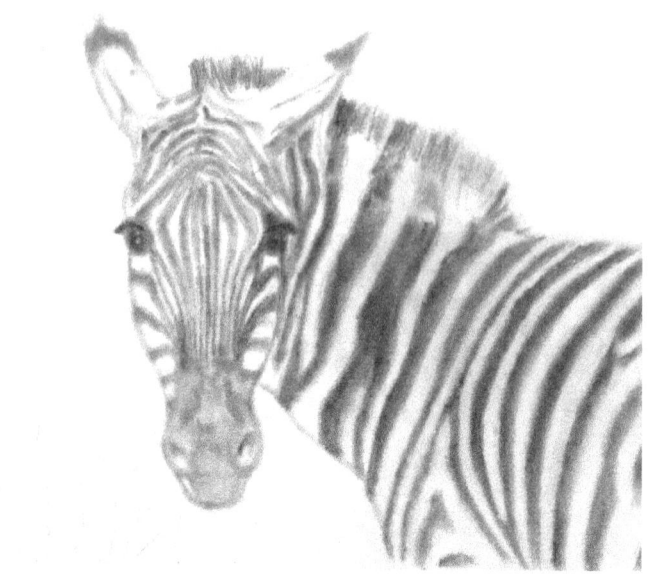

5. Finish the rest of the details using the Medium Charcoal Pencil: hair, ear, face, nose, and snout. Also apply highlights using kneaded eraser (just pull up some charcoal to make the white of the paper appear) eyes, nose, snout and ears.

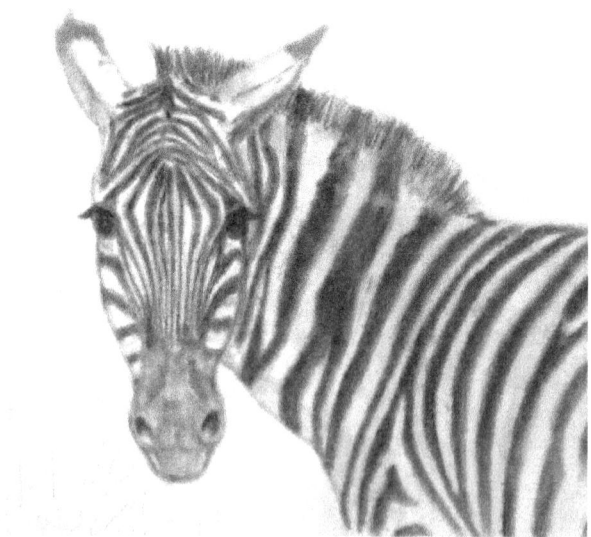

6. Let's work the details:
    - For the sky dab a Hard Charcoal S. using the Round Brush,
    - For the Mountain –dab using a Medium Charcoal S. again with Round Brush.
    - For the field (middle-ground)- use Medium Charcoal S. with Flat Brush apply it by shading it horizontally,

Apply highlights on the line between the mountain and field

- For the bushes near the foreground- use Medium and Soft Charcoal S. to render it using vertical strokes. Add highlights using kneaded eraser to add an effects.

    After that check for any corrections, add a tone if needed,and if you see that you applied a very dark tone to the light area erase it using your eraser. When finished spray fixative to your work and we're finished take a break before starting the next exercise.

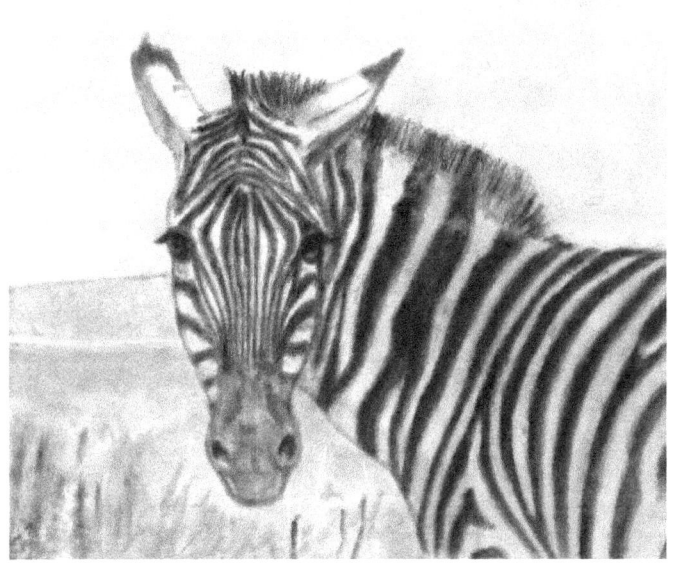

This is how it's really looks like if finished and with light over it.

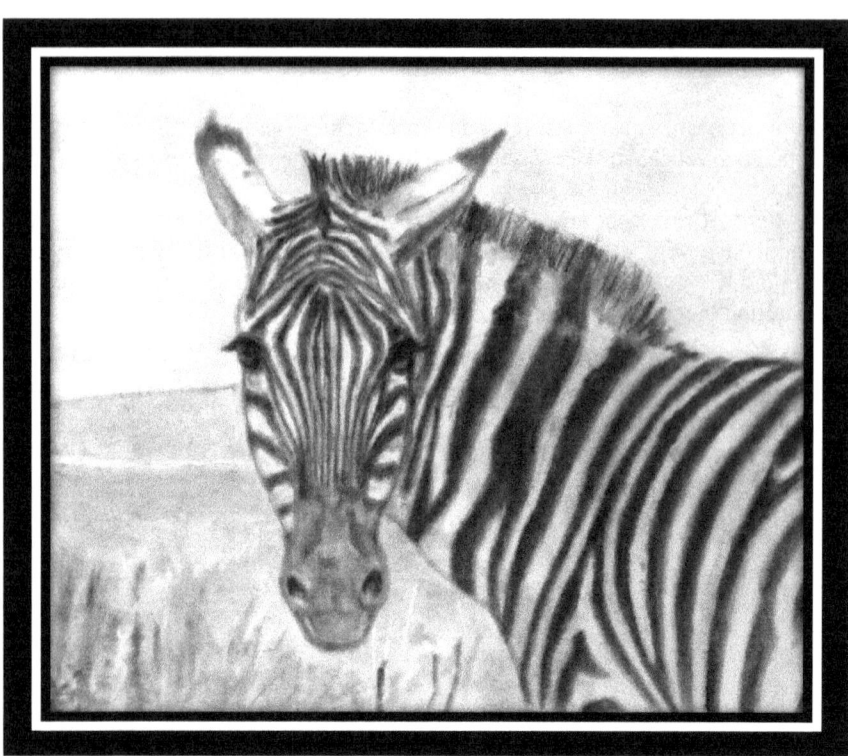

Giraffe

We're now in our second animal, our long neck friend looks so challenging to render, like the Zebra in our fist exercise, and they have distinctive patterns in their body, now before we start, imagine first how you will render this Giraffe, watch the shapes and take notes of the transition of the values.

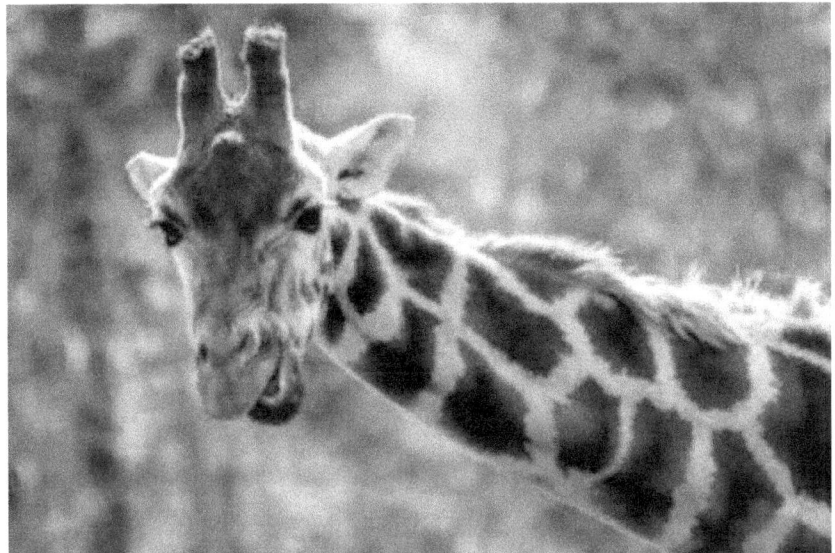

Transfer the outline to your working paper, the same method we used when we transferred the image of the Zebra.

Steps:

1.   Identify the Dark areas first, and using your Soft Charcoal S. with Flat Brush, shade it to those areas: inside the patterns or markings.

2.   Next is to shade the side of those pattern with Medium Charcoal S. again with Flat Brush, and also tone the face and the horns with this Medium Charcoal tone

with light pressure (if you are not confident with the pressure you're using practice if first to another paper, if you have enough practice then that's the time to apply it to your actual work-light and heavy pressure; light has light tone while the heavy tone has darker tone).

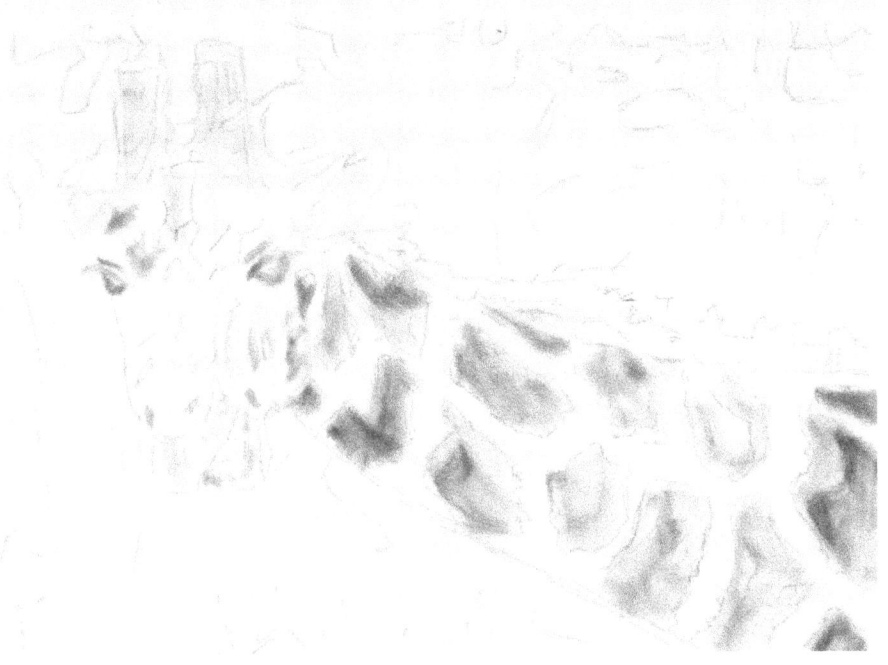

3.   Tone the neck with Hard Charcoal S. using Round Brush.

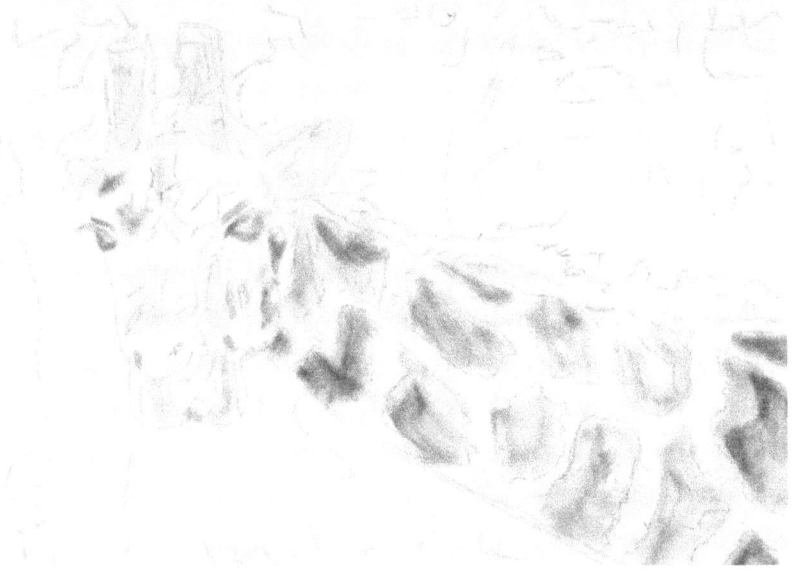

4. Add more definition to the face, by shading the face with Charcoal S. and using Charcoal Pencils, start using Dark Charcoal going to Light Charcoal. So the orientation should be Charcoal: Soft>Medium>Hard S. /Pencil (for tight and thin areas). Below is the guide of what to Shade to the areas.
    A. Soft Charcoal Shave
    B. Medium Charcoal Shave
    C. Hard Charcoal Shave

    Match the areas with tones you see below, you may apply another layer if needed.

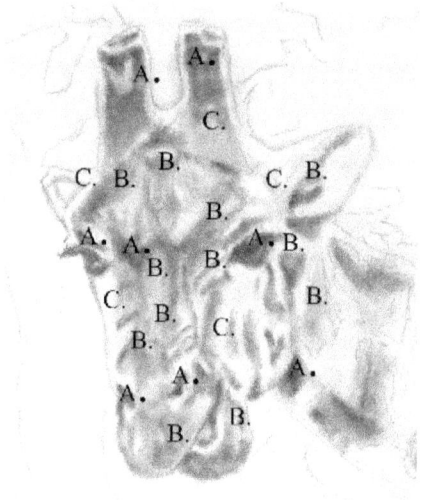

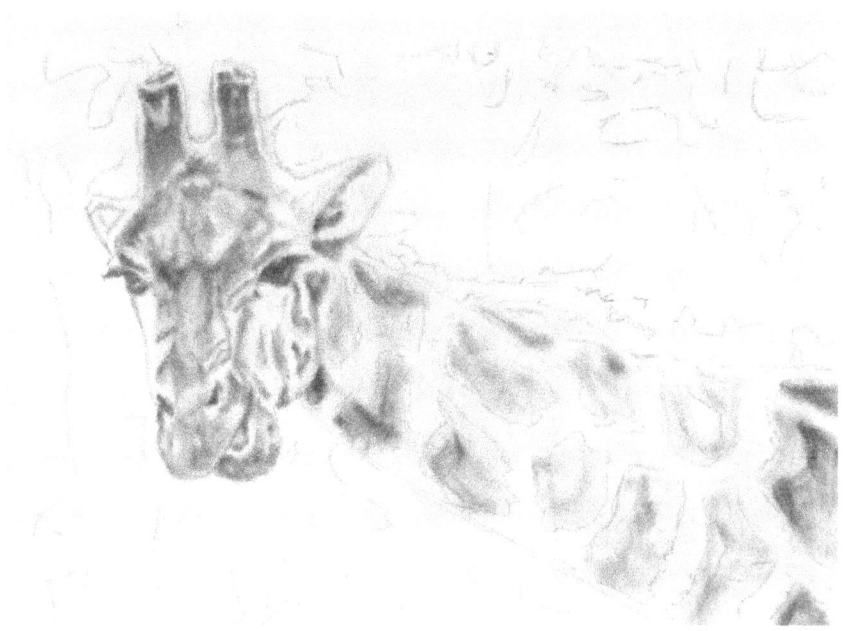

5.   Now time to work the neck, add more tone to the patches, apply another coat of Medium Charcoal S. to the light areas of the patches to make it more darker than before, also render the hair on the top of the neck, again use Soft Charcoal S. to dark areas, and shade the outline with Medium Charcoal S. or another trick is to draw the outline using Medium Charcoal Pencil and blend it with your Tortillon to make it soft edge. Apply highlights on the eyes, ears, nose, and lower lip below the neck.

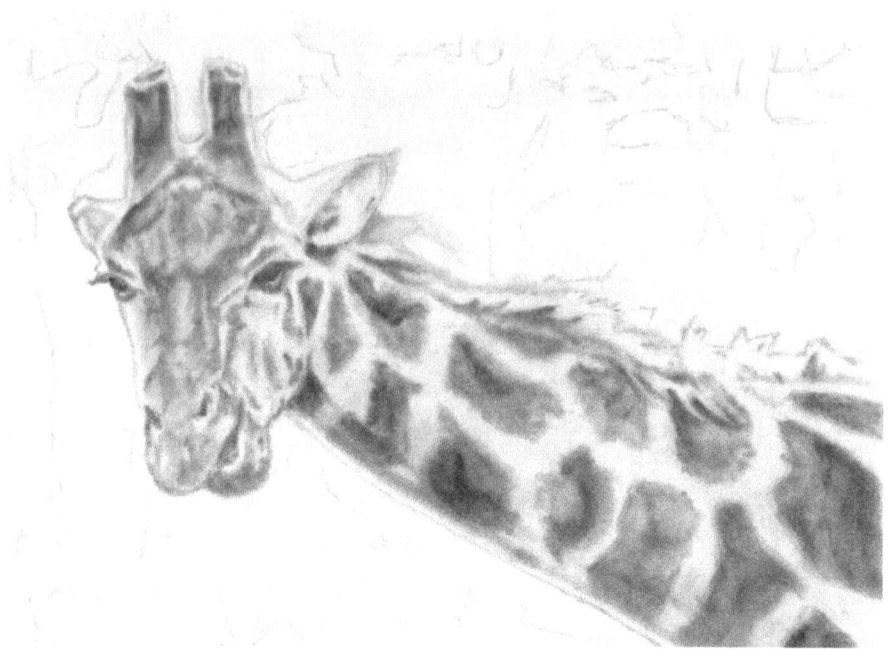

6.   Finish the background: Start shading the entire background with Lightest Value by dabbing it with Hard Charcoal S. with Large Round Brush, next apply dark values to the dark areas with Soft Charcoal S. using your Flat Brush use the picture below as a guide, and lastly dab a Medium Value using a Medium Charcoal S. to some areas to make it more diffuse or soft edge.
Check for any corrections and after that spray it with fixative.

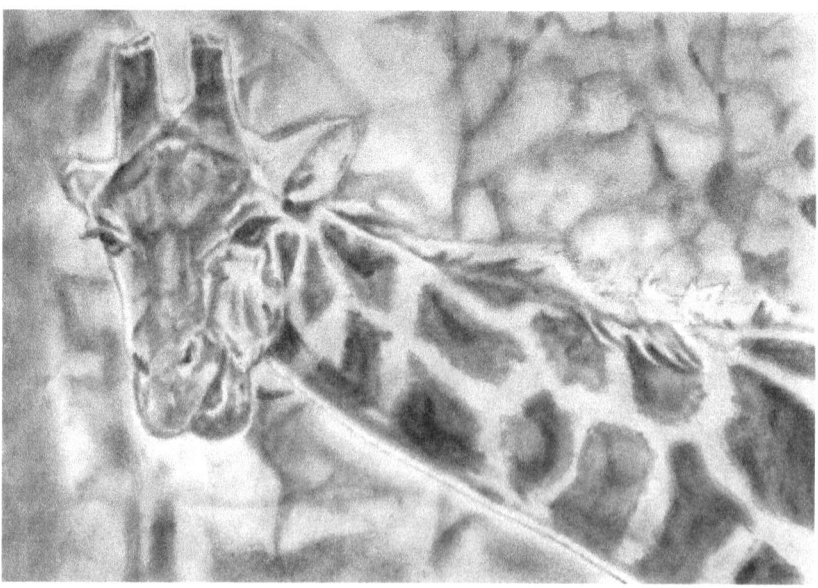

As you can see, the picture below looks alive.

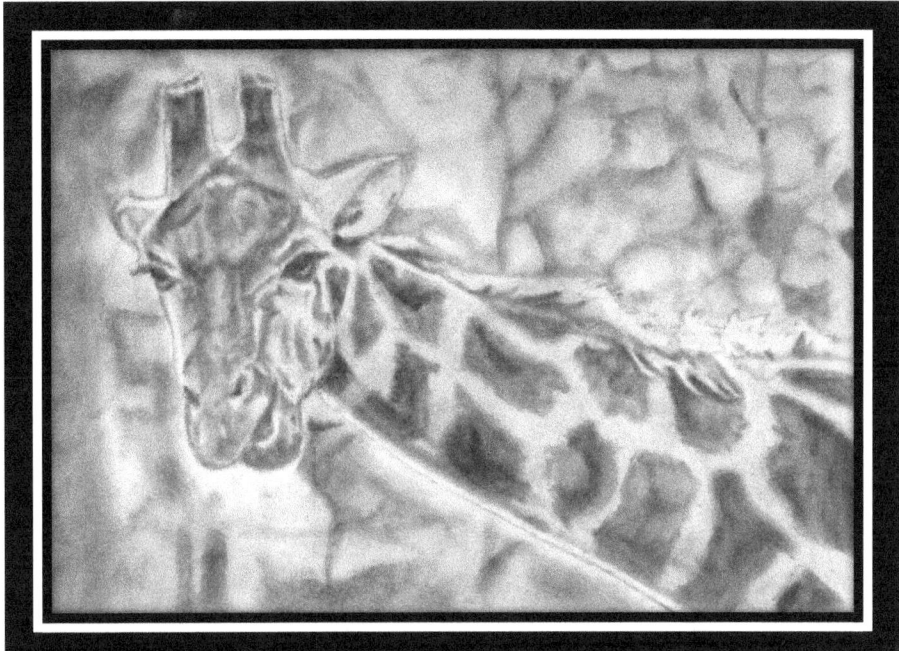

Elephant

For our third exercise, let's render this heavy mammal, who likes peanut, also for this challenge we're going to render it focus on its body texture as well the background. And don't forget to study the picture below before you begin.

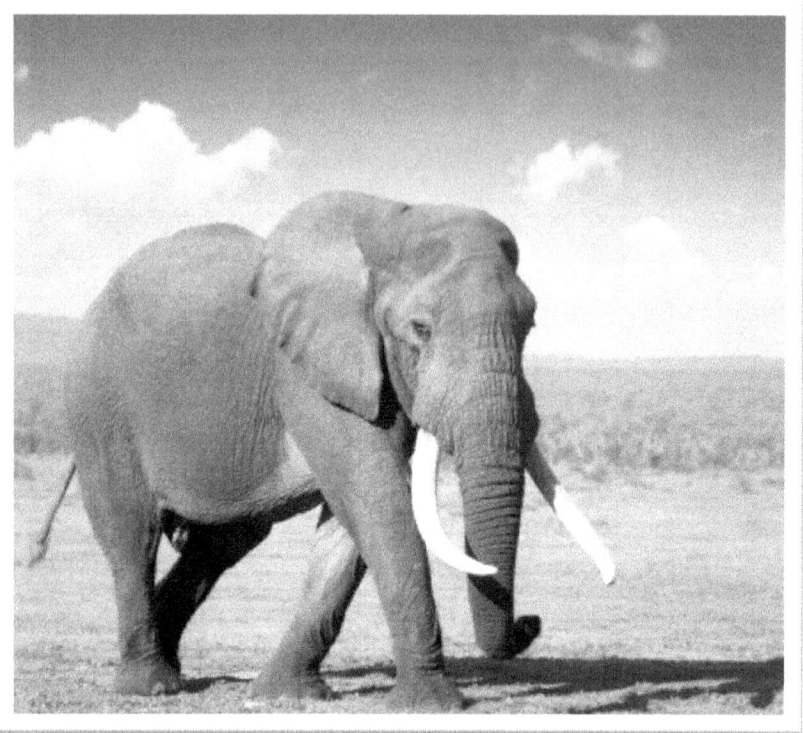

Again transfer this outline to your working paper, and we're set to go.

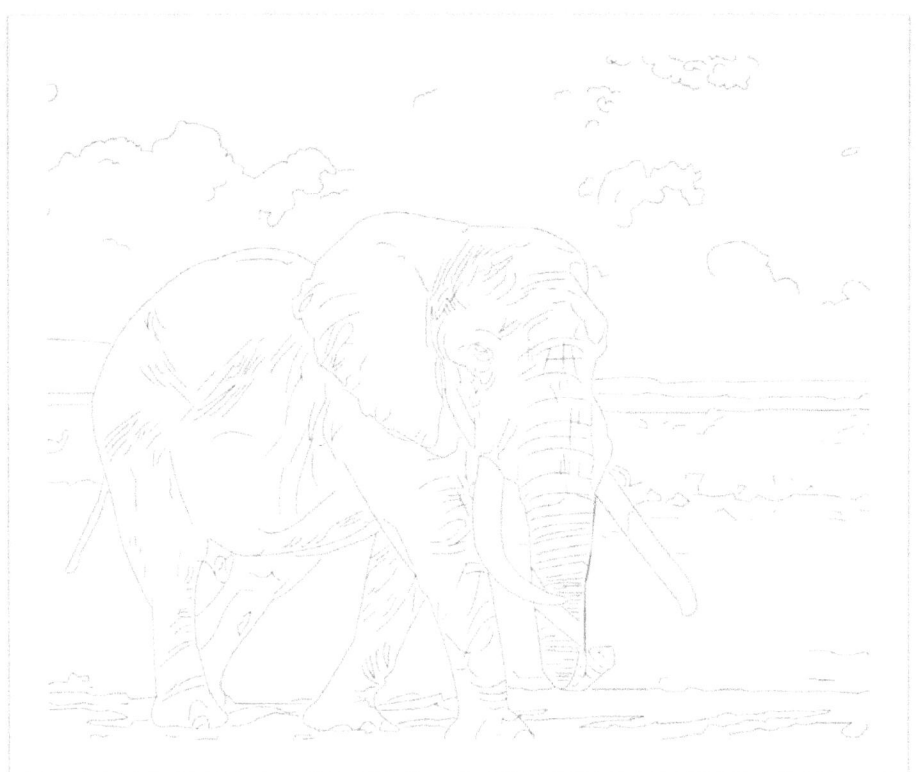

Steps:

1. Begin Shading the Dark areas, using the Soft Charcoal S. with your Flat Brush: left hind leg, shadow on the right ear and shadow on the left face.
And shade the shadow with the same Charcoal tone but use light pressure for this to be safe you can another layer later.

2.   To see the right contrast at this early stage we can begin working the background, using the guide below use Charcoal shave with Large Round Brush, use dabbing strokes when rendering the sky, work slowly but surely and working with the consistency of the value as well a good transition from dark(soft Charcoal) to light(hard Charcoal).

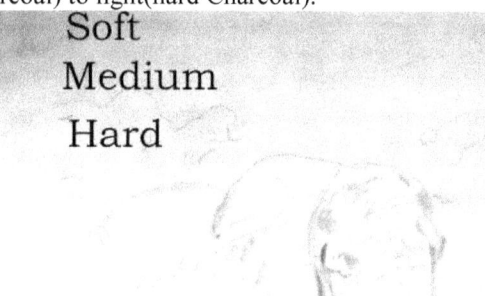

Soft
Medium
Hard

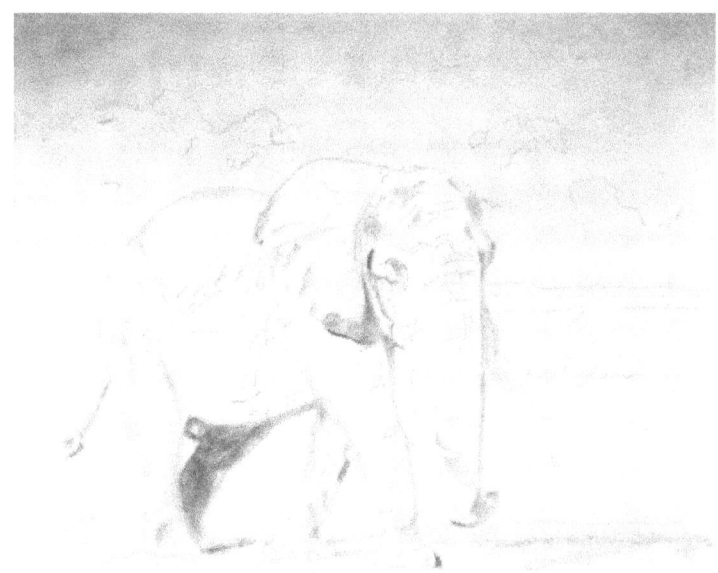

3. Next is to render the clouds in the sky, you can use your Vinyl eraser but if you have an electric eraser the better- it can erase deeper making the white of the paper more visible compared to any other eraser.

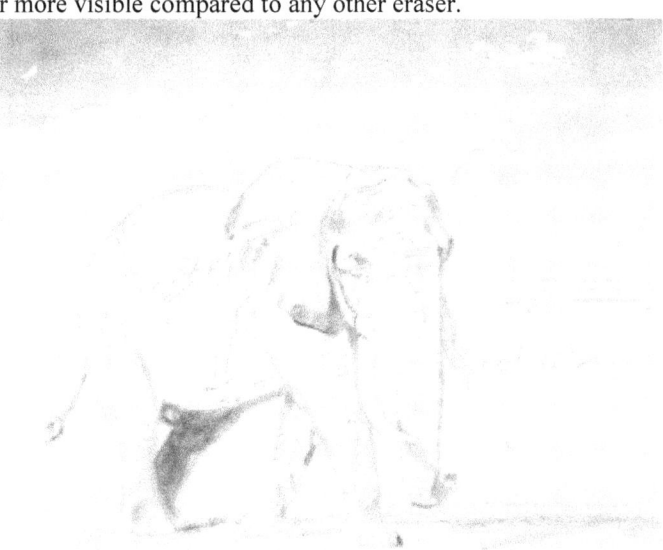

4. Finish the rest of the background using the guide below:
    A. Soft Charcoal S. with Flat Brush, use light pressure.
    B. Hard Charcoal S. with Round Brush
    C. Medium Charcoal S. with Round Brush

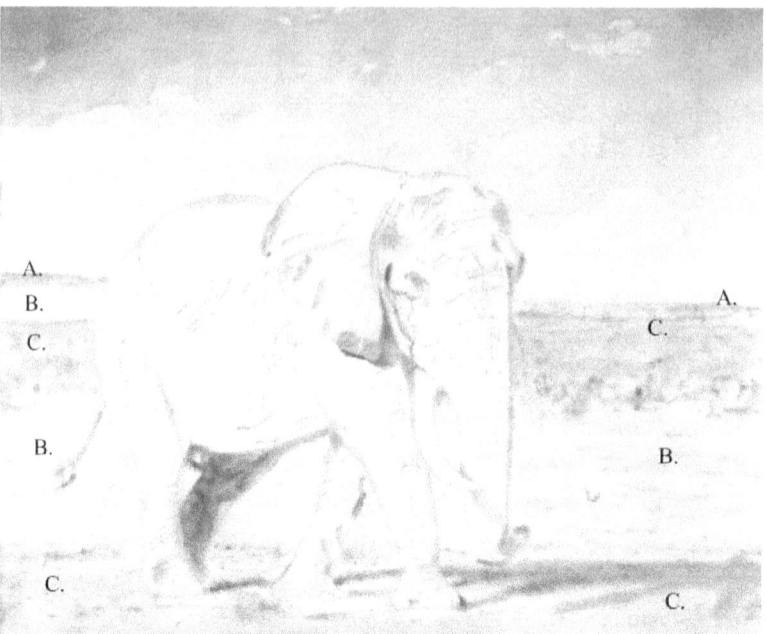

Note: For the middle ground area with C. add details using Medium Charcoal Pencil to add some effects and blend it with Tortillon to soften, for B. areas details draw light thin and short horizontal random lines with Medium Charcoal Pencil and again soften it with Tortillon.

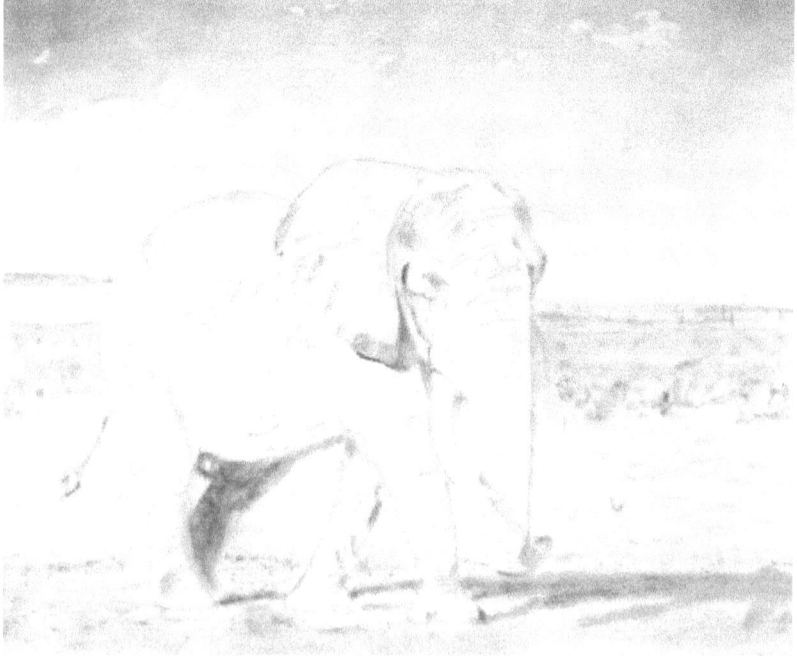

5.   Finish the details and texture of the subject:

First   Apply tone the body of the elephant by dabbing a Hard Charcoal S. with Round Brush.

Second Draw details like the eyes, lips and tusks using Hard Charcoal S. and soften it with tortillon, so that it will not look so sharp.

Third   Next add wrinkles to the following areas using Hard Charcoal Pencil: trunk, ear, body and legs,

Fourth Apply Highlights to the following areas using Kneaded eraser: ears, front face beside the trunk, body, tail and legs.

After you're finished, check your work for any corrections, and then spray it with fixative. And we're done. Wow you had finished half of the exercises in the eBook, good job and give yourself a pat in the back. Now take a break and after that get back and start the fourth exercise.

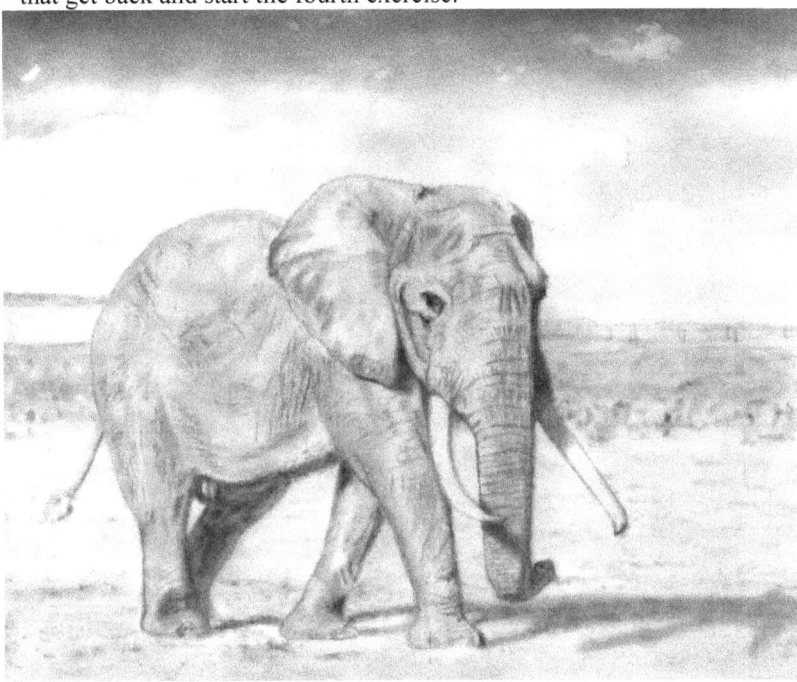

Hey! Look… it's like a scene from a movie, the part where the popular Jungle man calls his elephant ally.

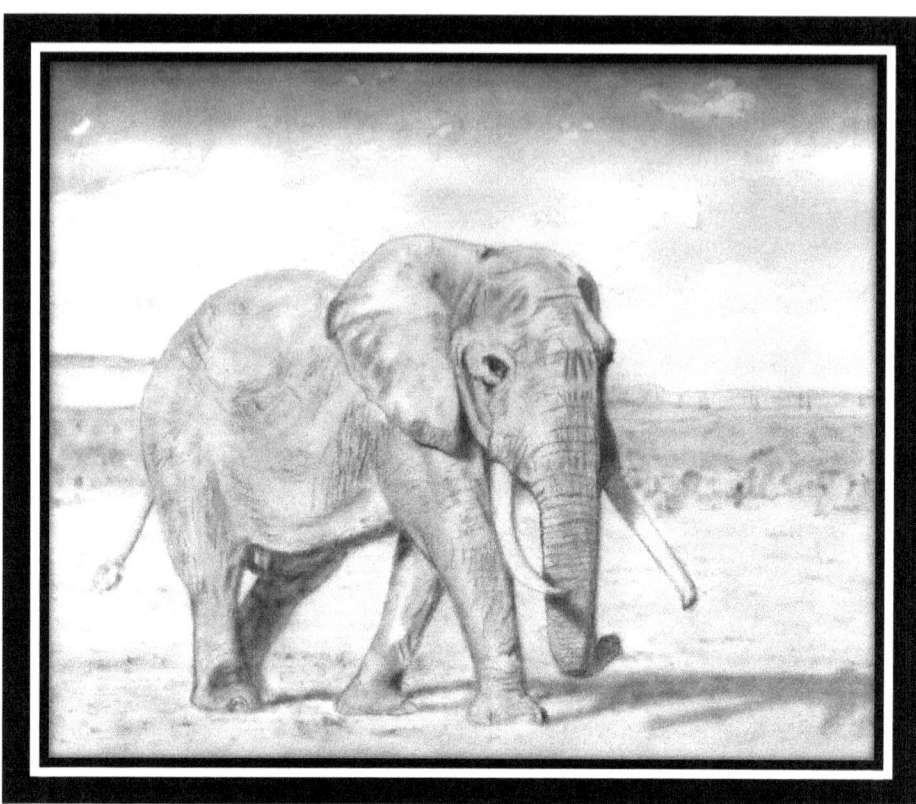

Baby Chimp

For our Fourth exercise let's render this cute little baby Chimp, the challenge is how to render it with consistent even tone, especially with hair covered to its body. Again let me remind you to study the picture first before you begin.

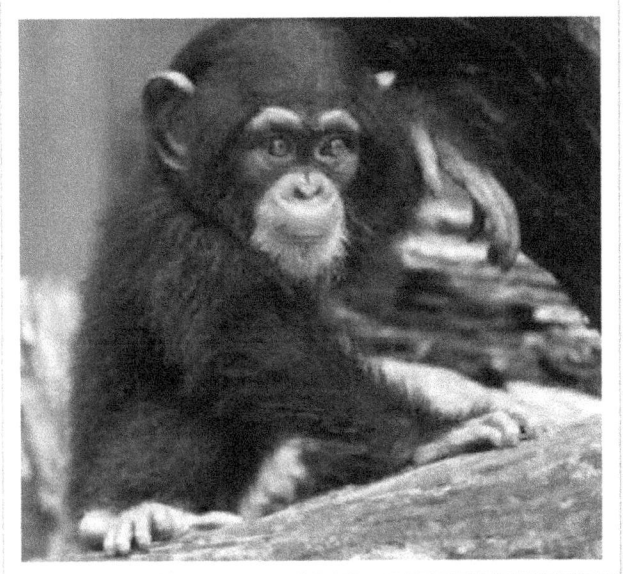

Transfer the outline and I'm sure you know what to do next.

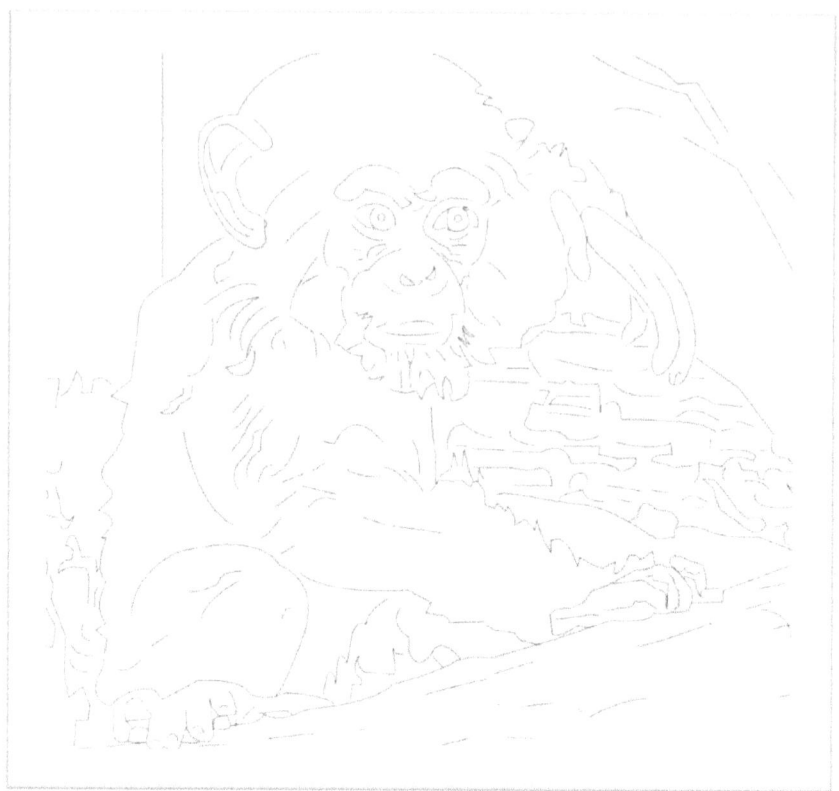

Steps:

1. Begin in the eyes, apply tone using Soft Charcoal S. (Shaved) with your small Flat Brush around the Iris, copy what you see in the picture below, use your Soft Charcoal Pencil to draw the pupil in the eyes, after that apply the tone to some areas to define the shapes: outline in the head, ears, nose, lips, hand and the body (outer outline) do it lightly so the pressure from your hand would be light also.

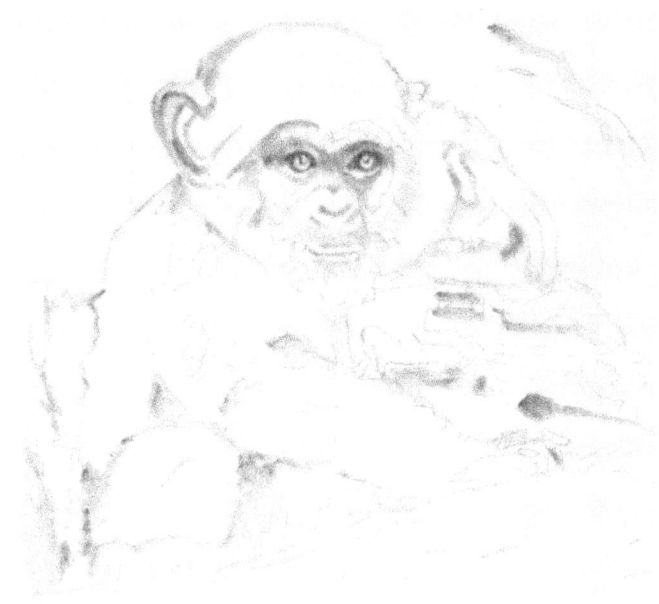

2. Refine the face by adding more tone using Medium Charcoal S. with your small Round Brush, dab it starting from the side going inward again using light pressure strokes. If you made a mistakes use your kneaded or Vinyl eraser.

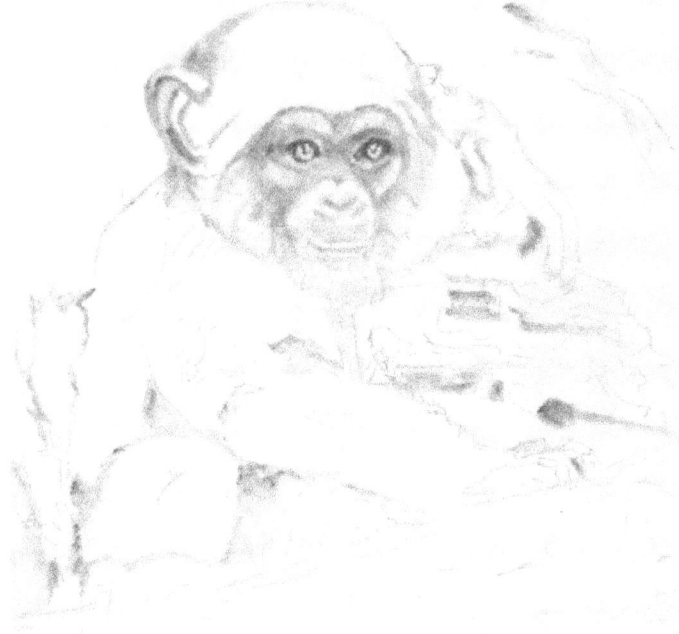

3.   Now apply a Medium Charcoal S. on the top of the head with your Flat Brush and sides of the face (hairy side) adding pressure to have a darker medium tone.

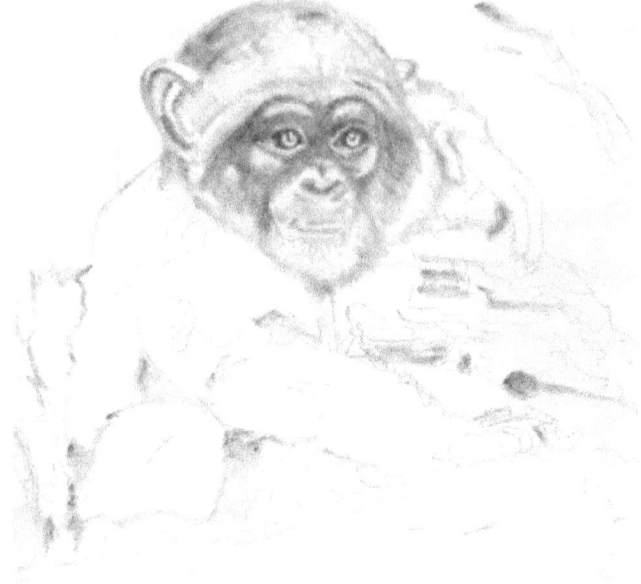

4.   Add details using your Medium Charcoal Pencil (make sure that point is sharp to make a thin detail lines). Define shapes by adding tones as what we did before in "Rendering using Charcoal".

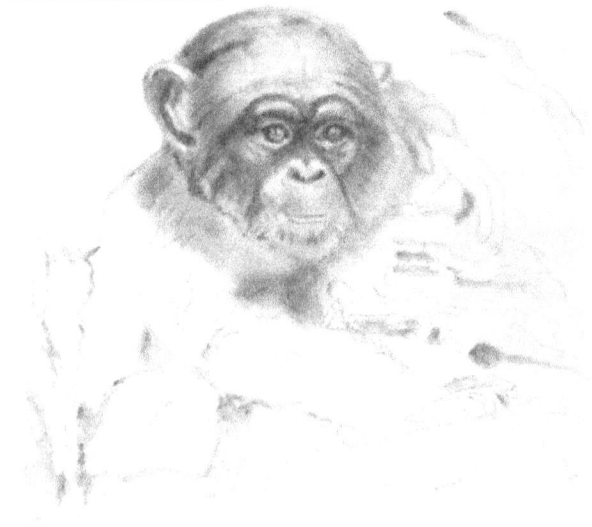

5.   Time to render the body, Apply Medium Charcoal S. with Large or Medium Round Brush.

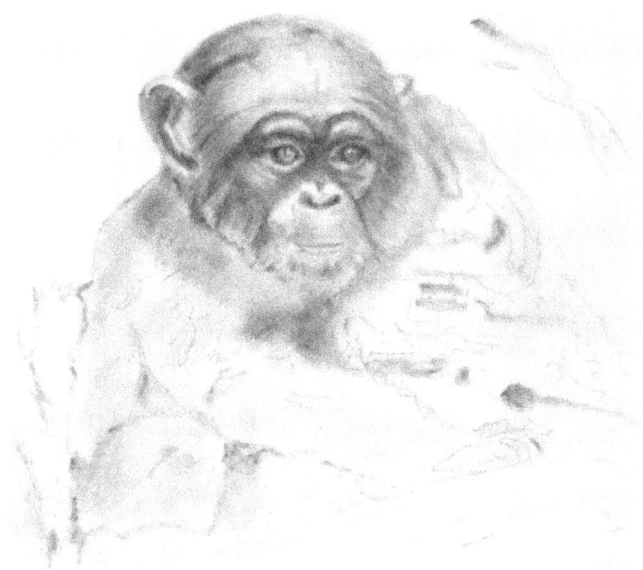

6. To darken the Hair in the body, apply a Soft Charcoal S. with Flat Brush to the dark areas like cast shadows (heavy pressure), and also apply to the rest of the body using same Charcoal but with Round Brush with dabbing strokes(light Pressure).

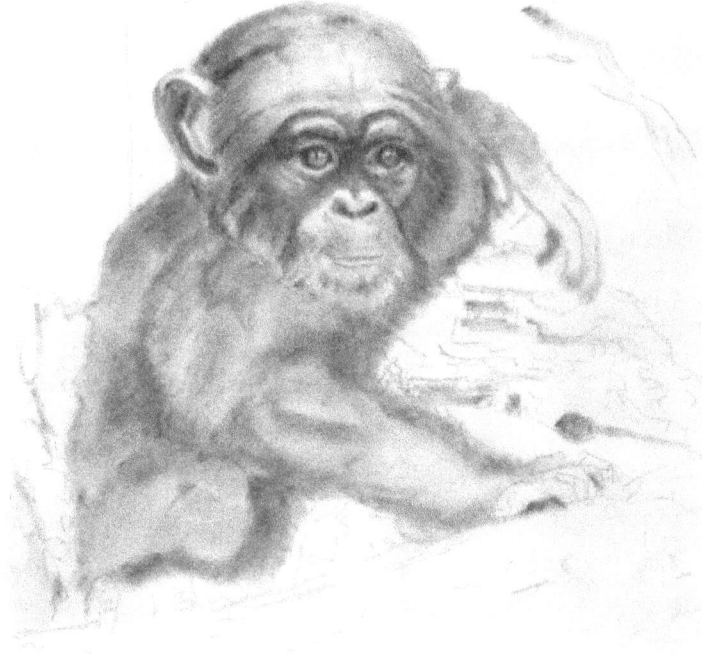

7. Let's work the background: dab the background with Hard Charcoal S. using large Round Brush for a light tone, then darken the left side with Soft Charcoal

S. using Flat Brush and blend it to the light tone using your tortillon, also draw a dark line behind the back of the chimp.

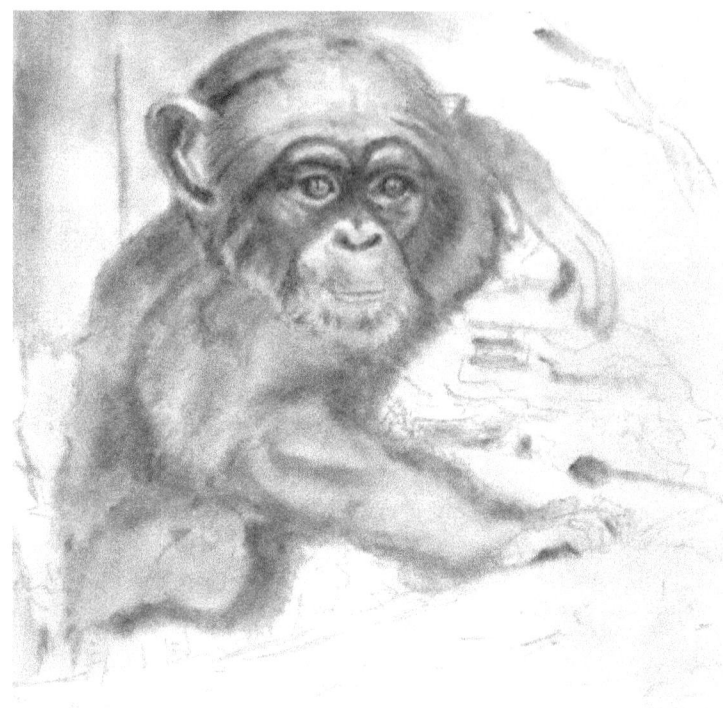

8.   Next would be the middle-ground, dab the area with Hard Charcoal S., again with large Round Brush, using your Medium Charcoal Pencil adds the details then shade it with your Flat Brush to make it soft edge (looks diffuse), an effect that tells the viewer the depth of the picture. Don't forget to fill the dark areas with Soft Charcoal S. or use pencil and just soften it with Flat brush with outward strokes.

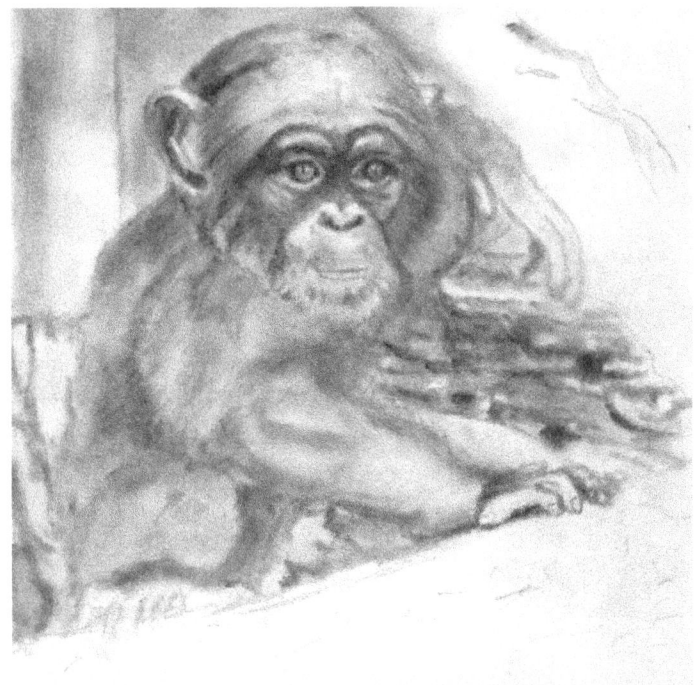

9. For the foreground(except for the chimp we're going to finish that later), Let's darken the dark areas of the branch on the right side by shading it using Soft Charcoal S. with Flat Brush and dabbing the rest of the area with the same Charcoal but using the round brush. Dab the bottom branch with Hard Charcoal S. with Round Brush.

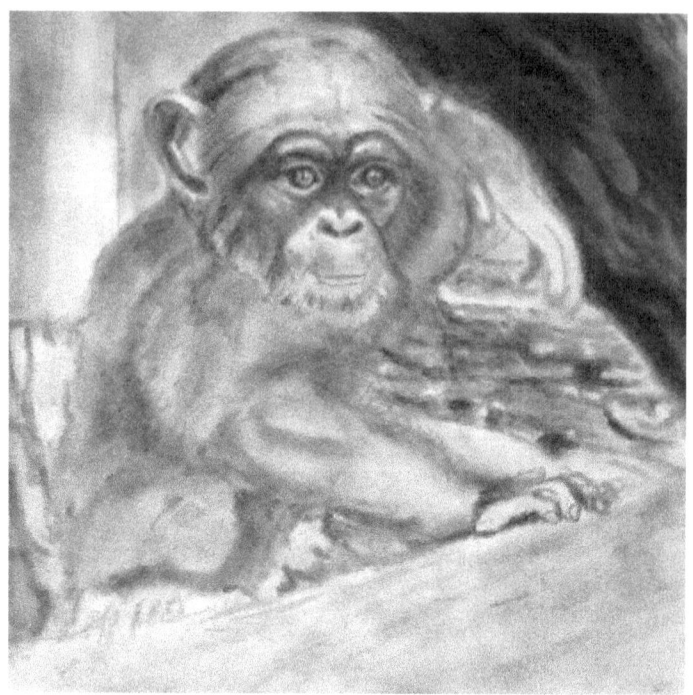

10.   Add details to the branch on the right side, using your kneaded eraser, lift up some tone so that the area will lighten up, note that this is not a highlight but more of a reflected light; you may add a tone lightly to the areas to give texture (a.). Add a highlight to the Top right corner using the Electric eraser (b.).

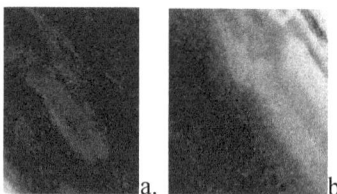
a.   b.

For the bottom branch, dab a Medium Charcoal S. with Round Brush to the area near the front, also using your Medium Charcoal Pencil draw some thin diagonal lines to give texture to it, you may thicken some of the lines to have a random texture, after that add highlights diagonally and some dots using kneaded Eraser.

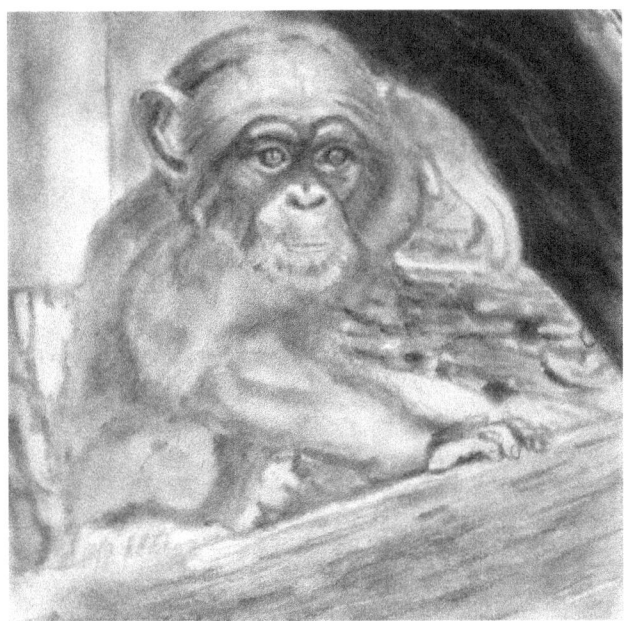

11. For the final step: Add another coat of Soft Charcoal S. with Round brush to the entire parts lightly and don't forget to tap the brush in the container, then add the rest of the details with Hard Charcoal Pencil, Draw thin hair lines of strokes to render the hair on the arms, legs, back and the rest of the body with hair that are evident (take note that not all areas are filled with hair) and also add details on the hands and feet. Check your work for any corrections, reminder: add a tone if needed,and if you see that you applied a very dark tone to the light area erase it using your eraser.

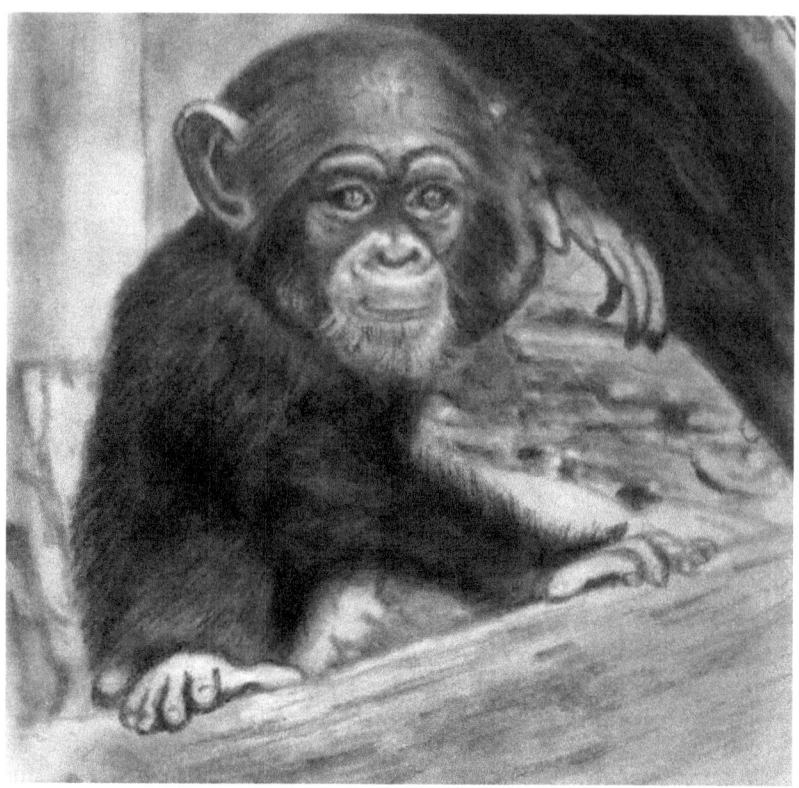

After that spray it with fixative, now it's finished and take a break, be back for the last challenge. Don't worry I'm sure you can do it.

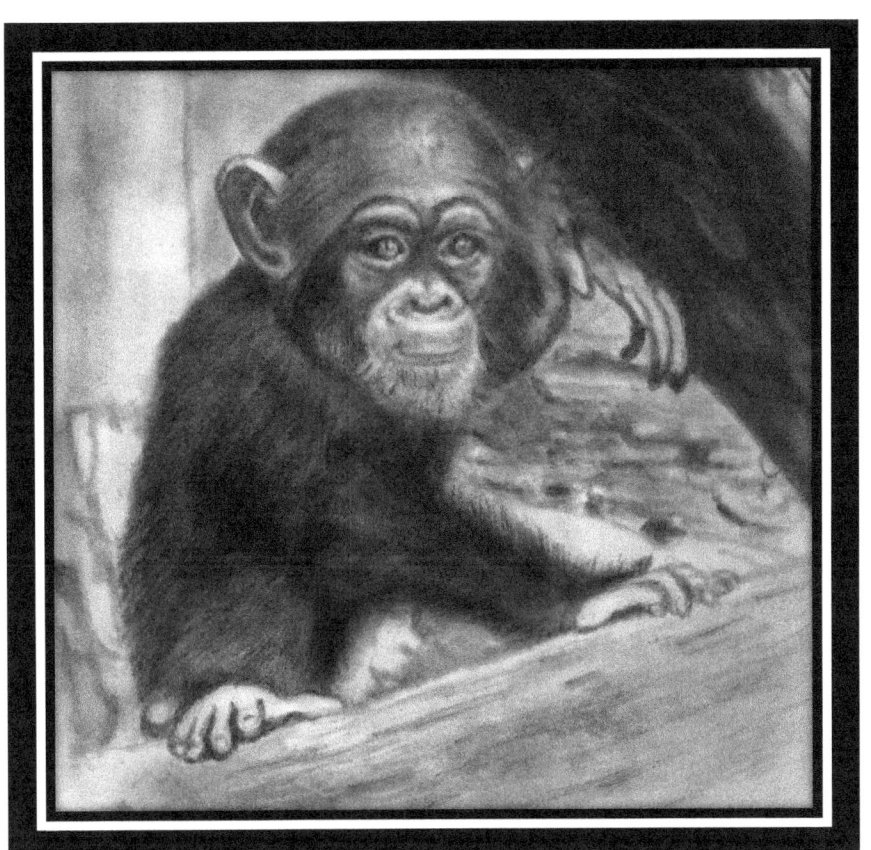

Lion

For our last exercise, we're going to render the King of the jungle, such royalty deserve a great artist to render the king and that's you. Study the picture of the Lion first, and if you ask me about the challenge it's how to render the mane and its texture, paws, grass and the rock texture in the foreground. So let's begin.

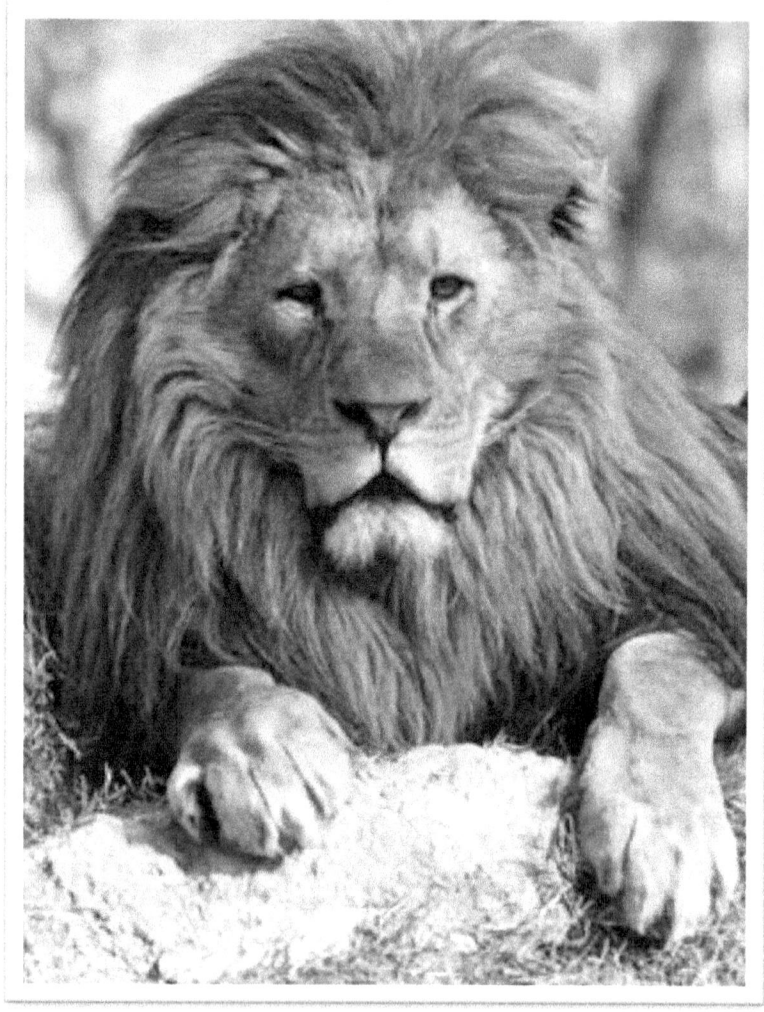

Transfer the image below to your working paper.

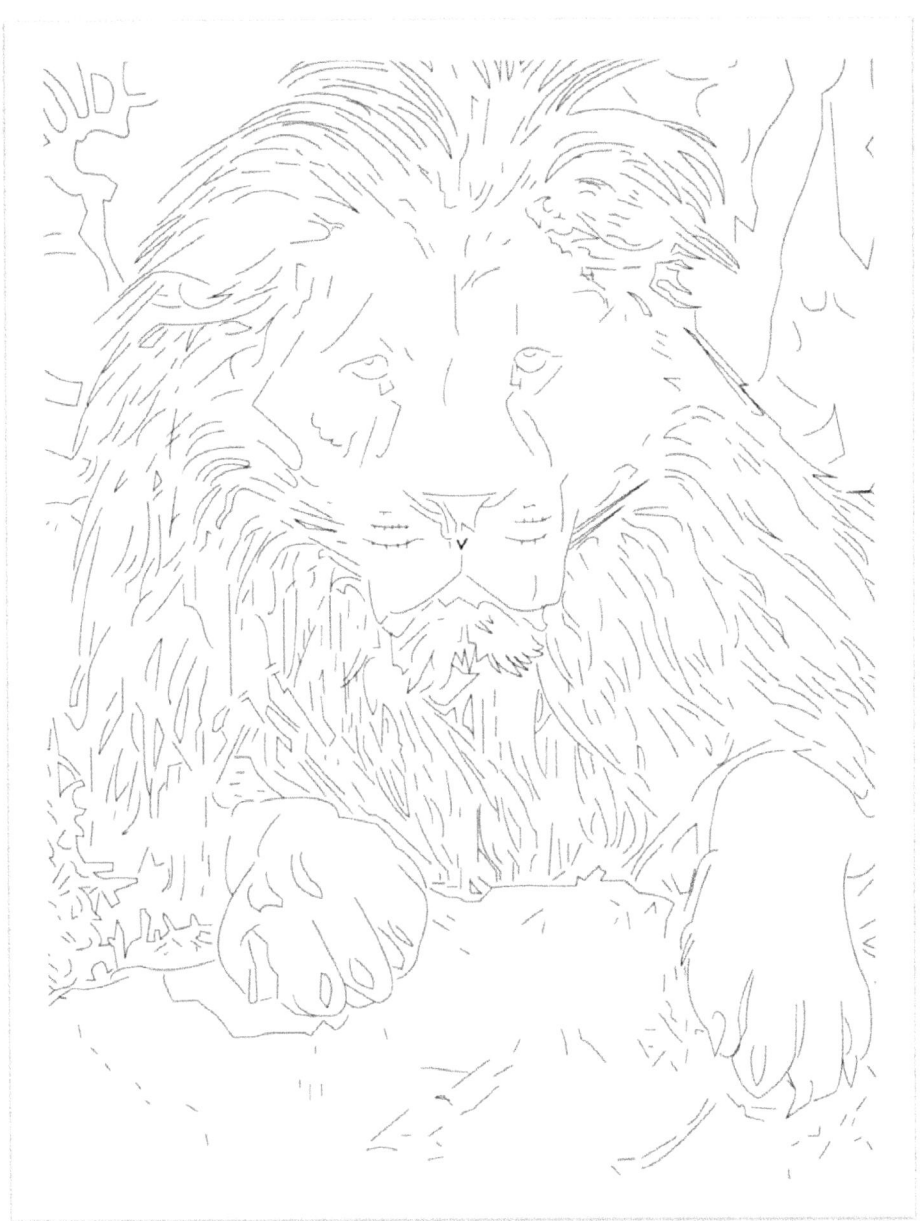

Steps:

1. As our first step start with the dark areas, let the picture below be your guide, use Soft Charcoal S. with Flat Brush.

2.   Next is to use Medium Value to your work, use Medium Charcoal S. with the Flat Brush again. Take note of the shapes, if you have a vivid imagination you can imagine it like you are making a sculpture, molding it bit by bit turning it into 3d.

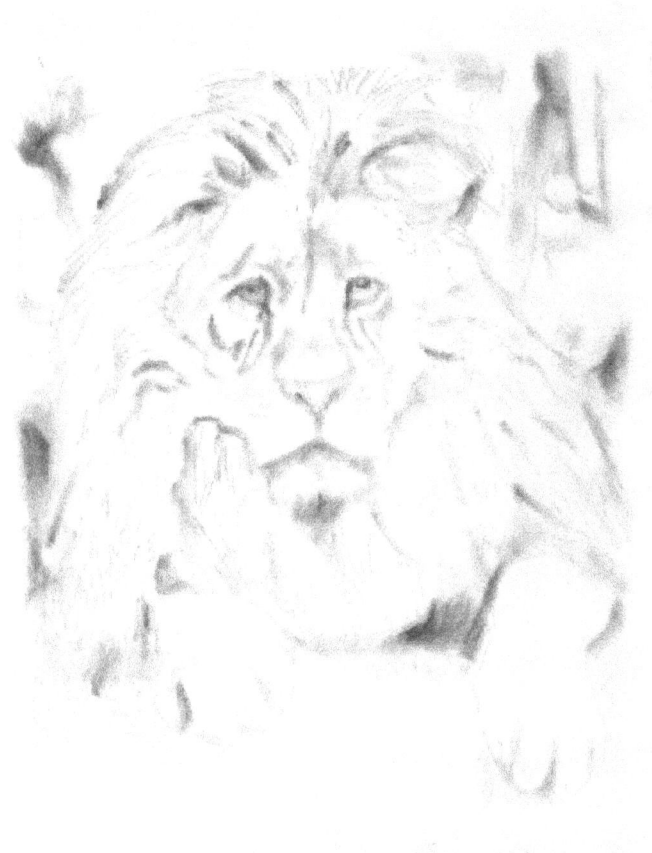

3.   Continue adding the same tones and defining the shapes, notice the mane how it was rendered using the Medium Charcoal S. with Flat Brush by following the strokes of the hair flow, also the left side of the face receive less light so you have to add more tone on that side, shade the details on the parts on the face: eyes, nose and mouth.

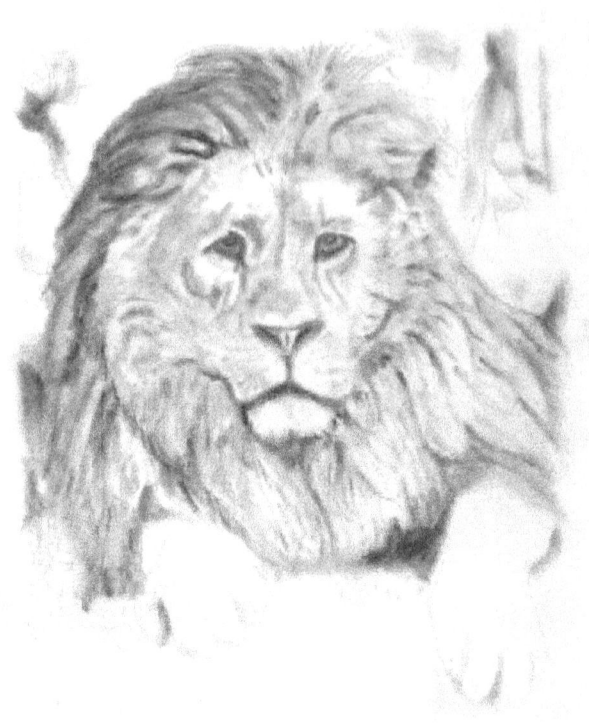

4. Add more value to the outer mane to look more bulky, render the paws again using Medium Charcoal S. with Flat Brush, and don't forget to render the shadow with the same Charcoal.

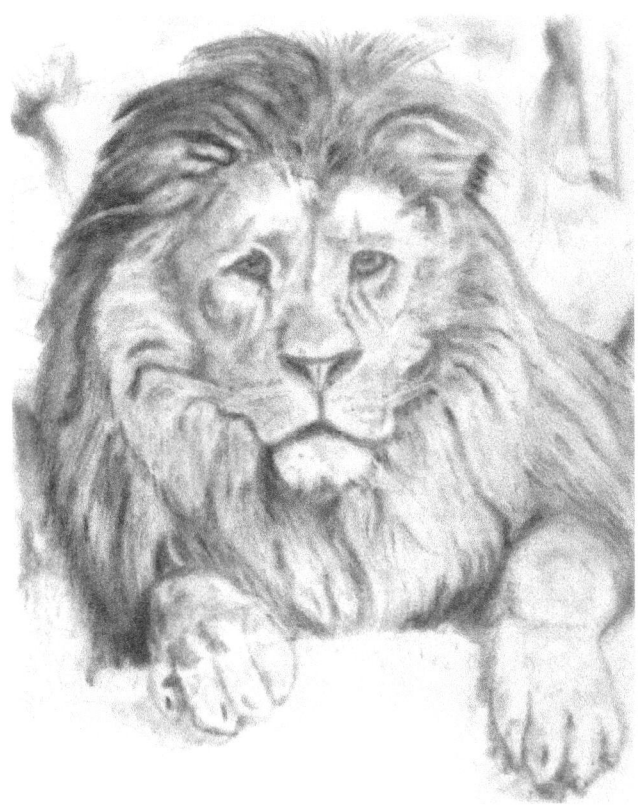

5.   Last step is to render the background and foreground:
   a)   Background- Shade the left side with Soft Charcoal S. with varying
        pressure when using your flat brush, the same thing on the right side.
   b)   Foreground- For the grass use Soft Charcoal S. with Flat Brush and
        also with Soft Charcoal Pencil for details, also highlights was added to
        create a good effect.
   c)   For the rock –Just use your Soft Charcoal Pencil to draw some detail
        lines and soften it with Tortillon, add dots with the Charcoal pencil, and
        add a tone on the rock with Hard Charcoal S. with Round Brush, apply
        slight highlights.

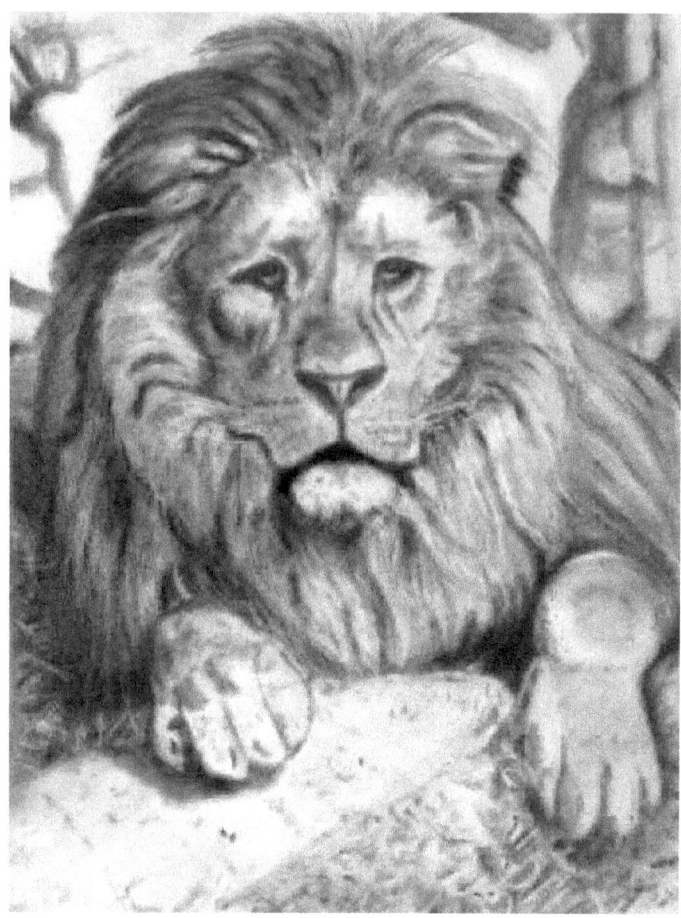

Check for any corrections if any, now we are almost finished, but first I want you to sign your Signature at the bottom of your work, as a sign of your accomplishment and finishing all the exercises, and time to spray it with fixative after that you can frame it, and hang it in your wall. - "Congratulations" you are now a great artist. Thanks for finishing this journey, and apply the new artistic skill for your benefit and also to all that surrounds you.

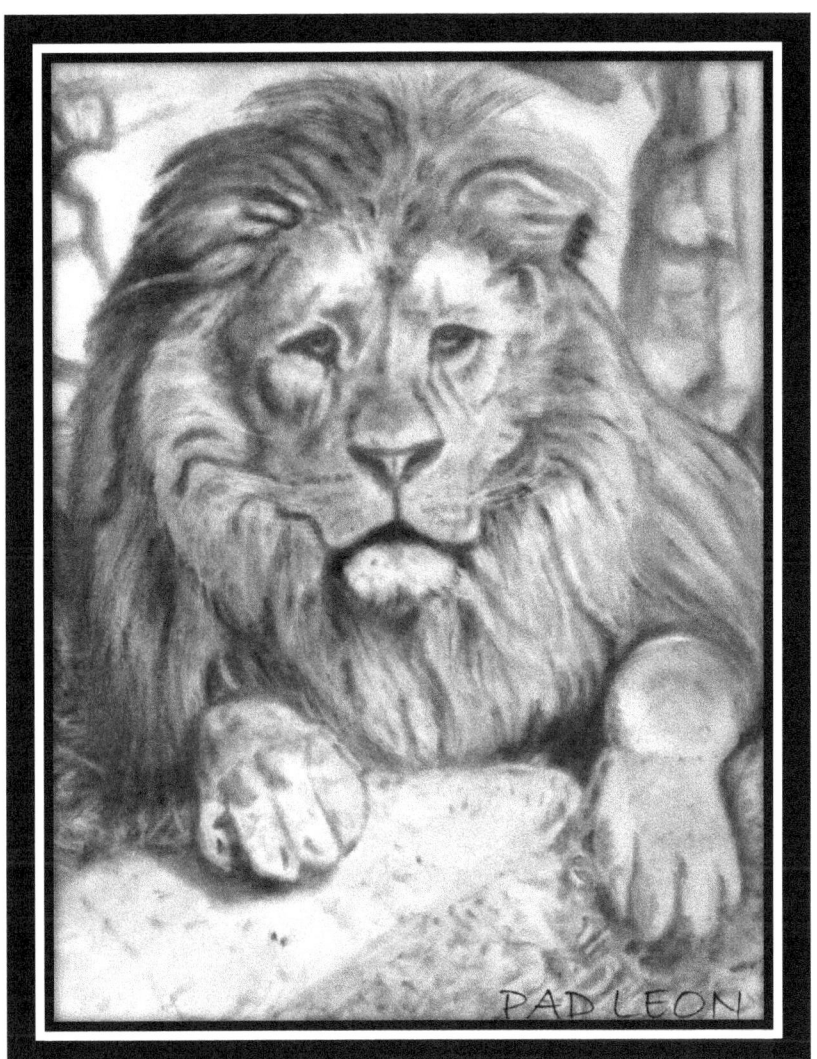

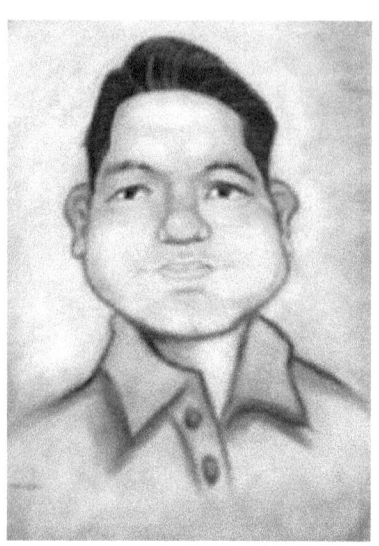

Author Bio

Paolo A. Lopez de Leon

A self taught Portrait Artist and Digital Illustrator, Experience in painting and drawing for more than 15 years. His works in various media like Pencil, Charcoal, Gouache, Watercolor, Acrylic (Air Brush), Oil and Digital Painting. He lives in Laguna,Philippines.

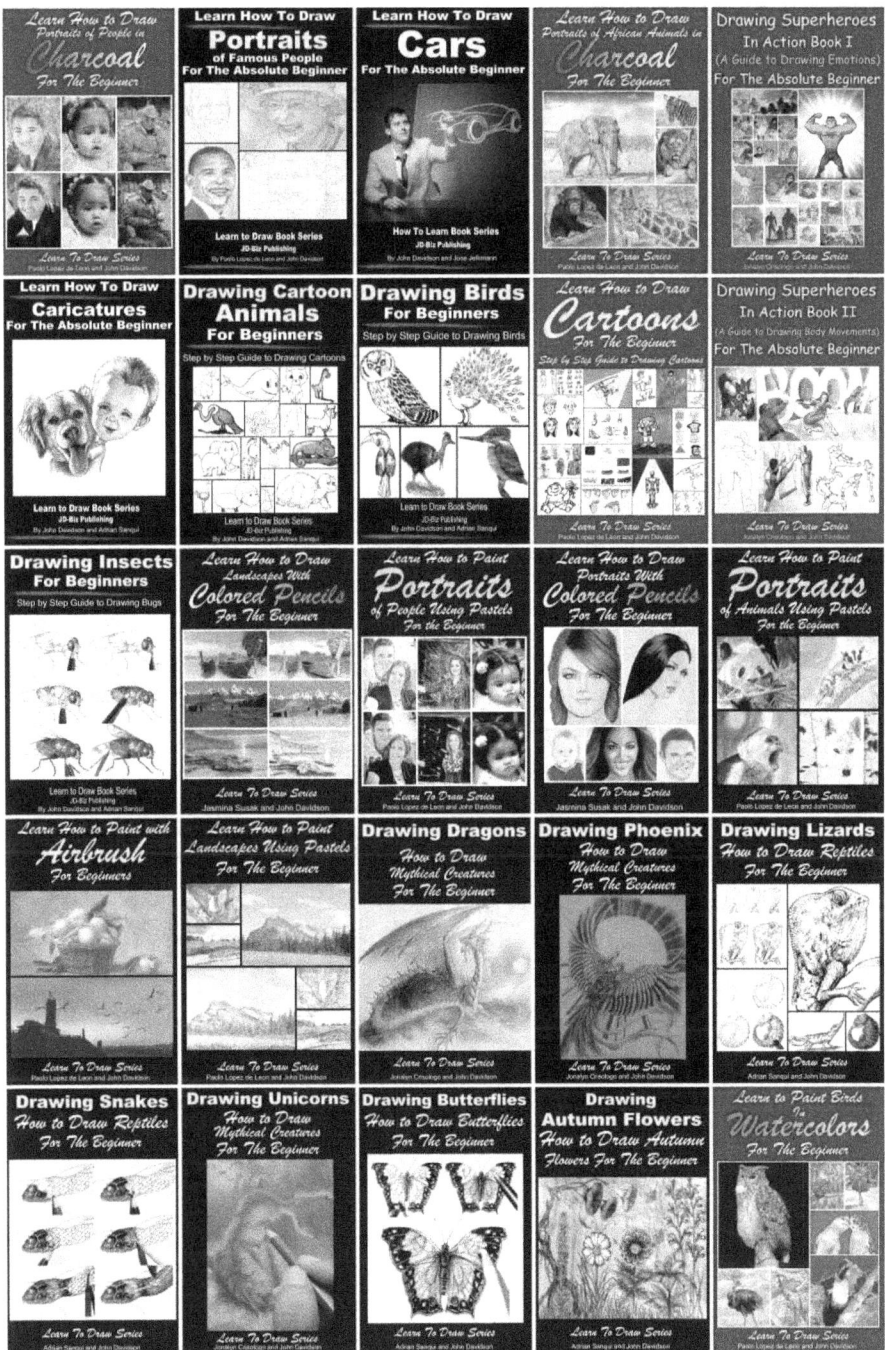

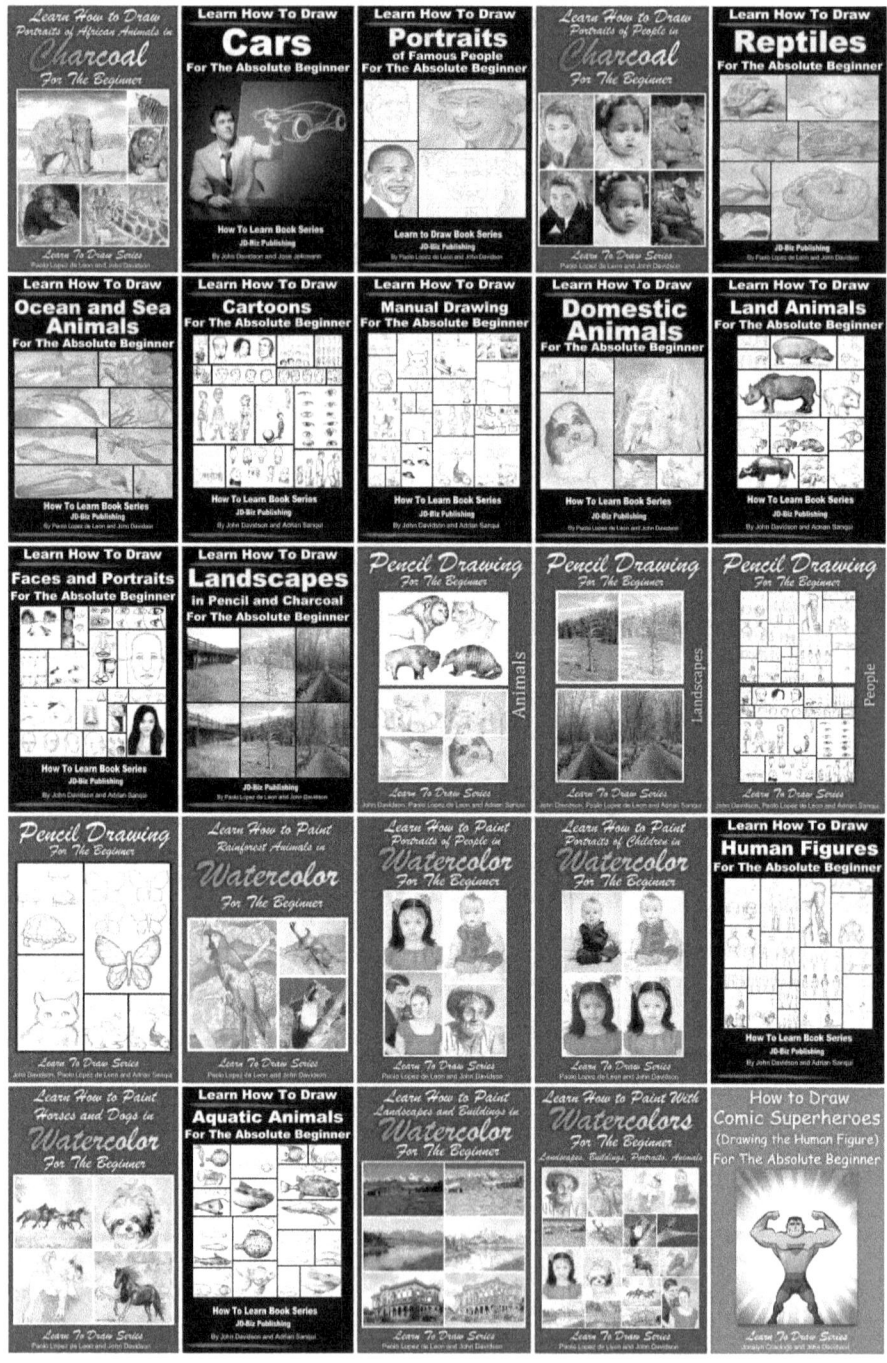

This book is published by

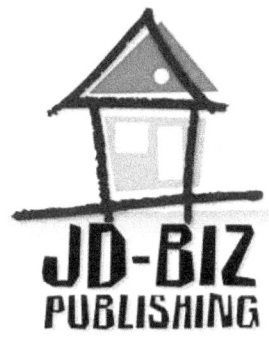

JD-Biz Corp

P O Box 374

Mendon, Utah 84325

http://www.jd-biz.com/

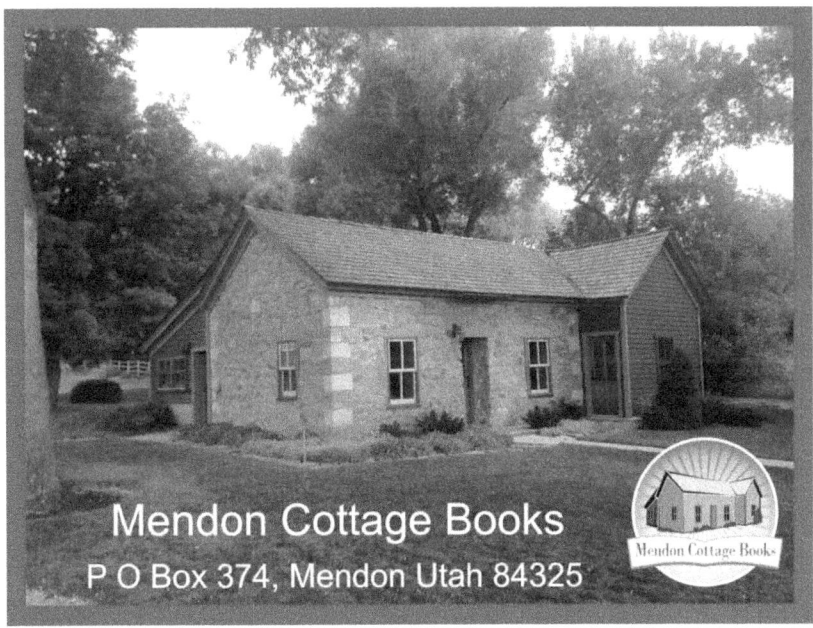

www.ingramcontent.com/pod-product-compliance
Lightning Source LLC
Chambersburg PA
CBHW051859170526
45168CB00001B/167